Dental School

D0861732

Preparation, Application, Admission

YOUR JOURNEY, YOUR FUTURE

**Leigh Moore, D.M.D.
and Rachel A. Winston, Ph.D.**

ISBN 978-1946432254 (hardback); 978-1946432230 (paperback - color); 978-1946432247 (e-book); 978-1946432292 (paperback - black and white)

LCCN: 2021906447

Lizard Publishing® 7700 Irvine Center Drive, Suite 800 Irvine, CA 92618 *www.lizard-publishing.com*

Lizard Publishing creates, designs, produces, and distributes books and resources to provide academic, admissions, and career information. Our mental process is fueled by three tenets:

- Ignite the hunger to learn and the passion to make a difference
- Illuminate the expanse of knowledge by sharing cutting edge thinking
- Innovate to create a world that makes the transition from dreams to reality

We work with academic leaders who transform the educational landscape to publish relevant content and advise students of their educational and professional options, with the aim of developing 21st-century learners and leaders. We also work with students to publish their books and present widely diverse ideas to the college/graduate school-bound community. With headquarters in Irvine, California, Lizard Publishing works virtually with authors to edit, publish, and distribute both hard copy and paperback books.

This book was published in the U.S.A. Lizard Publishing is a premium quality provider of educational reference, career guidance, and motivational publications/merchandise for global learners, educators, and stakeholders in education.

Book design by Michelle Tahan *www.michelletahan.com*

Book formatting by Obinna Chinemerem Ozuo

LIZARD PUBLISHING

This book is dedicated to Dr. Allison Blatt and is written in loving memory of Dr. Lea Ann Davenport Whelan.

ACKNOWLEDGMENTS

There is never enough room to acknowledge every person who contributed to an individual's perspective, assisted in the development of a person's knowledge base, or taught indelible lessons that last a lifetime. In this book, we gratefully acknowledge Michelle Tahan, Jasmine Jhunjhnuwala, and E. Liz Kim, as well as our family, friends, colleagues, and professors.

It is with profound gratitude that we mention the University of Louisville School of Dentistry in these acknowledgements. The support of Dr. Alma Llaljevik-Tucakovic, ULSD's Interim Dean for Student Admissions and Student Affairs, has been invaluable to us. During the busiest of seasons, Dr. Llajevik-Tucakovic enthusiastically supported our mission to provide a thorough, accurate guide for aspiring dentists. Dr. Paul Tran, former ULSD faculty member in Orthodontics, likewise, has been notably generous with his time and his insights.

Meaningful contributions to the book have been made indirectly by those faculty members who took a special interest in Dr. Moore's progress as a student, and by the dentists who studied and worked alongside her: Dr. Melanie Peterson, Dr. Sherrie Zaino, Dr. Margaret Hill, Dr. James Howell, Dr. Jack Morris (deceased), Dr. Marquetta Poynter, Dr. Richard Miller, Dr. Kim Hansford, Dr. Jason Bottoms, Dr. Jeff Feltzer, Dr. Perri Carnes, Dr. Brian Cook, Dr. Gene Beck, Dr. Scott Norton, Dr. Greg Smith, Dr. Troy Kerber, Dr. Chris Ward, Ms. Jackie Owen, Dr. Divya Raina, Dr. Doug Kirol, Dr. Ann Lang, Dr. Stephanie Poynter, and Dr. Jennifer McMeans.

"If I see so far, it is because I stand on the shoulders of giants."
– Isaac Newton

We would also like to thank the thousands of students we have taught, counseled, or supported in our decades of service. Isaac Newton once said, "If I see so far, it is because I stand on the shoulders of giants." A few of those giants whose broad shoulders lifted us higher and helped teach invaluable lessons include: Dr. James Dabrowiak, Dr. Ei-ichi Negishi, Dr. Marvin Druger, Dr. Sandra Savage, Michael Ortell, Dr. Zenobia Miro, Dr. David Waugh, Clifford Sobel, Steve Waugh, Karyn Holtzman, Anila Baseel, Nicky Ahad, Emily, Liu, Nick Walling, Bernice Li, Jenae Cervantes, Ann Kuga, Carlos/ Pauline Ruiz, Matt/Alfredo Robledo, Dante Rovere, Vincent Li, Skipper John, Charlie Cockerell, Leonard/Roberta Mirvis, and James Sullivan.

Finally, there would be no dental degree, no career in college admissions, no dental admissions book without the support of Dr. Moore's husband, Robert Moore, and her children--Bob, Mac, and Jane. Furthermore, there would be no Lizard Publishing or doctoral degree without the support of Robert Helmer.

ABOUT THE AUTHORS

Leigh Moore, D.M.D.

A Kentucky native, Leigh Moore earned a Bachelor of Science in Mathematics and Secondary Education from Vanderbilt University. After several years teaching high school, she enrolled at the University of Louisville School of Dentistry, where she also completed her Advanced Education in General Dentistry residency.

After having children, Leigh transitioned away from dentistry to educational consulting in order to help students achieve their goals. She is the co-founder of Real College Matters LLC, an integrative, team-based practice of postsecondary advisors. She and her husband Robert are the parents of Bob, Mac, and Jane.

Rachel A. Winston, Ph.D.

Rachel Winston has served as a university professor, college advisor, award winning author, and motivational speaker. As a leading expert in college counseling and an award-winning faculty member, Dr. Winston has spent her lifetime teaching, mentoring, and coaching students.

She has counseled thousands of students during her 35-year career. Working in D.C. and California gave her diverse experiences in politics, engineering, and mathematics. As an elected statewide leader, Academic Senate President and winner of the McFarland Literary Achievement Award, she earned her Ph.D. from the University of Texas and Master's degrees from Harvard, UChicago, CSUF, CSUDH, Claremont Graduate University, Pepperdine, and GWU.

AUTHORS' NOTE

You are reading this book because you are considering dental school. Whatever route you took to get to this point, you are in the right place. Right now, you need to gather information to make informed decisions. While many people offer advice, suggestions differ. Friends will tell you the 'right' way or the way their neighbor was accepted.

Graciously accept this anecdotal information while you commit to learning more. This is your future. Dig deeper to consider both expert and current information from counselors who have worked with hundreds of students. Changes in programs, curricula, requirements, and links happen each year. Double-check each program's specifics yourself. This guide is current as of 2021 with each school's website information. However, since researching this book, changes may have taken place.

> *"We are what we think. All that we are arises with our thoughts. With our thoughts, we make the world."*
> *— Buddha*

There are books on dental programs written by talented and experienced counselors. We admire and cheer on their efforts. This guide is different in that it provides maps, lists, timelines, and unique tidbits. We hope you find this information valuable.

Your job is to begin early by assembling information for the schools you are considering. Create a road map and set yourself on a clear path. If you see an error in this book or even a suggestion for a future edition, please write to Rachel Winston at collegeguide@yahoo.com or Leigh Moore at leigh@realcollegematters.com and we will fix the entry with the next printed version.

All of that said, this book was written with you in mind. There is a wealth of information on the Internet with free downloads, FAQs, testimonials, and offers to help you with your applications. Some of these advisors are knowledgeable and could help you. Students and parents hunt around the web, seeking the information they need. This book was designed to make your search easier.

For now, though, we will assume that you are reasonably confident that you want to attend dental school and are exploring this avenue as a possible way to take advantage of a program that will get you on your way toward your goal. We will also assume that you are a highly academic candidate who is willing to work very hard. You may have a fascination with the human body, passion for dentistry, and a commitment to serve others selflessly. These are virtually prerequisites for dental programs.

As you investigate colleges, you might find that some schools call these DDS or DMD programs; either way we will help you reach your goal. Applying to and writing essays for each application will require research to determine which is right for you. While you might believe that dental programs are relatively similar, each program's nuances make them very different. These small differences may seem confusing. Our goal with this book is to demystify the process.

CONTENTS

Part 3
Preparation

Part 4
Pre-Application: Testing and Recs

Part 5
Where and How to Apply

Part 6   213

Initial Application   213

Part 7   243

Application Process Continues   243

Part 8   269

Decisions, Decisions   269

Part 9 289
Dental Education 289

Part 10 317
College Profiles and Requirements 317

Part 11 419
Dental School Lists 419

Index 456

DENTAL SCHOOL ACRONYMS

100 WORDS TO KNOW

abutment: refers to a supporting element of a prosthetic dental structure, often denoting the end unit (that which abuts the natural teeth)

alloy: used interchangeably with "amalgam"; a mixture of metals

alveolar: the portion of the maxillary or mandibular bone which supports the tooth

amalgam: see "alloy"

analgesia: pain management

anesthesia: temporary and intentional blockage of neural function while a procedure is performed

arch, dental: the curved areas of the oral cavity where teeth exist, existed, or will exist

bicuspid: a two-cusped tooth between the incisors and the molars

bilateral: occurring on, or pertaining to, both right and left sides

bonding: using mechanical or chemical means to adhere components permanently

bruxism: tooth grinding; frequent cause of dental damage and/or pain

buccal: referring to the outer or cheek side of a tooth

calculus: tenacious, rigid mineral deposits on the teeth

cantilever extension: a portion of a prosthetic dental appliance that extends beyond the last supporting natural tooth

caries: tooth decay

cementum: hard connective tissue covering the outer surface of a tooth root.

cleft palate: congenital malformation; partial or full separation of the hard or soft palate

complete denture: a prosthetic device that replaces all teeth on the maxillary or mandibular arch

composite: a mixture of various dental materials used to fill and restore a tooth; unlike alloy, composites are very similar in color to the natural enamel

coronal: referring to the crown of a tooth.

crown: colloquially referred to as a "cap"; a prosthetic tooth which is permanently adhered to what remains of the natural tooth after preparation

cusp: the pointed aspect of a tooth

cuspid: aka canine; single cusped tooth located between the incisors and bicuspids

decay: aka caries; breakdown of tooth caused by acids, sugars, and bacteria

dentin: the layer of tooth between the pulp and the enamel

dentition: teeth; kinds of dentition are primary dentition (first set of teeth which exfoliate naturally), permanent dentition (second and last set of teeth), and mixed dentition (a combination of the two, usually present in the mouths of children older than five but not yet into the teens)

denture: artificial teeth; "denture" is commonly used by lay people to refer to a complete denture but it also exists as partial prosthetic devices

diagnostic cast: model of human teeth made by taking impressions which are then filled with a stone-like material to replicate the dentition

direct restoration: a repair, usually a filling, done inside the mouth (rather than something fabricated offsite)

distal: referring to the part of a tooth which is away from the center of the arch

dry socket: aka osteitis; painful inflammation of the site of a dental extraction, usually caused by bacterial infection or loss of the protective clotting of blood

enamel: the outer layer of the tooth; very hard material

equilibration: a systematic process of selective grinding of the teeth in order to rectify harmful dysfunction

excision: surgical removal of bone or other tissue

facial: see "buccal;" also known as "labial"

filling: the restoration of a tooth once all decay has been removed and the tooth has been primed for adherance to a new material

fixed partial denture: a permanent prosthetic replacement of one or more teeth

foramen: natural opening into or through bone

furcation: part of a bicuspid or molar where the roots diverge

gingiva: aka gums; the soft tissue of the oral cavity

graft: replacement of human tissue, either with tissue from another part of the patient's mouth or with man-made materials

immediate denture: a full denture which is delivered as soon as the remaining teeth on the arch have been extracted

impacted tooth: a tooth that is obstructed from normal eruption

implant: material inserted or grafted into tissue

incisor: a tooth for cutting or gnawing; located in the front of the mouth in both jaws

indirect: pertaining to a procedure, such as an inlay or prosthetic, which is manufactured apart from chairside dental treatment and later inserted orally

inlay: a dental restoration similar to a filling but fabricated indirectly

interproximal: between adjacent teeth

keratin: the protein found in hair, skin, nails (cuticular parts of the body)

labial: pertaining to or around the lip; see "facial"

lesion: an injury or wound; diseased tissue

lingual: the side of the tooth which faces the tongue; the inside aspect of a tooth

malocclusion: improper alignment of biting or chewing surfaces of upper and lower teeth

mandible: the lower jaw

mandibular canal: a tube-like space in the mandible for blood and nerve circulation

maxilla: the upper jaw

mesial: nearer the middle line of the body or the surface of a tooth nearer the center of the dental arch

mixed dentition: see "transitional dentition"

molar: largest and most posterior type of tooth

mucous membrane: lining of the oral cavity as well as other canals and cavities of the body; also called "mucosa"

occlusal: description of the biting surfaces of the teeth

occlusion: contact between upper and lower teeth

odontogenic: description of tissue in which teeth grow

onlay: an indirect (lab-made) dental restoration that covers at least one cusp of the tooth

operculum: the flap of tissue over an unerupted or partially erupted tooth.

osteitis: see "dry socket"

overdenture: a denture that is supported by tooth roots rather than solely by the periodontium

palate: the separation of the mouth from the nasal cavity; both soft and hard tissue comprise the palate

palliative: a treatment that only mitigates pain but does not resolve the underlying issue

panoramic radiograph: an x-ray taken by a machine outside the oral cavity that includes all teeth and supporting structures

papoose board: a surface on which patients are immobilized for dental treatment;

a behavior management technique sometimes used with children and with special needs adults

parafunctional: Other than normal function or use

partial denture: see "removable partial denture"; aka "RPD"

periapical radiograph: an x-ray taken with the objective of observing the entire length of the tooth

periapical: the area surrounding the end of the tooth root

periodontal: pertaining to the supporting and surrounding tissues of the teeth

periodontium: the system of supporting structures of the teeth--bone, cementum, periodontal ligament, gingiva

plaque: a soft, sticky substance that accumulates on teeth composed largely of bacteria and bacterial derivatives

pontic: the term used for an artificial tooth on a fixed partial denture (bridge)

posterior: teeth and tissues in the back of the oral cavity

premedication: administration of medicine prior to a procedure

preventive dentistry: the promotion of oral health, wise food choices, and effective hygiene of the mouth so that unnecessary pain and dental disease may be avoided

primary dentition: the first set of teeth; see deciduous and dentition

prophylaxis: in dentistry, the cleaning of the teeth; sometimes includes deep cleaning procedures like scaling and root planing

pulp: the tissue within the root canal; usually composed of blood and nerve tissue

pulpitis: inflammation of the dental pulp

radiograph: an image or picture produced on a radiation-sensitive film, phosphorous plate, emulsion, or digital sensor by exposure to ionizing radiation

removable partial denture: aka partial; a prosthetic replacement of one or more missing teeth; unlike crowns and bridges, partials can be removed by the patient for cleaning and rest

root canal: the tube-like inner portion of the tooth which contains the dental pulp (aka the "nerve")

root canal therapy: removal of organic pulp material from the root canal and replacement with inert material; root canal therapy is usually provided as the treatment for apical/pulp infection or abscess

root: the portion of the tooth that is typically embedded within the maxillary or mandibular bone

rubber dam: a stretchy material used to isolate a tooth for easier access by the practitioner

scaling: removal of plaque, calculus, and stain from teeth

sealant: a thin coating of material that is bonded onto molars to prevent decay

stomatitis: inflammation of the mouth

succedaneous tooth: the permanent tooth which erupts (usually) after a primary tooth exfoliates

supernumerary teeth: a condition when more teeth than the usual complement erupt into the arch

temporomandibular joint (TMJ): the joint between the maxilla and mandible

veneer: aka laminate veneer; a thin covering of the facial surface of a tooth usually constructed of tooth-colored material used to restore discolored, damaged, misshapen or misaligned teeth

xerostomia: aka dry mouth; the condition of having too little saliva in the mouth

Adapted from the ADA's Glossary of Clinical Terms

PART 1

THE PRE-DENT JOURNEY

"

Education is the most powerful weapon which you can use to change the world.

— Nelson Mandela

CHAPTER 1

THE LANDSCAPE OF DENTAL EDUCATION AND DENTISTRY: WHY DENTAL SCHOOL?

Dentistry is rewarding, respected, and fascinating. Skills like team building and teamwork gained in dental school aid in providing the skills to build a private practice with the staff members who make up your team. Dentistry is a career choice with a significant initial investment and numerous positive future rewards. The income and intellectual potential are only limited by the time invested.

Fortunately, the positive outcomes eclipse the negative. The cons include long years spent in undergraduate science classes and additional years in dental school. Dangers exist, including infections from needle pricks, scalpels, and other equipment used in practice. Other challenges to overcome include unruly patients, crying children, and difficult cases.

However, these problems can be avoided by being extra careful and understanding how to work with the diversity of patients. Despite these challenges, the effort is worth the outcome in service, lifestyle, balance, flexibility, autonomy, and opportunity.

Dental health is crucial to overall health and self-image. Interestingly, the average woman smiles 62 times a day while the average man smiles 8 times a day. It is also intriguing that a child laughs about 400 times a day.[1] Smiles are important to people. Many individuals are self-conscious just because of the shape, alignment, and color of their teeth. Choosing to join the noble profession of dentistry is a guaranteed means to help people to smile and laugh while at the same time offering a rewarding experience and career.

IS DENTAL SCHOOL THE RIGHT CHOICE?

Have you ever had a terrible toothache? Or perhaps, have you broken a tooth by biting on a nut? If you have, then you are not alone. Many people have experienced either gum pain, a chipped tooth, or the inability to bite down. The excruciating pain can be debilitating. If you have not yet had one of these experiences, rest assured, a dentist's magic is enough to provide relief.

However, at this juncture, the question remains whether or not dental school is the right choice. Much needs to be done before you can help others, serve the community, and provide relief from toothaches. Dental school is between you and your future. If you love the sciences, problem-solving, and are also willing to put in the many extra years of education, you may consider becoming a dentist.

No doubt, you will have to work hard, study incessantly at times, and prepare for exams, including the DAT. You will need to submit applications and go through the application process, including essays and interviews. However, if this is your passion, pursue the journey with all of your heart.

FORECAST FOR CAREERS IN DENTISTRY

Your future career in dentistry is rock solid if you dedicate yourself to your craft and build your practice. There will always be a need. Use creative marketing and networking skills to let people know you are available. Many people never go to a dentist, forget to go, do not have insurance, or forego their dental needs. Millions of people need a dentist and do not see one. Thus, numerous people have put off seeing a dentist and are merely waiting to find someone they trust.

If you are determined, dedicated, and talented, you should have no problem. Besides, at this moment, you are reading this book because you are considering this future. Maybe you have gone through an episode of severe pain or appreciated the work of your orthodontist. Perhaps you dreamed of helping out the tooth fairy

---

1   Children's Dental Village, "Interesting Facts about Teeth and Dentistry," *Children's Dental Village*, n.d., https://www.childrensdentalvillage.net/patient/resources/interesting-facts

or being a toothache savior. Whatever your reasons, dentistry is a bright career with numerous opportunities. You are in the right place to find out more about this aspiration.

WHAT DO DENTISTS DO?

Dental care dates back about 25,000 years. Evidence exists from thousands of years ago that 'specialists' aided others who suffered from tooth problems. By 1700, dentistry became a profession unto itself.[2] Dentistry established a strong foothold in healthcare since 1867 when Harvard University Dental School was established.[3]

Dentistry offers numerous avenues, rewards, and hurdles at the same time.[4] Dentists remain on the front lines of the healthcare profession while also being involved in disease prevention, medical intervention, and health promotion.

Dentistry is a highly reputable profession with continuing academic opportunities. Lifelong education continues to be essential with changes in technology, materials, resources, and techniques. Dentists offer dental checkups of the oral cavity and advice on oral health information in general. They perform essential treatments, including filling a tooth, minor surgical procedures, cleaning and polishing teeth, and tooth extraction.[5]

AREAS OF SPECIALIZATION OPTIONS

Endodontics – The word, endodontics, comes from the Greek word 'endo', meaning inside, and 'dontics', meaning tooth. Endodontics is the examination and treatment of internal tissues or 'pulp' of the tooth. Endodontists perform root canals and related surgical procedures as well as the assessment and care of the inner tooth.[6]

Orthodontics – An orthodontist is involved in the straightening and alignment of the teeth and jaw. They fit, align, and tighten braces and treat disorders

---

2   American Dental Education Association, "History of Dentistry," *American Dental Education Association*, n.d., https://www.adea.org/GoDental/Health_Professions_Advisors/History_of_Dentistry.aspx

3   Alyssa Walker, "Six Reasons to Become a Dentist," *Keystone Healthcare Studies,* March 6, 2019, https://www.healthcarestudies.com/article/six-reasons-to-become-a-dentist/

4   Lake Erie College of Osteopathic Medicine, "Why Choose a Career in Dental Medicine," *Lake Erie College of Osteopathic Medicine,* March 16, 2021, https://lecom.edu/dental/dental-career/

5   Your Free Career Test, "What Does a Dentist Do?," *Your Free Career Test,* n.d., https://www.yourfreecareertest.com/dentist/

6   American Dental Association, "Endodontics," *Mouth Healthy,* n.d., https://www.mouthhealthy.org/en/az-topics/e/endodontics

involving misaligned teeth. They will also deal with problems of the bones in and around the mouth area. They correct misaligned bite patterns and can also focus on modifying facial growth, known as dentofacial orthopedics.[7]

Periodontics - Periodontists are involved in treating gingival diseases and ailments. They assess and manage inflammatory diseases of the gums, cementum, periodontal membranes, and alveolar membrane.[8]

Prosthodontics - Prosthodontists consider various cosmetic dentistry options, including braces, artificial teeth, and tooth removal. They fit implants to replace removed teeth and make artificial replacements for missing parts of the mouth and jaw.[9]

Pediatric Dentists - Pediatric dentists serve the dental needs of children. Like adults, children need consistent dental care and education on better oral health, prevent gingivitis, and care for problems related to the teeth, gums, and mouth. Pediatric dentists help prevent dental disease in children from birth to adolescence.[10] Their work involves researching, teaching, and applying therapeutic and oral health care for children and adolescents.[11]

REQUIREMENTS TO BECOME A GOOD DENTIST

Before enumerating the compelling reasons to pursue dentistry, it is essential to have insight into the necessary qualities and personality traits. To be an outstanding dentist, an individual should possess or develop the following ten characteristics.[12]

- Empathy - caring and considerate of how others feel
- Personable - amiable and able to be in close personal contact with people
- Unambiguous – ability to make explicit decisions
- Communication – open conversations without shying away from difficult discussions

7   Yvette Brazier, "How Can Orthodontic Treatment Help?," *Medical News Today*, May 24, 2018, https://www.medicalnewstoday.com/articles/249482

8   American Dental Association, "Periodontics," *Mouth Healthy*, n.d., https://www.mouthhealthy.org/en/az-topics/p/periodoncia

9   WebMD, "What is a Prosthodontist?," *WebMD*, n.d., https://www.webmd.com/a-to-z-guides/what-is-a-prosthodontist

10   CareerExplorer, "What Does a Dentist Do?," *CareerExplorer*, n.d., https://www.careerexplorer.com/careers/dentist/

11   Health Education and Improvement Wales (HEIW), "Paediatric Dentistry," *Health Education and Improvement Wales (HEIW)*, n.d., https://heiw.nhs.wales/education-and-training/dental/training-programmes/specialty-training-in-dentistry/paediatric-dentistry/

12   Kaplan Test Prep, "Is Dental School Right for You?," *Kaplan Test Prep*, December 15, 2020, https://www.kaptest.com/study/dat/is-dental-school-right-for-you/

- Problem solver – the capability to creatively think through new situations and quickly find solutions
- Passion – curiosity, fascination, and intellectualism for the field of dentistry
- Servant Leader - transforming the lives of people in need[13]
- Perceptive – being able to sense how people feel when they do not express their feelings
- Visually Attuned – able to understand and execute patient's aesthetic needs
- Self-Starter – showing the enterprise to initiate, facilitate, and manage operations

Aspiring dentists should not be worried if they do not have all of these qualities at the onset. Some attributes are learned, and others are intuitively discovered. However, a few of these traits are essential to start. As a prospective dental student, capabilities and commitments become more critical. However, on a closer look, most of these qualities are also valuable for those who desire to become physicians, pharmacists, nurses, or most other healthcare practitioners.

Dentistry is not your only option. However, if you are passionate about this work, the profession is rewarding. On the other hand, if you are interested in medicine, in general, you have choices. The exact reason you may choose dental school may be different than someone else. This book presents the what, where, why, and how.

---

13 American Dental Education Association, "Why Be a Dentist?," *American Dental Education Association*, n.d., https://www.adea.org/godental/dentistry_101/why_be_a_dentist_.aspx

*Use the talents
you possess, for
the woods would
be very silent if
no birds sang
except the best.*

– Henry Van Dyke

CHAPTER 2

INTELLECTUAL AND BEHAVIORAL COMPETENCIES

Before you begin the active phase of your clinical career, your educational experiences lay a foundation for your future. Consider what you would want to see in a dentist. How do you envision a clean, safe, and friendly office? Great dentists get to know you, listen to your concerns, and consider your needs while taking the time to explain both preventative care and potential problems. They respect your time, money, and situation while also following up and valuing your long-term relationship.

Success as a dentist is different from success in dental school. A person who masters biomedical education and quantitative analysis is not necessarily the best individual to support your practical needs. Intellectual and behavioral competencies in both are necessary to complete dental school and have a successful dental practice.

Dental school coursework is complex and often more demanding than the most strenuous undergraduate classes. The comprehensive and detailed nature of the dental school curriculum sharpens the student and prepares them to address stressful clinical experiences in a broad context. It's never just a tooth; dental tissues are inexorably connected to the rest of the human body. As such, every dental procedure must be performed to the best of the clinician's ability.

COMPETENCIES FOR SUCCESS IN DENTAL SCHOOL

Intellectual/Academic Competencies	Behavioral Competencies
Biomedical Foundation	Self-Awareness
Information Assimilation	Respect
Planning	Persistence
Visualization	Commitment
Quantitative/Qualitative Data Analysis	Self-forgiveness/ability to move past mistakes
Research/Assessment	Affability
Problem Solving	Easy Going Nature
Critical Thinking	Balance
Active Participation	Altruism
Multicultural Awareness	Empathy
Prioritization	Trust and Honesty
Collaboration	Focus and Attention
Support	Compassion
Organization	Resilience
Punctuality	Reliability
Openness to new people	Determination
Leadership	Social Accountability

Embrace technology while also recognizing and compensating for its limitations. Digital planners may be helpful, but you might find that the paper versions of the Franklin Planner, Planner Pad, Blue Sky, Erin Condren, or Panda Planner are equally useful for managing lists, reminders, and appointments. Online calendars and reminders are essential. However, the drawback of various systems is that there is little room for notes.

COMPETENCIES FOR SUCCESS AS A DENTIST

Comprehensive Knowledge of Oral Healthcare

Assessment, Image Analysis, Diagnosis, Treatment

Technical Psychomotor Skills

Patient-Centered Professionalism

Ability to Successfully Perform in Emergency Situations

Understand Mental and Physical Limitations

Interpersonal Skills with Diverse Populations

Listening, Informing, and Expression in Difficult Situations

Ethical and Moral Behavior

Know the Limits to Professional Expertise

Referring Patients to Appropriate Specialists

Recordkeeping, Organization, and Financial Management

Quality Assurance and Risk Assessment

Compliance and Legal Obligations (OSHA, HIPAA, HR)

Commitment to Lifelong Learning

Adapting to New Technologies and Continuous Improvement

Professional Obligation to Staff, Profession, and Community

Competencies are not limited to dental expertise. Knowledge of the laws and responsibilities is essential. Dental students will learn the provisions of HIPAA (Health Insurance Portability and Accountability Act). This bill, signed into law on August 21, 1996, was written to protect patients from disclosing personally identifiable information. In modernizing healthcare information flow - presentation, documentation, sharing, and distribution – protection mechanisms are put in place to secure patient information from access, fraud, theft, and abuse. A code of ethics and responsibilties binds dentists, and they must put the needs of their patients ahead of their own.

The American Dental Association published the "Principles of Ethics & Code of Professional Conduct," revised November 2020, which provides a guide to the ADA rules for ethical behavior and practices.[1] The Commission on Dental Accreditation (CODA), established in 1975, is the agency that oversees post-secondary dental education. CODA provides additional competencies students must achieve through their study of dentistry.

---

1   American Dental Association, "Principles of Ethics & Code of Professional Conduct," *American Dental Association*, November 2020, https://www.ada.org/~/media/ADA/Member%20Center/Ethics/ADA_Code_Of_Ethics_November_2020.pdf?la=en

> *It does not matter how matter how slowly you go as long as you do not stop.*

– Confucius

CHAPTER 3

UNDERGRADUATE JOURNEY AND PREPARATION

Academic focus, passionate pursuit, and career vision are the mainstays of dental school. The process of planning, applying, and completing dental school is not easy and requires a full dose of dedication. Yet, each step leads to the next. Persistence is one of the most critical elements in completing the hardest of classes with your sanity. Working in a dental clinic is helpful to put on your resume, but the experience is even more valuable for you to clarify in your mind where you are headed and why.

You are on a journey. The destination is just ahead, past the hurdles and roadblocks – financial, academic, social, experiential, and the admissions process. Your life encompasses a bit of purpose and a bit of mystery. The sleepless nights are just as monumental as you take strides toward your goal. The professors you endure in subjects you do not enjoy are as indelible as the dreams you have for your future.

Your journey has a story. That story should be part of your personal statement, complete with the triumphs and pitfalls. Each anecdote is an intriguing problem you resolved, the serendipity that led to your research, and the intentional act of unsuccessfully applying to fifty internships until the last attempt. You do not need to use the word 'persistence' in your story when you can demonstrate its existence in your narrative.

Stress, anxiety, and overwhelm can be debilitating to a dental school student. With the enormous amount of material to cover, if you are concerned about being engulfed with subject matter you do not know, buy the books ahead of time. Dedicate time to learning the details before you begin your classes. Some students suffer from the elusive 'Imposter Syndrome'. They feel unsure if they are good enough or if the shortcuts they took will be 'discovered'.

Prioritization is a crucial element in the pursuit of dental education. Ask yourself, "What is most important today, and how can I squeeze in sports, clubs, service, or spiritual activities that will maintain my sanity and close relationships?"

While some people describe this as balance, compromise, or sacrifice, it is useful to think of your relationships as supportive or helpful for your education, commitment, and attitude. One can aid the other rather than consider the process a zero-sum concession. You are more humane and more compassionate because you care, laugh, and engage in new experiences. However, you must not lose track of time. Assignments still need to be a high priority. Your work as a dentist will demand focus, attention, and time consciousness.

Always be mindful of your mental and physical health. Students are often so engrossed in their studies that they miss or ignore signs of exhaustion, anxiety, ulcers, or weight fluctuations. Ironically, a dentist is trained to be cognizant of others' mental health challenges while often missing their own as a student. Within that realm of physical awareness, proper nutrition and water consumption are equally important. What goes into your body impacts your mental and physical health. You may consume a dozen energy drinks a week or a pot of coffee a day, but there are long-term effects.

Frequently, a balanced diet is not available or not quickly attainable during very long study sessions when only junk food is offered in vending machines. This note of caution may seem blatantly obvious to students on the road to dental school. However, after four hours of study, some students will not take an hour to go to a store or restaurant, cook or eat a meal, and then return to studying. As much human science as students know, pizza delivery or chips from a machine may seem most sensible, when a refrigerator with fruit and salad fixings might be more prudent.

Patience is a skill to be practiced and appreciated. In a hectic life, where every moment seems to count, patiently waiting for a book, elevator, or even a website to load is not as easy as it sounds. As a dentist, you will need to be patient with those who come for your services, but equally important is to be patient with yourself. A certain amount of emotional intelligence is required to process complex situations while also managing your own emotions.

Many people or stressors can complicate a given day. Instructors may criticize while patients complain or dental materials fail and create anxiety. The dental student must digest feedback humbly without losing confidence.

Competencies that are often under-acknowledged are trust, loyalty, and honesty, first within the dental school community and later in your career. These go hand-in-hand with respect. By being honest, demonstrating transparency, and building trust, a root canal, bridge, or referral to an oral surgeon or orthodontist will be appreciated rather than questioned. Showing that you care, listening attentively, and modulating between very different personalities in a family can make all the difference. At this point, academic knowledge takes a backseat to interpersonal relationship building.

Being proactive rather than reactive is essential. If you have assignments that you know must be done, you are better off finishing them ahead of time – well ahead of time. There is an adage, which fits well here.

"There's no time like the present."

Finishing a paper, online quiz, or research project in the present moment relieves stress. First, there is one less thing to remember. Second, less brain space is required trying to remember the task. Third, you can proceed to other projects with less mental burden. Fourth, something may come up at the last minute. Thus, why worry when you can finish what you need to accomplish? Some people are procrastinators and have numerous justifications for delaying projects until the last minute. After all, it worked the last few times, so it should work this time too. However, emergencies can occur at the last minute, and getting caught off-guard with a professor who is unwilling to give an extension can be detrimental. You would not want your patients to see you only for emergencies and not have routine checkups to prevent a problem. Walk-the-walk means that you, too, should be proactive with your assignments.

Finally, be observant and avoid pitfalls. Be keenly aware of challenges and opportunities from those around you. You can learn from other people's mistakes and take advantage of academic and clinical opportunities. Shadowing dentists is one of the best ways to learn. See what works best and what does not. Rather than doing your work by trial and error, learn from your classmates who have diverse backgrounds and experiences. Learn from dentists who have been in practice for decades. Attend school and gain experiences without regret.

"

To accomplish
great things, we
must not only
act, but also
dream; not only
plan, but also
believe.

—Anatole France

CHAPTER 4
PLANNING CALENDAR – THE ADMISSIONS CYCLE

APPLICATION CALENDAR - MAY THROUGH FEBRUARY

The 2020-2021 and 2021-2022 dental school admission cycles were novel due to the pandemic. A good strategy is to apply early for 2022 and 2023 to help counter delays caused by closed test centers, rescheduled DAT tests, and revised admission requirements. Pre-dental shadowing experiences are severely impacted for all applicants.

The pandemic resulted in unprecedented hurdles for dental school admissions that will probably redefine the admission process for many years.

DENTAL SCHOOL ADMISSION PROCESS

Studying dentistry in the United States is very attractive, with nine universities ranking among the top 25 dental schools in the world. U.S. dental schools offer a 4-year Doctor of Dental Surgery (DDS) or Doctor of Medicine in Dentistry (DMD) degree.[1]

The primary application method in the U.S. is through the American Dental Education Association's Associated American Dental Schools

---

1   Komal Yadav, "Dentistry in USA: Top Colleges, Cost, Eligibility, Scholarships, Scope," *Collegedunia*, March 18, 2021, https://collegedunia.com/usa/article/dentistry-in-the-us-why-us-deadlines-application-process-and-cost

Application Service (ADEA AADSAS). Exceptions to the AADSAS dental school application process include foreign-trained dentists and Texas residents. The former apply through the American Dental Education Association Centralized Application for Advanced Placement for International Dentists (ADEA CAAPID). The latter apply through the Texas Medical & Dental Schools Application Service (TMDSAS).

These services allow students to submit standardized applications to their preferred dental school choices by collecting, collating, and distributing submitted credentials, including grade point average (GPA), Dental Admission Test (DAT) results, letters of recommendation, essays, personal/demographic data, and experiences.[2]

UNDERGRADUATE COURSEWORK

While the prerequisites for dental school admissions vary, the general requirements for undergraduate coursework include one year of each of the following:[3]

- Biology with Lab
- Physics
- English
- General Chemistry with Lab
- Organic Chemistry with Lab

Modifications brought about by the pandemic, such as online learning, have affected students' curriculum and performance in some of these required courses. Studies have shown that online learning has many challenges both for learners and faculty. These challenges could be technological, social, or motivational.[4] As a result of social distancing regulations, most students could not perform in-person laboratory experiments. Instead, many schools transitioned to virtual reality demonstrations, videos, and previously formulated datasheets.[5] These changes resulted in some schools altering their grading system from letter grades to pass/

---

2   South Eastern Louisiana University, "Time Line for Dental School," *South Eastern Louisiana University*, n.d., http://www2.southeastern.edu/orgs/DOA/Dline.html

3   American Dental Association, "Career Resources," *Mouth Healthy brought to you by the American Dental Association*, n.d., https://www.mouthhealthy.org/en/resources/lesson-plans/career-resources

4   Papia Bawa, "Retention in Online Courses: Exploring Issues and Solutions – A Literature Review," Sage Open 6, no. 1 (2016), https://doi.org/10.1177/2158244015621777

5   P. Klein, L. Ivanjek, M.N. Dahlkemper, K. Jeličić, M.-A. Geyer, S. Küchemann, and A. Susac, "Studying Physics During the COVID-19 Pandemic: Student Assessments of Learning Achievement, Perceived Effectiveness of Online Recitations, and Online Laboratories," *Physical Review Physics Education Research 17*, no. 1 (2021), https://doi.org/10.1103/PhysRevPhysEducRes.17.010117

fail.[6]

PRE-DENTAL ACADEMIC REQUIREMENTS ADJUSTED

Some dental schools agreed to temporarily accept pass/fail grades and online courses taken during the pandemic, including, but not limited to:

- School of Dentistry, University of California, San Francisco
- School of Dentistry, University of California, Los Angeles
- Western University Of Health Sciences College Of Dental Medicine
- Southern Illinois University School of Dental Medicine
- University of Kentucky College of Dentistry
- A.T. Still University Arizona School of Dentistry and Oral Health.[7]

DENTAL ADMISSION TEST (TYPICALLY TAKEN FROM THE PREVIOUS JULY TO AUGUST OF THE APPLICATION CYCLE)

As part of dental school admission requirements, prospective dental students take the Dental Admission Test (DAT). The DAT evaluates the applicant's understanding of science, perceptual ability, and academic aptitude. With six subjects and a standard scale of 1-30, the average score is about 17, and a score of 20-22 is preferable for admissions in most schools.[8]

Each year, over 8,000 applicants take the computer-based, multiple-choice DAT at Thomson/Prometric testing center in the United States.[9] Safety measures were put in place at Prometric test centers in response to the COVID-19 pandemic. Some test centers closed, while others operated at a limited capacity.[10] In anticipation of new COVID-19 restrictions, DAT test takers were urged to schedule their tests as early as possible and keep abreast of the latest developments by double-checking the site. This proactive approach attempted to mitigate situations caused by canceled or rescheduled appointments.

---

6   Robert Farrington, "Colleges Go To Pass-Fail Due to Coronavirus Concerns: What Does This Mean for Students," *Forbes*, December 15, 2020, https://www.forbes.com/sites/robertfarrington/2020/03/30/colleges-go-to-pass-fail-due-to-coronavirus-concerns-what-does-this-mean-for-students/?sh=3d3813a77eaa

7   American Dental Education Association, "COVID-19 Application Updates by Dental School," *American Dental Education Association*, n.d., https://www.adea.org/GoDental/AADSAS-Update/

8   Tests.com, "The DAT Test Guide," *Tests.com*, n.d., https://www.tests.com/DAT-Testing

9   Psychometric Success, "Dental Admission Test (DAT)," *Psychometric Success*, n.d., https://psychometric-success.com/university-graduate-admissions/dat

10   Prometric, "Corona Virus Update," *Prometric*, n.d., https://www.prometric.com/covid-19-update/corona-virus-update

INTERVIEWS

Personal interviews remained part of the admissions process for the 2020-2021 admissions cycle and will continue for 2022 and 2023. Many schools offered virtual interviews due to COVID-19, although in-person interviews will likely resume for 2022-2023 and beyond. On-campus interviews allow admissions staff and faculty to get to know students while students also had the opportunity to learn more about the campus environment, academic atmosphere, and student life.

Virtual interviews limited the spread of the virus, accounting for social distancing and travel restrictions. While some schools continued in-person interviews, video conferencing offered a reasonable alternative. Those universities that held in-person interviews observed safety protocols, including face masks, hand sanitizers, and social distancing.

CLINICAL EXPERIENCES

Shadowing opportunities, typically expected, were not required for the 2020-2021 cycle. Though many dental offices were closed in 2020, for 2021-2022 and beyond, shadowing experiences will be highly recommended, even if the hours are virtual.

OTHER REQUIREMENTS

Applicants to dental schools are required to provide a maximum of four letters of recommendation or evaluation. Letter types include individual letters, committee letters, and composite letters. For the individual letters, schools usually require one or two letters from an applicant's science professor, one from a dentist you shadowed, and one from an advisor.[11]

This requirement remains unaffected by the pandemic.

---

11   American Dental Education Association, "Letters of Evaluation," *American Dental Education Association*, n.d., https://www.adea.org/GoDental/Application_Prep/The_Admissions_Process/Letters_of_evaluation.aspx

"

To learn something new, you need to try new things and not be afraid to be wrong.

— Roy T. Bennett

CHAPTER 5
CONSIDERING A GAP YEAR

GAP YEAR AND THE PANDEMIC

The 2020-2021 pandemic provided significant challenges to dental school applicants whose education was complicated by the change in learning environments, pass-fail grading, and laboratory courses that discontinued traditional, syllabus-described outcomes. As a result, many research projects and volunteer opportunities were curtailed, though some students recalibrated by devising innovative ways to support the underserved in their communities.

With the adjustment to online learning and the use of Zoom, which was unfamiliar to most faculty at the beginning, students and faculty were concerned about the depth of learning in academic courses. This situation was true, especially with science courses with labs (e.g., biology, chemistry, organic chemistry, and physics), raising dental schools' concerns about preparedness. As a result, some students needed to retake these courses.

Many students were unable to take the DAT. The American Dental Association canceled tests numerous times as students scrambled to find new sites. This scenario amounted to students spinning in a frustrating runaround of register-study-cancel-re-register and repeat. For students who took the DAT and plan to take a gap year, schools will accept test scores taken within two to three years. Check the school to see their requirements.

Alternative testing options were made available in 2021, which improved this predicament. However, many students earned low scores during the pandemic given their frustration, canceled tests, and need to retake the exam. While there is a stigma associated with students who retake the exams, you should retake the test if your score is low. An uncompetitive score is likely to eliminate your chances, and the show of improvement shines a positive light on your capabilities and potential to bounce back.

Shadowing and other clinical experiences were unavailable, and virtual platforms lacked the veracity for HIPAA requirements. With quarantines, COVID-19 concerns, and risks to students, patients, and local residents, most specialized study abroad and overseas medical mission trips were canceled. Students constructed alternative plans of action to complete courses, gain experiences, devise research projects, and support the healthcare needs of their community. Some decided to attend graduate school as a gap year option to gain a stronger foundation and await opportunities that had previously been unavailable.

GAP YEAR PLAN

Applying to dental school during a busy junior and senior year is incredibly challenging. Thus, taking a gap year to work at a dental practice is helpful for students to finish college, prepare for tests, and apply to school while also gaining skills and experiences. This period between undergraduate and dental education can also assist in improving foundational skills and prepare for the DAT exam. In addition, some students choose to work for a year in the healthcare profession to earn money and immerse themselves in the field. Most students, particularly during the pandemic, used their gap year to strengthen their application.

Whether you work on your personal and mental health, conduct research, serve your community, or take additional classes, use this opportunity to become more focused, aware, and prepared. If you work with a mentor closely, they may be willing to write one of your letters of recommendation. Continue to communicate with your former professors, lab supervisors, and volunteer coordinators who you may ask to write a recommendation. Keep them informed about your current pursuits and that you would like to receive a recommendation from them later.

While you are pursuing your gap year, take the time to volunteer and shadow dentists. A year away from the classroom may be necessary, but it is also an excellent opportunity to take advantage of new experiences that deepen your understanding of dentistry. Non-dental healthcare experiences, scribing, and hospital work are also valuable along your journey to dental school. A paid position in the dental field would also provide you with a broader understanding of the field.

Certifications can also be a valuable pursuit. Options include CPR certification, Basic Life Support, First Aid, Emergency Medical Technician, and phlebotomy. To gain national certification as a phlebotomist, you need to complete a training program and take the Certified Phlebotomy Technician Certification Exam.

Another option is to build your language and cultural skills by traveling abroad. Options like Dentists without Borders and For World Wide Smiles are excellent options. Read about Dr. Sherwin Shinn for an inspiring story about the importance of global service opportunities in dentistry. Dr. Shinn commented, "When you work for money, you can have all the things money can buy. When you give unconditionally, you get to have all the things money can't buy!' Having a good measure of both experiences is what brings broad and lasting fulfillment to Life."[1]

POST-BACCALAUREATE PROGRAMS

Two predominant types of post-baccalaureate programs serve as intermediaries between undergraduate degree programs and dental school, including a one-year post-bacc foundation-strengthening program. Often, these programs include a component whereby applicants prepare throughout the year for the DAT and retake the exam if they have taken it before. The other is a master's program in a scientific area like public health, healthcare administration, human physiology, molecular genetics, or biochemistry. These are typically one to two years and can be completed with or without a thesis and research project.

In both cases, students demonstrate continued interest in the sciences, the discipline to continue learning, and a stronger foundation to build upon for dental schools. Needless to say, high grades in either of these types of programs is essential to be a competitive applicant.

ADVICE FROM YOUR PRE-HEALTH ADVISOR

Pre-Health advisors' advice can be invaluable. They typically know about regional jobs, internships, scholarships, honors programs, college activities, leadership development, service organizations, shadowing opportunities, and

---

1   Aseptico, "Dentistry Without Borders: An Interview with Dr. Shinn," Aseptico, April 2, 2014, *https://aseptico.com/dentistry-without-borders-an-interview-with-dr-shinn/*

professors looking for students to assist with research. They can also provide advice on courses, professors, sum, and gap year options.

While a gap year may seem like a waste of time or a delay in your long-term plan to attend dental school and become a dentist, this is an excellent opportunity to regroup and gain a much-needed break from intense studying. Unsurprisingly, taking a gap year was more common during the pandemic, given the multitude of roadblocks. However, with a renewed spirit and healthcare experiences, data show that students who begin dental school a year later are more excited to get back to work and eager to learn.

> *Student, you do not study to pass the test. You study to prepare for the day when you are the only thing between a patient and the grave.*

— *Mark Reid*

CHAPTER 6

LOOKING AHEAD: DAT, LETTERS OF REC, ESSAYS

From the moment you know that you plan to pursue dentistry, you should set up a plan. Preparation is essential so that you do not miss required or desirable courses, activities, or considerations along the way. Think about what is required around the corner before you get there. At some point, you will apply. To do so, you will need to:

1. Meet with your pre-health advisor

2. Map out your academic curriculum so that you complete the required courses

3. Get involved on campus – leadership, ambassador, social, academic, science, spiritual, athletic, art, music, theater, etc.

4. Gain language skills and basic health certifications (CPR, AED, BLS, EMT, Phlebotomy, etc.)

5. Plan your volunteer work, tutoring, shadowing, clinical experiences, scribe position

6. Consider summer and school-year research opportunities

7. Consider study abroad, dental support abroad, or work in a dental clinic in an underserved area

8. Prepare and take the Dental Admissions Test (DAT)

9. Request transcripts to be sent from each school

10. Determine the people who will write your letters of recommendation

11. Consider the schools to which you want to apply and determine

their requirements

12. Write your personal statement
13. Prepare your application

COURSE PREPARATION AND GRADES

You will need high grades. Some of your classes will be exceptionally difficult. Most colleges have free tutors. Seek them out even if you are not terribly behind. They may know better ways to study for classes or prepare for specific professors' tests. Tutors can be invaluable to help you get unstuck from a problem or clarify a concept that could take you hours to figure out.

Your GPA is possibly the single best predictor of success in dental school. Focus on being organized and efficient. One technique that helps students enter a class on the first day feeling more confident and prepared is to buy textbooks and begin reading ahead of time. If the book is on an audio file, listen to the books before classes start. If you are required to memorize large volumes of information, like the nomenclature in organic chemistry, put the material on flashcards, posters, or digital files to learn ahead of time.

You can make your studying more efficient and more manageable. With a plan and determination, success will follow.

DENTAL ADMISSION TEST (DAT)

You will have a hard time mastering the material on the DAT without the knowledge of the four subject areas covered on the test: (1) natural sciences (biology – 40q, chemistry – 30q, organic chemistry – 30q), (2) perceptual ability, (3) reading comprehension, and (4) quantitative reasoning. Consider retaining your knowledge and practicing your skills in biology and chemistry by tutoring those subjects to first- and second-year students. You win because you continue to remind yourself of the material while you help other students and essentially study for the DAT.

You may want to also prepare for the DAT by obtaining a DAT study guide with practice tests from an online or on-ground bookstore. Students in the Pre-Health Advising Club may have a practice book you can use. There are also numerous private in-person and virtual test prep centers where you can practice in individual and group settings to master the topics on the exam. As of May 2021, Khan Academy did not have free DAT test prep, but there may be other free sources.

LETTERS OF RECOMMENDATION

In each class you take, you want to think, "Could this professor be one of my recommenders?" Of course, this is not why you should be punctual, responsible, and attentive in class, but literally, any of your professors could be a recommender. This means that you need to show up prepared and ready to be engaged in discussions in every class. You always need to finish your homework and, if you are stuck, you need to get help so that you can follow and not get behind.

As you finish a class, consider whether that professor is a person you might ask to be a recommender. If so, remain in contact. You may ask that professor to recommend you for a leadership position, scholarship application, or some other opportunity before you apply to dental school.

PERSONAL STATEMENT AND OTHER ESSAYS

Your personal statement is an essay on your journey to dental school and how you came to the realization that this career is your future. Although there are many ways to tell your story and lots of anecdotes you can include, as you begin your pursuit of dental school, you want to consider the activities you want to have along the way. Your goal is for the admissions committee to have a robust understanding of who you are, where you came from, what is important to you, how you made your life choices, and where you envision your journey heading.

Looking ahead at what you might write, plan what you will do over the rest of your college experience so that your actions match your intention. What values do you hold? What is most meaningful to you? Since life is a matter of choices, you will need to decide what pursuits make the most sense and how you want to portray these to dental schools when you write your personal statement.

Benjamin Franklin once said,

"If you fail to plan, you are planning to fail."

Without data, you are just another person with an opinion.

– W. Edwards Deming

CHAPTER 7

SHOW ME THE DATA!

D ata is often helpful in boiling down some of your most pressing questions into succinct answers.

Dental Schools

- 68 accredited U.S. dental schools
- 10 accredited Canadian dental schools
- 1 or 2 new dental schools expected to open in July/August 2021
- High demand for dental school faculty – Consider teaching at a dental school
- 708 graduates of international dental schools were admitted to U.S. dental schools w/advanced standing in 2019-2020
- 627 graduates of international dental schools were admitted to U.S. dental schools w/advanced standing in 2018-2019

Dental Applicants and Students

- 2020 – 10,965 students applied; 6,257 first-time, first-year students enrolled
- 2018 – 11,298 students applied; 6,163 first-time, first-year students enrolled
- 2018 – average student applied to 10 dental schools
- 2019-2020 – 25,807 total dental students enrolled (51.6% female)
- 2018-2019 – 25,381 total dental students enrolled
- GPA Average 3.58/4.0 in 2020; 3.55/4.0 in 2018 (science GPA – 3.45/4.0)
- DAT Average 28.8 in 2020; 20.5 in 2018 (First-Time, First Year)
- 58.33% Penn admits took 1-2 gap years (2018-2019)

Dental School Graduates Over Time

- 2019 – 50.6% female
- 2009 – 46.2% female
- 1999 – 35.3% female
- 1989 – 27.6% female
- 1979 – 11.7% female

Average Cost of Dental School

- 2019-2020 - $55,395 for state residents; $72,219 non-residents; $75,161 private school

Snapshot of US dental admissions stats for the class entering in Fall 2020

Total applicants: 10,965
Total enrollees: 6257

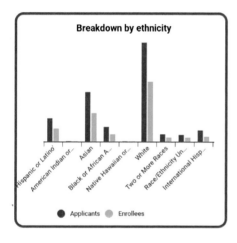

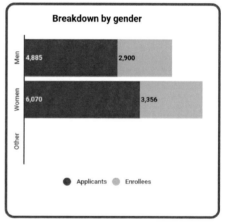

Average GPAs (once uniformly calculated)		
	Applicants	Enrollees
Science	2.54-3.95	2.77-3.95
Overall	2.89-3.98	3.04-3.98
(5th-95th percentile range)		

DAT scores			
	Academic Average	Perceptual Ability	Total science
Science	16-24	15-25	15-24
Overall	18-25	17-25	17-24
(5th-95th percentile range)			

Source: ADEA Official Guide to Dental Schools (2021-22), p 53

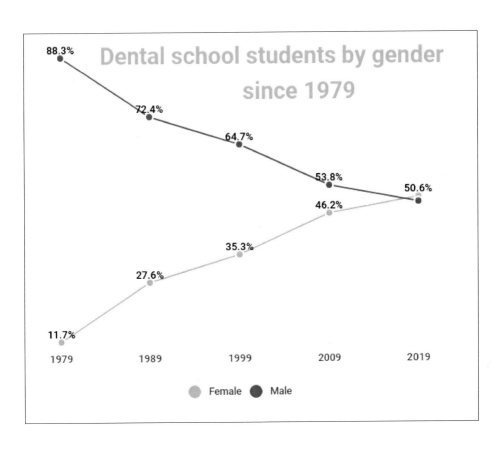

Dental school students by gender since 1979

88.3%
72.4%
64.7%
53.8%
50.6%
46.2%
35.3%
27.6%
11.7%

1979   1989   1999   2009   2019

Female   Male

Develop a passion for learning. If you do, you will never cease to grow.

–Anthony J. D'Angelo

CHAPTER 8
SPECIAL NOTE FOR INTERNATIONAL STUDENTS

INTERNATIONAL STUDENTS VS. FOREIGN-EDUCATED DENTIST

The admissions process is distinctively different for international students and for those students who completed their dental education in a foreign country.

INTERNATIONAL STUDENTS

Dental Admissions – First-Time, First-Year 2020-2021

580 International Applicants – 248 Students Enrolled in Fall 2020

Students who are not U.S. citizens or do not hold permanent residency in the U.S. are considered international students whether they earned their undergraduate degree in the U.S. or in a foreign country. All international students will require a student visa to attend dental school in the United States.

International students may apply to dental schools and study dentistry in the United States and Canada. For most dental schools, diversity is an important component of their incoming class. Being from an underrepresented minority at a particular dental school may actually give you an advantage. However, check the charts at the back of this book, which show that about a dozen of the schools do not accept international students. Also, cross-reference the results with each of the college websites to see if changes were made after May 2021.

The process to apply for dental school in the United States requires a few additional steps than a domestic application to assure schools of English competency, comply with visa requirements, and verify the ability to pay.

- Students must take the Test of English as a Foreign Language (TOEFL), the International English Language Testing System (IELTS), or another English language competency exam. English proficiency is critically important in dentistry since dentists must be able to communicate and develop a relationship with their patients.

- F-1 Visa – This is the visa required to study in the United States for high school or college (undergraduate and graduate school). You can only apply for an F-1 visa after you have been accepted to a Student Exchange and Visitor Program (SEVP) approved school. You must have your visa before you begin, but you may not travel to the U.S. until the month before you start school.

- Financial Aid is difficult to obtain for international students, though there are scholarships. International students typically need to send a verification of finances from a bank, signed by both the bank and parents. This document is proof that the student has enough funds to pay for school.

Each school has slightly different policies for international student admission. Continue your research to learn more about each college's process.

ADVANCED STANDING FOR INTERNATIONALLY TRAINED DENTISTS

Students who completed their training to become a dentist in a foreign country other than Canada, whether or not they are U.S. citizens, must apply for advanced standing in a U.S. dental school.

Dental Admissions – First-Time, First-Year 2019-2020

708 graduates of international dental schools were admitted to U.S. dental schools w/advanced standing in 2019-2020

Foreign-educated dentists who wish to practice in the U.S. must review the specific requirements for state licensure. Many states require a DDS or DMD degree from an American Dental Association (ADA) Commission on Dental Accreditation (CODA) accredited dental education program.

Internationally-trained dentists can gain the requisite skills by entering a dental program in the United States with advanced standing. This means that the training could take two additional years (occasionally three) to complete the DDS or DMD. Student applicants wanting to pursue this advanced standing option can apply through the American Dental Education Association Centralized Application for Advanced Placement for International Dentists (ADEA CAAPID).

Applicants can apply to multiple advanced standing programs simultaneously, although it is important to note that not all advanced standing programs participate in ADEA CAAPID. This streamlined process includes only one standardized application in which programs receive the same information.

ADEA CAAPID APPLICATION CYCLE:
MARCH 4, 2021 – FEBRUARY 22, 2022

Some programs take a couple dozen students who are internationally trained dentists. Boston University accepted trained dentists from 24 countries in their current DMD program. Boston University's program is two years and provides students opportunities for cancer research, community outreach programs, mentorship, and state-of-the-art patient care.

SCHOOLS PARTICIPATING IN ADEA CAAPID IN THE 2021-2022 ADMISSIONS CYCLE INCLUDE:[1]

University of Alabama at Birmingham School of Dentistry

Herman Ostrow School of Dentistry of USC

Loma Linda University School of Dentistry

University of California, Los Angeles, School of Dentistry

University of California, San Francisco School of Dentistry

University of the Pacific Arthur A. Dugoni School of Dentistry

Western University Health Sciences College of Dental Medicine

University of Colorado School of Dental Medicine

Howard University College of Dentistry

University of Florida College of Dentistry

Nova Southeastern University College of Dental Medicine

The University of Iowa College of Dentistry & Dental Clinics

Southern Illinois University School of Dental Medicine

University of Illinois at Chicago College of Dentistry

Indiana University School of Dentistry

University of Louisville School of Dentistry

Louisiana State University School of Dentistry

Boston University Henry M. Goldman School of Dental Medicine

Tufts University School of Dental Medicine

University of New England College of Dental Medicine

University of Michigan School of Dentistry

University of Minnesota School of Dentistry

University of North Carolina at Chapel Hill, Adams School of Dentistry

University of Nebraska Medical Center College of Dentistry

Rutgers, The State University of New Jersey School of Dental Medicine

University of Nevada, Las Vegas School of Dental Medicine

Columbia University College of Dental Medicine

---

1   ADEA, "ADEA CAAPID Directory," *ADEA*, 2021, https://www.adea.org/CAAPIDapp/deadlines-and-requirements.aspx

New York University College of Dentistry

University at Buffalo School of Dental Medicine

University of Oklahoma College of Dentistry

The Maurice H. Kornberg School of Dentistry Temple University – International Program

University of Pennsylvania School of Dental Medicine

University of Pittsburgh School of Dental Medicine

University of Puerto Rico School of Dental Medicine

Meharry Medical College School of Dentistry

Virginia Commonwealth University School of Dentistry

University of Washington School of Dentistry

Marquette University School of Dentistry

"
"You're braver than you believe, stronger than you seem, and smarter than you think."

– Christopher Robin

CHAPTER 9

BS/DDS – EARLY ASSURANCE DENTAL PROGRAMS

Interested in an early start? As of May 2021, 16 dental schools in the United States participate with undergraduate institutions to offer combined degree programs. Admitted students begin their college careers at an undergraduate institution that may or may not be at the same university as the cooperating dental school. Details vary in terms of assurance policies for dental admission and the ability to complete one's studies a year early. We encourage you to check institutional websites for more information.

Colleges with Combined Bachelors-Dental Degree Programs
Case Western Reserve University School of Dental Medicine
Dental College of Georgia at Augusta University
Lake Erie College of Osteopathic Medicine School of Dental Medicine
Nova Southeastern University College of Dental Medicine
NYU College of Dentistry
Rutgers, The State University of New Jersey, School of Dental Medicine
Stony Brook University School of Dental Medicine
The Maurice H. Kornberg School of Dentistry, Temple University
Tufts University School of Dental Medicine
University at Buffalo School of Dental Medicine
University of Connecticut School of Dental Medicine
University of Detroit Mercy School of Dentistry
University of Florida College of Dentistry
University of Louisville School of Dentistry
University of Pennsylvania School of Dental Medicine
Virginia Commonwealth University School of Dentistry

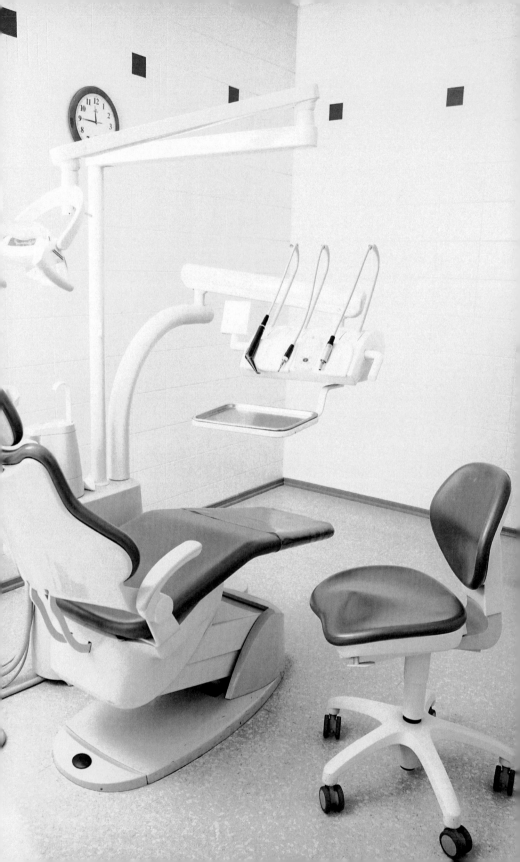

PART 2

DENTISTRY PAST AND PRESENT

"

You were designed for accomplishment, engineered for success, and endowed with the seeds of greatness.

– Zig Ziglar

CHAPTER 10
CAREER OUTLOOK AND OPTIONS

OVERVIEW

According to the Bureau of Labor Statistics, the median income for dentists in the United States in 2020 was $164,010. The growth rate of the profession is rated "average", with several thousand new dentists joining the job market each year.[1]

Training and Licensure

Dentists must graduate from an accredited school of dentistry and pass both written and clinical exams. Afterward, they must be licensed in the state where they practice dentistry. Licensure requirements vary by state.

Upon Graduation from Dental School

On the other side of dental school, there are a myriad of career pathways to choose from, including: individual practice, partnerships, group clinics, and hospitals. Options abound for the new dentist and hundreds of decisions must be made.

A few options that must be considered before graduation:

1. Will you begin practice immediately after graduation?
2. Would you prefer to gain additional expertise within a training program?
3. Do you want to practice in a specialty field?

---

1   Bureau of Labor Statistics, U.S. Department of Labor, "Occupational Outlook Handbook, Dentists," *Bureau of Labor Statistics,* Updated April 9, 2021, https://www.bls.gov/ooh/healthcare/dentists.htm

Students who are ready to begin their career as a dentist are free to apply for licensure in a state so that they can secure employment or establish a practice.

Distribution of U.S. Dental Specialists in 2021

All Other Specialists 12,157	Pediatric Dentists 6,321	Oral Surgeons 5,758
Orthodontists 8,320	Periodontists 4,400	Endodontists 4,379

Source: American Dental Association per special request from KFF.org

Beyond Formal Training: To Own or Not to Own

At some point, every dentist reckons with their capacity to own a practice. Arguably the biggest change in the business of oral care is the corporatization over the past several decades. It was once customary for new dentists to set up shop in a solo or small group practice, but 21st-century dentists increasingly find work as employees for a larger entity. Dental franchises can be spotted in most cities. Numerous private equity firms have pivoted their focus toward dental practice buyouts.

Whether during dental school itself or in the context of part-time employment afterward, the new dentist should consider "trying on" practices of multiple types. Ultimately, the decision to own one's practice is usually a function of individual preferences, the ability to lead others, and the financial ability to cover expenses.

RESIDENCES

Residencies for General Dentists

You do not have to specialize to take advantage of further training after dental school. General dentists have two options for residency experiences: Advanced Education in General Dentistry (AEGD) and General Practice Residency (GPR).

AEGDs and GPRs are popular with new dentists who can choose from almost a hundred AEGD programs and nearly 200 GPR programs.

AEGDs and GPRs are typically year-long experiences, but some run for two years. They both build on the foundational knowledge and expertise acquired in dental school. Then, what's the difference? The ADA website nicely contrasts the two, observing that the "major distinction between the AEGD and GPR programs is the emphasis that the AEGD program places jon clinical dentistry in contrast to the emphasis on medical management in the GPR program." AEGDs focus more on the practice of dentistry, from office management to techniques and materials. Meanwhile, GPR residents often treat patients whose dental care must be contextualized in light of systemic medical challenges.

According to the Commission on Dental Accreditation, 924 dentists were enrolled in 93 AEGD programs during the 2019-2020 academic year and 1237 dentists were enrolled in 177 GPR programs.

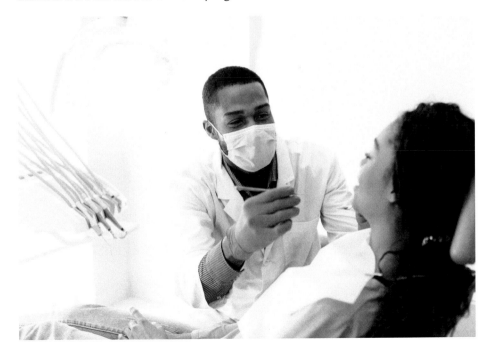

Specialty Areas of Practice

There are twelve areas of specialty which vary in numbers of practitioners, selectivity, and potential salary. Some of the most common dental specialties include:

Dental Anesthesiology (DA) – *36-month residency* – 9 CODA Accredited DA Programs

- Advocate Aurora Health - Department of Dentistry - Chicago, IL
- Jacobi Medical Center - Department of Dentistry/OMFS - Bronx, NY
- NYU Langone Hospital – Brooklyn - Division of Dental Medicine - Brooklyn NY
- St. Barnabas Hospital - Department of Dentistry - Bronx, New York
- Stony Brook University Medical Center - Division of Dental Anesthesiology - Stony Brook, NY
- The Ohio State University Medical Center - Section of Dental Anesthesiology - Columbus, OH
- University of Pittsburgh Medical Center - Department of Dental Anesthesiology Pittsburgh, PA
- University of Toronto - Faculty of Dentistry - Department of Anesthesia - Toronto, Ontario, Canada
- Wyckoff Heights Medical Center – Dental Anesthesiology Residency Program - Brooklyn, New York

Dental Public Health (DPA) – *Average 14 Months* (Varies by Program) – 15 CODA Accredited DPA Programs

- A.T. Still University - 25 months
- Boston University Goldman School of Dental Medicine – 12 months FT; 24 months for MSD; 36 months for DScD
- Case Western Reserve University – 12 months certificate; 24 months MPH
- Centers for Disease Control and Prevention – 12 months
- Columbia University College of Dental Medicine – 12 months
- Faculty of Dentistry, University of Toronto – 24 months
- Harvard School of Dental Medicine – 23 months - MMSc (3 years), DMSc (4 years)
- National Institute of Dental and Craniofacial Research – 12 months
- New York State Dental Public Health Residency Program – 12 months
- North Carolina Division of Public Health – 12 months
- Temple University, The Maurice H Kornberg School of Dentistry – 12 months

- UT Health San Antonio – 12 months MPH
- Texas A&M College of Dentistry – 12 months
- The University of Iowa College of Dentistry – 25 month MS Program
- University of California, San Francisco – 12 months MPH with UC Berkeley

Endodontics – *Average 26 Months* (Varies by Program) – 55 Accredited Programs

Oral and Maxillofacial Pathology – *Average 37 Months* (Varies by Program) - 15 Accredited Programs

- University of Florida College of Dentistry
- University of Iowa College of Dentistry
- University of Maryland School of Dentistry
- Naval Medical Leader and Professional Development Command
- Harvard University School of Dental Medicine
- University of Buffalo School of Dental Medicine
- New York-Presbyterian Queens Dental Service
- Zucker School of Medicine at Hofstra/Northwell at Long Island Jewish Medical Center
- Mount Sinai Hospital Medical Center
- New York Presbyterian Hospital
- University of North Carolina at Chapel Hill Adams School of Dentistry
- Ohio State University College of Dentistry
- University of Pittsburgh Medical Center/School of Dental Medicine
- Texas A&M University College of Dentistry
- The University of Texas School of Dentistry at Houston

Oral and Maxillofacial Radiology – *24 to 36 Months* – 9 Accredited Programs

- University of California at Los Angeles School of Dentistry
- University of Connecticut School of Dental Medicine
- University of Florida College of Dentistry
- University of Iowa College of Dentistry
- Stony Brook University Medical Center
- University of North Carolina at Chapel Hill Adams School of Dentistry
- Texas A&M University College of Dentistry
- UT Health San Antonio School of Dentistry
- University of Washington School of Dentistry

Oral and Maxillofacial Surgery – *4 to 6 years* – 101 Accredited Certificate or MD Programs

Oral Medicine - *24 to 36 Months* – 6 Accredited Programs
- University of California at San Francisco School of Dentistry
- Tufts University School of Dental Medicine
- Harvard University School of Dental Medicine
- Carolinas Medical Center-Dept. Oral Medicine
- University of Pennsylvania School of Dental Medicine
- University of Washington School of Dentistry

Orofacial Pain – *12 to 36 Months* – 12 Accredited Programs
- University of California at Los Angeles School of Dentistry
- Herman Ostrow School of Dentistry of the University of Southern California
- University of Kentucky College of Dentistry
- Naval Medical Leader and Professional Development Command
- Tufts University School of Dental Medicine
- Massachusetts General Hospital
- University of Michigan Health Systems
- University of Minnesota School of Dentistry
- Rutgers School of Dental Medicine
- University of Buffalo School of Dental Medicine
- University of Rochester Eastman Institute of Oral Health
- University of North Carolina at Chapel Hill Adams School of Dentistry

Orthodontics and Dentofacial Orthopedics - *24 to 36 Months* – 67 Accredited Programs

Periodontics – *Average 35 Months* (Varies by Program) - 57 Accredited Programs

Pediatric Dentistry - *24 to 36 Months* – 82 Accredited Programs

Prosthodontics - *Average 36 Months* (Varies by Program) - 47 Accredited Programs

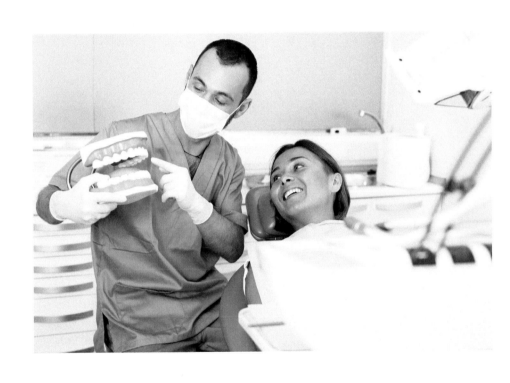

"

I do not know anyone who has gotten to the top without hard work. That is the recipe. It will not always get you to the top, but it will get you pretty near.

– *Margaret Thatcher*

CHAPTER 11

WHAT TO EXPECT IN A DENTAL CAREER

REPUTABLE PROFESSION

As a scientist, artist, and technician, dentists are highly skilled. The number of years of schooling is enough to earn a positive reputation. However, working in a community of established professionals, dentists are respected and highly reputable. Dentists charged with the duty of eliminating excruciating tooth pain and providing aesthetics to a smile is appreciated. Dentistry is among the most valued professions in the health sector. However, to build a good image, time must be invested along with education, mastery, and commitment to the community.[1]

STABILITY

Dentists will always be needed. While patients may come twice a year or just when they have a problem, there will always be a need. Now and in the future, dentists will be essential for humanity. The skill levels may even need to increase with technological changes. Will the services no longer be required? Will this profession become extinct? Dentistry ticks 'No' to these questions. The field of dentistry is stable and will continue to be in demand.

---

1   Chahita Lalchandani, "Answer to: Is Dentistry a Good Career? What are the Pros and Cons of Dentistry?," *Quora*, 2016, https://www.quora.com/Is-dentistry-a-good-career-What-are-the-pros-and-cons-of-dentistry

After all, humans will continue to have teeth that decay and a mouth that requires maintenance and care. The demand for cosmetic dentistry continues to increase as people appreciate artificial teeth. Furthermore, many seek to improve their smiles which offer career and personal advantages. Techniques in straightening teeth have also improved, and access is more widespread. Rest assured, dentistry will continue long into the future.[2]

ABILITY TO HELP PEOPLE

The joy derived from putting a smile on people's faces, restoring lost self-confidence, taking away the pain of toothaches, and helping to ensure the ability to eat are rewarding aspects of dentistry. Assisting people comes easy as dentists naturally come to the aid of people who need help. The painful part is temporary, but the long-term benefits are great. Most people are grateful either at that moment or in a few days.[3]

Dentistry is, in essence, a service-oriented profession.[4] What is also applause-worthy is that dentists help patients improve their oral health while improving their overall wellbeing. Smiling also boosts the body's immunity. Dentists will also inform you of the need to brush and floss twice a day, reduce sugar consumption, and have regular oral checkups to prevent tooth decay and gum disease. They educate patients and the general public of all ages, cultures, and lifestyles on how to take proper care of their oral health. All walks of life are served, even dogs and cats.

BALANCED LIFESTYLE

A treasured value of many people is living a balanced life. Dentistry offers a job that allows people to enjoy family, social, and intellectual life. Dentists typically choose their own opening and closing times. There is great flexibility in how to operate an individual dental practice. Services are primarily by appointment, though occasionally dentists are called for serious emergencies. Thus, dentists do not work round the clock, and few work outside of traditional office hours.

---

2   Kip Nielsen, "What You Should Know Before You Become a Dentist," *Crush the DAT*, Updated April 15, 2021, https://crushthedatexam.com/what-you-should-know-before-you-become-a-dentist/

3   Career Alley, "5 Reasons Why a Career as a Dental Hygienist Will Have You Smiling," *Career Alley*, n.d., https://careeralley.com/5-reasons-why-a-career-as-a-dental-hygienist-will-have-you-smiling/

4   The Dentists Dorridge, "So You Want to be a Dentist," *The Dentists Dorridge*, n.d., https://thedentistsdorridge.co.uk/so-you-want-to-be-a-dentist/

Additionally, compared to other professions, dentists spend less time at work. Therefore, dentistry offers a high-paying job with time to spend with family and still have time for recreational activities. This profession is the quintessential job for a balanced life.

SELF-EMPLOYMENT

Independence offers freedom. Self-employment offers flexibility, autonomy, and self-regulated life choices. Dentists often say this is the best aspect of the job. Dentists have the privilege of deciding how to operate, when to take patients, and how much to charge. Self-employment also means that an individual must be organized, disciplined, and able to set goals. Dentists must abide by professional ethics while also serving as their own boss. Income is determined by skill, reputation, self-image, effort, and the amount required. Dentists support patients while building a reputable name.

JOB SECURITY AND AUTONOMY

Since dentists establish their own practices or work under the auspices of an experienced professional, time and the acquisition of patients determine success. However, most dentists build a successful practice not long after dental school. Financing for an office, equipment, and staff can speed up the establishment of a dental office workspace. The profession of dentistry also enjoys some level of autonomy. Dentistry requires skill, and only the well-trained can provide dental care. Education in business and law is a plus.

ATTRACTIVE INCOME

In honest appraisal, many students are motivated by the income commanded in dentistry. Even when consumed with studying and grueling final exams, the knowledge that the outcome is a high salary, autonomy, stability, balance, and professionalism are enough to motivate students to press onward.

However, if that is the only motivation, then this is the wrong profession. Passion for the work is essential. There will be times during school, with a difficult patient, or a complex dental emergency when an individual may question whether they made the right career choice. However, the love for serving others, making a difference, and the craft of dentistry should be the true motive.

There is a saying that says, "Do what you love, and the money will come." This statement is particularly true with dentistry. If you love what you do and hunger to stay abreast of the latest techniques, others will appreciate what you do, and you will be successful. Nevertheless, there are financial benefits. The salary is impressive, though there are variables including location, skill level, experience, specialty, and clientele. Successful dentists who invest in their practice and life are millionaires within a few years of gaining a full complement of patients. Dentists earn an average of over $150,000 in a year. Private practitioners typically earn a higher income.

CREATIVITY

Dentistry not only requires a mastery of science and technical skills, but practitioners also need to be able to think creatively. Innovation, ingenuity, and resourcefulness are imperative. Situations may require taking a new or innovative approach to patient care, emergency situations, and business growth. Dentists employ creativity in solving a variety of dental problems. Many health, medicine, and business opportunities require thinking outside the box to provide solutions to new clinical problems.[5] Creativity is even more important when dealing with children, which offers challenges and opportunities. Enjoying the company of kids is a plus.

SPECIALIZATION

Dentists often obtain advanced education.[6] Dentists can specialize in a variety of fields discussed elsewhere in this book. Specializations allow dentists to be exceptionally good in a particular area and well known for solving specific types of problems. Additionally, advanced skill levels increase opportunities. This additional education also boosts community image, reputation, and professional opportunities.

WORK AS PART OF A TEAM

One benefit of being a dentist is the chance to be part of a team. Particularly in dental school, collaborative learning and diverse experiences increase the understanding of common and rare situations and conditions. By working as a team member, dental students learn from other professionals, especially those who have significant experience. Dental students also gain from talents displayed

---

5   Dr. Sunil, "Is Dentistry and Creativity Inter-related? Find Out Here," *Dr. Sunil Dental Blog*, August 3, 2016, http://www.drsunildental.com/dental-blog/creativity-dentistry-relation/

6   Ibid.

by senior members of the profession. This cooperation and situational learning is a double benefit while working with others.[7]

7   NetNewsLedger, "Ten Reasons Dentistry is the Right Career Choice for You," *Net News Ledger,* September 17, 2019, http://www.netnewsledger.com/2019/09/17/ten-reasons-dentistry-is-the-right-career-choice-for-you/

It doesn't matter what others do. It only matters what you choose to do.

– unknown

CHAPTER 12
ALTERNATE MEDICAL-RELATED CAREER PATHS

MEETING THE NEED FOR HEALTHCARE WORKERS

According to the Bureau of Labor Statistics (BLS), the healthcare industry is expected to grow faster than the average for all other occupations. With a projected increase of 14 percent from 2018 to 2028, approximately 1.9 million new jobs will be available for those interested in medicine. The demand for healthcare will only increase in the post-pandemic environment. However, increases are also anticipated due to the aging population in a demographic shift sometimes referred to as the "gray tsunami."

According to the U.S. Census Bureau, baby boomers, born between 1946 – 1964, are turning 65 at a rate of about 10,000 per day. By 2030, when the next census is taken, all baby boomers will have crossed that threshold. This information is critical to understanding careers in healthcare and is the key reason why the healthcare profession will have a surge of jobs. Hospitals, emergency services, home healthcare, nursing homes, and mental health services will require professionals to meet the rising need. Wages are likely to rise in this arena during the next decade.

WHAT MEDICAL PROFESSION IS RIGHT FOR YOU?

When students ponder the pursuit of medicine in general, they tend to consider medical school as the quintessential career and life objective. No doubt, medical school is the right pursuit for many students. Yet, there are many rewarding options, and there is more than one road to reach your goal.

In the 1990s, a Harvard interviewer asked one of my very talented Hispanic students why she would want to attend a liberal arts school if she wanted to pursue nursing. My student answered the question without hesitation, explaining that her mom had a DNP but always wished she had started her road with a rigorous liberal arts education. However, I never stopped thinking about that question. Sure, specialized undergraduate nursing education is a more direct pathway and this route would extend her timeline, but she was committed to expanding her knowledge base. After we talked, I came to understand her long-term objective. She did not get accepted to Harvard, but she did attend Columbia, and she is now a nurse practitioner.

There are numerous possibilities for students who find medicine, dentistry, healthcare, and human biology fascinating. Popular choices for those who complete graduate school include the following: allopathic medicine (MD), osteopathic medicine (DO), podiatrist (DPM), dentist (DDS), veterinarian (DVM), pharmacist (PharmD), psychologist (M.A., Ph.D., Psy.D.), psychiatrist (MD), optometrist (OD), chiropractor (DC), physician's assistant (PA), physical therapist (PT), speech pathologist, nurse practitioner (MSN, DNP), occupational therapist (MSOT, DOT), nurse anesthetist (MSN).

OCCUPATION/DEGREE	ASSOCIATIONS, CERTIFICATION ORGANIZATIONS	BUREAU OF LABOR STATISTICS DATA (2018)
Medical Doctor (MD) Allopathic Medicine – AMCAS - 154 accredited colleges in the U.S.; 17 in Canada	*American Association of Medical Colleges (AAMC) *American Medical Association (MDs & DOs)	Median Annual Salary – $208,000 Number of Physicians & Surgeons (2018) – 756,800 Projected Job Change (2018 – 2028) – 7% inc. Job Openings (2018 – 2028) – 55,400
Physician (DO) Osteopathic Medicine – AACOMAS - 36 accredited colleges in the U.S.	* American Association of Colleges of Osteopathic Medicine (AACOM) *American Osteopathic Association (AOA) *Bureau of Osteopathic Specialists (BOS) *Certifying Board Services (CBS)	Median Annual Salary – $208,000 Number of Physicians & Surgeons (2018) – 756,800 Projected Job Change (2018 – 2028) – 7% inc. Job Openings (2018 – 2028) – 55,400

OCCUPATION/DEGREE	ASSOCIATIONS, CERTIFICATION ORGANIZATIONS	BUREAU OF LABOR STATISTICS DATA (2018)
Podiatrist (DPM) – CPME - 9 accredited colleges in the U.S.	*American Association of Colleges of Podiatry Medicine (AACPM) * Council on Podiatric Medical Education (CPME)	Median Annual Salary – $129.550 Number of Podiatrists (2018) – 10,500 Projected Job Change (2018 – 2028) – 6% inc. Job Openings (2018 – 2028) – 600
Dentistry (DDS) – ADEA AADSAS – 67 ADA accredited dental schools in the U.S.; 10 in Canada	*American Dental Education Association (ADEA) *American Dental Association (ADA)	Median Annual Salary – $156,240 Number of Dentists (2018) – 155,000 Projected Job Change (2018 – 2028) – 7% inc. Job Openings (2018 – 2028) – 11,600
Veterinary Medicine (DVM) – VMCAS - 30 accredited veterinary medical schools in the U.S.; 5 in Canada	*Association of American Veterinary Medical Colleges (AAVMC) *American Veterinary Medical Association (AVMA)	Median Annual Salary – $93,830 Number of Veterinarians (2018) – 84,500 Projected Job Change (2018 – 2028) – 18% inc. Job Openings (2018 – 2028) – 15,600
Pharmacist (PharmD) – PharmCAS - 144 full or candidate accredited pharmacy schools in the U.S.	*Accreditation Council for Pharmacy Education (ACPE) *American Pharmacists Association (APhA)	Median Annual Salary – $126,120 Number of Pharmacists (2018) – 314,300 Projected Job Change (2018 – 2028) – 0% inc. Job Openings (2018 – 2028) – (-100)
Psychologist (MA, Ph.D., Psy.D) – numbers vary by type	*American Psychological Association (APA)	Median Annual Salary – $79,010 Number of Psychologists (2018) – 181,700 Projected Job Change (2018 – 2028) – 14% inc. Job Openings (2018 – 2028) – 26,100
Psychiatrist (MD)	See MD	Median Annual Salary – $208,000 Number of Physicians & Surgeons (2018) – 756,800 Projected Job Change (2018 – 2028) – 7% inc. Job Openings (2018 – 2028) – 55,400
Optometrist (OD) - 23 accredited optometry schools in the U.S. and 2 in pre-accreditation	*Association of Schools and Colleges of Optometry (ASCO) *Association of Optometrists (AOP)	Median Annual Salary – $111,790 Number of Optometrists (2018) – 42,100 Projected Job Change (2018 – 2028) – 10% inc. Job Openings (2018 – 2028) – 4,000

OCCUPATION/DEGREE	ASSOCIATIONS, CERTIFICATION ORGANIZATIONS	BUREAU OF LABOR STATISTICS DATA (2018)
Chiropractor (DC) - 20 chiropractic schools in the U.S.	*Association of Chiropractic Colleges (ACC) *American Chiropractic Association (ACA) *Council on Chiropractic Education	Median Annual Salary – $71,410 Number of Chiropractors (2018) – 50,300 Projected Job Change (2018 – 2028) – 7% inc. Job Openings (2018 – 2028) – 3,700
Physician's Assistant (PA) - 254 ARC-PA accredited PA programs in the U.S.	*Accreditation Review Commission on Education for the Physician Assistant (ARC-PA) *American Academy of Physician Assistants (AAPA)	Median Annual Salary – $108,610 Number of PAs (2018) – 118,800 Projected Job Change (2018 – 2028) – 31% inc. Job Openings (2018 – 2028) – 37,000
Physical Therapist (PT) - Over 400 CAPTE accredited PT schools	*American Physical Therapy Association (APTA) *Commission on Accreditation in Physical Therapy Education (CAPTE)	Median Annual Salary – $87,930 Number of PTs (2018) – 247,700 Projected Job Change (2018 – 2028) – 22% inc. Job Openings (2018 – 2028) – 54,200
Speech Pathologist – 230 accredited programs	*American Speech–Language–Hearing Association (ASHA)	Median Annual Salary – $77,510 Number of Speech Pathologists (2018) – 153,700 Projected Job Change (2018 – 2028) – 27% inc. Job Openings (2018 – 2028) – 41,900
Nurse Practitioner (NP) MSN, DNP - Approximately 400 NP programs	*American Association of Colleges of Nursing (AACN) *American Association of Nurse Practitioners (AANP)	Median Annual Salary – $113,930 Number of NPs (2018) – 240,700 Projected Job Change (2018 – 2028) – 26% inc. Job Openings (2018 – 2028) – 62,000
Occupational Therapist (MSOT, DOT) - 37 fully accredited DOT programs	*American Occupational Therapy Association (AOTA) * Accreditation Council for Occupational Therapy Education (ACOTE)	Median Annual Salary – $84,270 Number of Occupational Therapists (2018) – 113,000 Projected Job Change (2018 – 2028) – 18% inc. Job Openings (2018 – 2028) – 23,700
Nurse Anesthetist (MSN)	See NP	Median Annual Salary – $113,930 Number of NPs (2018) – 240,700 Projected Job Change (2018 – 2028) – 26% inc. Job Openings (2018 – 2028) – 62,000

ALLIED HEALTH PROFESSIONS

The medical profession would not be able to serve the public without the talented and dedicated service of allied health professionals who support, assist, record, evaluate, and rehabilitate patients. From intake and testing to nutrition and maintenance, if it 'takes a village', the village that is needed to treat patients is multifaceted, multilingual, and multitalented. These careers often require interpersonal skills in communication and listening along with recordkeeping, problem-solving, and critical thinking. In addition to healthcare administrators, managers, and insurance professionals, the following presents a list of some of the many professionals in the medical support community.

- *Athletic Trainer*
- *Audiologist*
- *Cardiovascular Technologist*
- *Clinical Laboratory Technician*
- *Clinical Laboratory Technologist*
- *Diagnostic Medical Sonographer*
- *Emergency Medical Technician*
- *Exercise Physiologists*
- *Dental Assistant »*
- *Dietician (RD, RDN)*
- *Dispensing Optician*
- *Genetics Counselors*
- *Health Information Technician*
- *Home Health Aide*
- *Kinesiologist*
- *Massage Therapist*
- *Medical Assistant*
- *Medical Records Assistant*
- *Medical Transcriptionist*
- *Midwife*
- *MRI Technologist*
- *Nuclear Medicine Technologists*
- *Nursing Assistant (CNA)*
- *Nutritionist*
- *Occupational Therapy Assistant*
- *Orderly*
- *Orthodontists*
- *Orthotists*
- *Paramedics*
- *Pharmacy Technician*
- *Phlebotomist*
- *Physical Therapy Assistant*
- *Prosthetists*
- *Psychiatric Aide*
- *Recreational Therapist*
- *Radiation Therapists*
- *Radiologic Technologist*
- *Registered Nurse (RN, BSN)*
- *Respiratory Therapist*
- *Ultrasound Technician*
- *Veterinary Assistant*
- *Veterinary Technologist*

"

Cure sometimes,
treat often and
comfort always.

— *Hippocrates*

CHAPTER 13
ORGANIZATIONS/ASSOC. YOU SHOULD KNOW

LIFELONG DENTAL EDUCATION

A concept you will encounter many times in your professional career is the idea of being a lifelong learner. All dentists are required to complete a certain amount of continuing education to maintain their licenses. Some dentists embrace professional development far beyond what is mandated, often building reputations as experts in their distinct areas of interest.

Organizations are key to the dentist's growth. Associations offer networking opportunities, collaboration on cases, and online facilitated forums. Some provide coursework, certifications, and continuing education units (CEUs). Many also hold national and/or regional conferences. There are often also professional journals, providing the latest research in the field.

Depending on one's type of dental practice, at times, the job can feel isolating. Involvement in and commitment to organized dental associations can provide a hub, friend group, or colleagues who are asking the same types of questions and seeking to resolve challenges by sharing information. In dentistry, there are new discoveries around every corner—and, often, new adventures to explore.

Even knowing the various dental organizations that one might join can help relieve concerns. Dentistry is an evolving profession and demands ongoing engagement. Technological change has introduced novel approaches to the field like 3D printing, wireless technologies, and equipment. Additionally, the speed with which all information multiplies ensures a multitude of dynamic organizational opportunities for the dentist and the student dentist. Some organizations in the field are listed below.

ADA - AMERICAN DENTAL ASSOCIATION (ADA.ORG)

The most widely recognized organization of dental professionals is the ADA. The *Journal of the American Dental Association*, or JADA, is a popular resource for professional development and is encountered by most students during their dental education.

ADEA - AMERICAN DENTAL EDUCATION ASSOCIATION (ADEA.ORG)

The first dental organization a student will encounter and join will likely be the American Dental Education Association. As its name suggests, ADEA is a clearinghouse for information about all things related to dental training, from allied fields such as dental assisting to post-doctoral education.

One does not have to be a dentist or even a dental student to be a member of ADEA—and most prospective dentists discover the organization in the process of learning about the common dental school application which it hosts. The scope of content provided by ADEA would be hard to overstate; it consists of several dozen special interest sections. From tobacco education to the oversight of a dental hygiene clinic, almost every topic related to the mouth and teeth finds some space on the ADEA platforms.

AADSAS – ADEA Associated American Dental Schools Application Service
This service in which you will submit your application is part of ADEA.

TMDSAS – Texas Medical & Dental Schools Application Service
This application is for Texas residents who plan to apply to Texas dental schools.

CAAPID – ADEA Centralized Application for Advanced Placement for International Dentists
Foreign-educated dental graduates apply to U.S./Canadian dental schools who participate in the CAAPID service through this application that offers the chance for advanced standing. The CAAPID is a shorter application than the AADSAS and is specifically for those who plan to practice dentistry in the U.S. or Canada. The dental training is typically a shorter route to the DDS and DMD

ASDA - AMERICAN STUDENT DENTAL ASSOCIATION

Another organization the prospective dentist will find sooner rather than later is the American Student Dental Association, which is the student-governed arm of the American Dental Association. Every U.S. and Canadian dental school holds membership in ASDA, with each school represented by two delegates.

CODA – THE COMMISSION ON DENTAL ACCREDITATION

You want to ensure that the program you have chosen or training programs afterward are accredited. CODA delineates strict guidelines to which dental schools, training facilities, and associations must adhere. CODA serves students and professionals by developing and setting accreditation standards to encourage and monitor the quality of dental education programs.

INTERNATIONAL ASSOCIATION FOR DENTAL RESEARCH

IADR, along with its member associations, such as the American Association for Dental Research, supports clinical, scientific, and policy-related research initiatives. The AADR also consists of its own smaller, statewide groups.

SPECIALIST ASSOCIATIONS

American Society of Dentist Anesthesiologists (ASDA) – 5,000 members

American Association of Public Health Dentistry (AAPHD) – 5,000 members

American Association of Endodontists (AAE) – 7,400 members

The Academy of Oral and Maxillofacial Pathology (AAOMP) – 619 members; 276 fellows

The American Academy of Oral and Maxillofacial Radiology (AAOMR)

The American Association of Oral and Maxillofacial Surgeons (AAOMS) – 5,085 members

The American Academy of Oral Medicine (AAOM)

The American Academy of Orofacial Pain (AAOP)

American Association of Orthodontists (AAO) – 19,000 members

The American Academy of Periodontology (AAP) – 7,500 members

The American Academy of Pediatric Dentistry (AAPD) - 10,800 members

The American College of Prosthodontists (ACP) – 3,900 members

Consider getting a student membership (if available).

Hard work may have opened the door, but it is hard work, self-care, and mental fortitude that is going to get you through.

– Unknown

CHAPTER 14

THE BUSINESS OF DENTISTRY – SKILLS NEEDED

KNOW THYSELF

The practice of dentistry and small business ownership demands two distinct skill sets. A dentist can own and operate a dental practice, but they should understand the myriad duties that come with each role. Buying an existing practice, in whole or in part, effectively commits the dentist to the ethical, clinical, management, and fiduciary responsibilities of both roles.

Dentistry requires technical and scientific mastery along with compassion and humility. On the other hand, business ownership necessitates a different focus. Owners must tend to property security, location maintenance, contracts, quality control, recordkeeping, and accounting. A healthy dose of assertiveness is needed to be an effective leader/manager-dentist/practitioner. One must not only be able to lead, but also be willing to make tough decisions, to hire and fire staff as needed, and to accept the necessary financial risks associated with practice ownership.

BUSINESS KNOWLEDGE AND ACUMEN

The owner of a dental practice needs to understand the principles of sound business relationships as well as legal requirements ubiquitous to healthcare provisions. The skills in treating a patient are not the same as the skills in working with legal entities, property managers, and employees. Employees and contractors do not share business risk, so caution must be exerted in making choices that affect other people.

If bookkeeping or accounting responsibilities are assigned to an employee, the owner must exercise due diligence in ensuring that all functions are completed. In the end, the buck stops with the dentist – whether legal, ethical, or fiduciary. Even when delegated, the responsibilities lay with the dentist. From big-picture concepts like the state of the economy to the tiniest details of insurance deductibles, dentists must understand, analyze, make course corrections, and execute.

Acumen is essential too. Not all dentists who want to own a business have the 'sixth sense' to anticipate the unexpected and stay on task with both the practice of dentistry and the management of the practice. Business organization is very different from dental care.

PERSONALITY TRAITS—ARE YOU AN EXTROVERT?

Extroverts derive energy from the presence of other people. Introverts, on the other hand, need time alone for restoration when fatigued. One can nurture extroversion if nature does not grant this ability naturally. However, a comfort level with people in varied situations is necessary for a practice owner.

DO YOU NEED THE APPROVAL OF YOUR EMPLOYEES?

Dental practice owners must be confident and believe in their capacity for sound decision-making. You will not always be liked. Because you are human, you will stumble in any number of ways. Perhaps you fail to communicate effectively about a procedure to be done. Maybe you unwittingly put a staff member in the position of managing an unpleasant patient. Whatever the case, your staff may complain, criticize, or even quit. Frankly, even if you miraculously managed never to make mistakes, your administrative decisions could be misinterpreted by your employees. The point is, you must respect your staff members and treat them well without giving them power over your confidence as a practitioner.

When agendas conflict, there can only be one boss. As with effective parenting, dentist-managers must forsake the temptation to prioritize popularity over responsibility. Dentists must learn to delegate responsibilities efficiently and hold employees accountable to performing the tasks required.

LISTENING TO STAFF MEMBERS

On the other hand, just as the boss must hold a high standard, he or she must also understand the stressors faced by employees. In the business of your practice, it will not be just you whose family depends on the income generated. The practice must succeed in the interest of everyone. Listen to those who work for you so that you can be attentive and flexible.

BEYOND THE OFFICE WALLS

Practice owners must build a relationship with the community to ensure a steady stream of patients.

Within a society, people share information with one another, and referrals are the best way to attract patients. We also live in a digital community. The internet age has changed businesses and business practices. Websites can provide both positive and undesirable feedback from the public. This internet glow of satisfaction or even the perception of lackluster care cannot be stopped. This wave of commentary means that every patient can write about you, your associates, your staff, and your practice. All dentists—but especially business owners—must accept the risk of being negatively portrayed on medical review sites.

In general, a dental practice needs to establish an online presence. Your staff members can tend to the details of social media posts and replies. However, again, it is the dentist's name and reputation on the line. It is the dentist who is praised or criticized. A shy person or someone afraid of public opinion will find it difficult to be a practice owner.

Some dentists truly enjoy entrepreneurship. They embrace the challenges of owning a business. Others, though, may find that their quality of life could be improved by working for another entity—a hospital, another dentist, the government, or a dental service organization.

Decisions determine destiny.

– *Thomas S. Monson*

CHAPTER 15

DDS VS. DMD

DDS – DOCTOR OF DENTAL SURGERY
DMD – DOCTOR OF DENTAL MEDICINE

The dental education for students in DDS and DMD are the same. There is no functional difference in their curricula, and they are considered equal degrees. The ratio of dental schools granting DDS degrees to those granting DMD degrees is almost 1:1, both in the United States and in Canada. In the U.S. there are 35 DDS- and 33 DMD-granting programs. The map below shows which degrees (DDS and DMD) are offered around the United States.

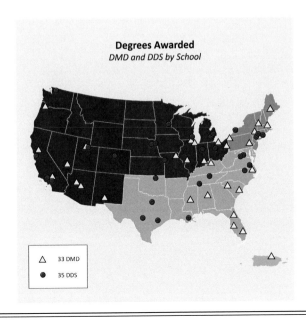

Degrees Awarded
DMD and DDS by School

△ 33 DMD

● 35 DDS

Life is short, art long, opportunity fleeting, experience treacherous, judgment difficult.

– Hippocrates

CHAPTER 16
BRIEF HISTORY OF DENTISTRY

DENTISTRY'S ETYMOLOGICAL ORIGINS

The word 'dentistry' comes from the Latin word 'dens', meaning tooth or the Greek word 'odous', meaning tooth. Dentistry is the healing art and science concerned with the anatomy, physiology, pathology of the oral-facial complex. According to the Oxford dictionary, surgery comes from the Old French word *surgerie* and the work involves the treatment of injuries, diseases, and disorders by manual or instrumental means. Dentistry and dental surgery are often used interchangeably. Surgery, in essence, means repair by manipulation. Dental surgery is the manual manipulation of the teeth. The teeth and mouth are the entrance to an individual's interior and is thus important in one's all-around healthcare.[1]

EARLY YEARS OF DENTISTRY

Dentistry dates back at least 7000 BC, with evidence found in the Indus Valley civilization. In 5000 BC, a Sumerian text described dentistry and dental decay, explaining that tooth worms are responsible for dental decay, though this was proven inaccurate in the 1700s.[2] In Ancient Greece,

1 Sisir K. Majumdar, "History of Dentistry: An Overview," *National Library of Medicine* 32, no. 1 (2002), https://pubmed.ncbi.nlm.nih.gov/15307211/

2 Alyssa Walker, "Six Reasons to Become a Dentist," *Keystone Healthcare Studies*, March 6, 2019, https://www.healthcarestudies.com/article/six-reasons-to-become-a-dentist/

Hippocrates and Aristotle wrote about the treatment of decaying teeth. Their writings explained that dental problems arise from a natural susceptibility to tooth decay or genetic weaknesses. The earliest dental filling made of beeswax dates back 6500 years. The first mention of dentists is in an Egyptian text from 2700 BC. The foremost known reference to an identified dental practitioner was Hesy-Ra, an Egyptian Scribe who lived around 2600 BC.[3]

Toothpaste was utilized first in China, Rome, and India as far back as 500 BC. Soot, honey, and crushed eggshells were contained in the toothpaste used during this period. As far back as 200 BC, Chinese people practiced dentistry using silver amalgam as fillings.[4] In 100 BC, Celsus, the writer of a medical compendium, described oral hygiene, the stabilization of loose teeth, and treatments for toothache. In 166-201 AD, the Etruscans began to replace missing teeth using gold crowns, artificially fixing bridgework.[5]

DENTISTRY TO THE 19TH CENTURY

By the 1300s to the 1500s, Europeans in the Middle Ages practiced oral hygiene. Liquids were formulated to make teeth look white. Ironically, the poor had less tooth decay compared with the rich since they consumed less sugar. People treated tooth pain using homemade medications. Barber-surgeons served as local dentists. The first dental anatomist, Barto Lommeno Eustachio, published a pamphlet, *On The Teeth*, covering anatomy and histology of the teeth.

The bristle toothbrush was invented in 1498. The bristles of the brush were made of stiff hairs from the back of a pig's neck. The pig-hair brush was used until 1938, when nylon bristles were invented. John Baker was one of the first recorded dentists in America.

Barber-surgeons whose red and white towel hung outside their shops signified their profession. They pulled teeth, performed minor surgery, cut hair, and applied leeches. Tooth decay was treated by pulling out impacted teeth. They also filled in tooth holes and crafted false teeth. In 1530, Artzney Buchlein published a book in Germany entitled, "The Little Medicinal Book for All Kinds of Diseases

3   O.S. Michael, "Book Appraisal: History of Dentistry in Nigeria," *Annals of Ibadan Postgraduate Medicine* 14, no. 1 (2016): 44-46, https://www.ncbi.nlm.nih.gov/pmc/articles/PMC5049602/

4   Colgate, "The History of Dentistry," *Colgate*, n.d., https://www.colgate.com/en-us/oral-health/dental-visits/the-history-of-dentistry

5   PDF Drive, "History of Dentistry Chapter 1," *PDF Drive*, 2010, https://www.pdfdrive.com/history-of-dentistry-chapter-1-history-of-dentistry-e51844953.html

and Infirmities of the Teeth",[6] wholly dedicated to dentistry. Buchlein's book was written for barber-surgeons who treated the oral cavity. Topics included mouth and teeth care, tooth extraction, drilling, and placement of gold fillings. In 1575, France's Ambrose Pare, known as the 'Father of Surgery', published his 'Complete Works', which included practical information about dentistry such as tooth extraction and the treatment of tooth decay and jaw fractures.

In 1699, L'Ecole Dentaire (dentistry school) was founded in France. In 1700, a law was enacted to govern dental practice. By the 1700s, dentistry became a more defined profession. In 1723, Pierre Fauchard, a French surgeon, published a book called "The Surgeon Dentist", formulating a treatise in teeth. Pierre Fauchard is generally acknowledged as the Father of Modern Dentistry.[7]

Living in Boston in the 1700s, his comprehensive book described a system to care for and treat teeth, while introducing the idea of fillings and the use of dental prosthetics. He identified that acid produced by ingesting sugar was responsible for tooth decay. He expounded on the need for patients to sit on chairs instead of on the floor. In 1839, the creation and use of false teeth was advanced using vulcanized rubber that strongly affixed false teeth. Nevertheless, today's artificial teeth are much improved with ceramic or plastic.

In 1746, Claude Mouton described how a gold crown and post could be retained in the root canal and recommended white enameling for gold crowns. By 1760, John Baker immigrated from England to set up his practice in Boston, training Paul Revere in making and fitting artificial teeth.[8] In 1789, Frenchman Nicolas Dubois received the first patent for porcelain teeth.

In 1790, John Greenwood constructed the first known dental foot engine for drilling. John was the son of Isaac Greenwood, one of George Washington's dentists. That same year, Josiah Flagg, a renowned American dentist of the time, constructed the first chair for dental patients. The chair had an adjustable headrest and armrest to hold instruments.

DENTISTRY FROM THE 19TH CENTURY ONWARD

In 1801, Richard C. Skinner composed the "Treatise on the Human Teeth", the

---

6   American Dental Education Association, "History of Dentistry," *American Dental Education Association*, n.d., https://www.adea.org/GoDental/Health_Professions_Advisors/History_of_Dentistry.aspx

7   Carefree Dental, "A Brief History of Dentistry," *Carefree Dental*, June 8, 2016, https://www.carefreedental.com/resources/28-your-life/206-a-brief-history-of-dentistry

8   *Boston Gazette* advertisement in 1770, Paul Revere publicizing his dental prosthetic practice.

first dental book published in America. By 1825, porcelain teeth were commercially available, beginning with Samuel Stockton, who owned S.S. White Dental Manufacturing Company who held the dominant marketshare throughout the 19th Century.

The first reclining chair was devised in 1832 by James Snell. By 1838, the world's first dental journal, *The American Journal of Dental Science*, began publication. Modern dentistry included numerous improvements, led by the 'founders of modern dentistry', Horace Hayden and Chapin Harris. Baltimore College of Dental Surgery was the first dental college established in 1840. In 1923, the school united with the University of Maryland. In 1840, the American Society of Dental Surgeons was founded as the world's first national dental organization (closing in 1856).

In 1841, Alabama passed a law regulating the practice of dentistry in the United States, though it was never put into effect. In 1859, about 20 years later, twenty-six dentists met in Niagara Falls, New York, and created the American Dental Association (ADA). Hayden and Harris also developed the curriculum for the current Doctor of Dental Surgery (DDS) degree, the degree held by most of today's dentists. In 1866, Lucy Hobbs became the first woman dentist, graduating from Ohio College of Dental Surgery.

In 1846, William Morton openly showcased in a public demonstration the use of ether as an anesthesia for surgery. Although Horace Wells carried out a similar event the preceding year, he failed to attract the same attention. Even earlier, in 1842, Crawford Long, a physician, was purported to have used ether as an anesthetic in an operation, but the results of his work were not published.

In 1864, Sanford C. Barnum developed the 'rubber dam', a piece of elastic rubber fitted over a tooth by employing weights. The rubber dam insulated the tooth from the oral cavity, which had previously posed problems for dentists.

In 1867, Harvard University Dental School established the first university-affiliated dental institution. In 1871, James B. Morrison patented the first produced foot-treadle dental engine, which made dental burs at an adequate velocity to quickly and evenly cut enamel. George F. Green received the first patent for an electric dental engine.

In the 1880s, a collapsible metal toothpaste tube was produced with soap and chalk, a variation of the dentifrice available in liquid and powder form. In 1873, Colgate released the first toothpaste prepared with a minty taste. The collapsible toothpaste tube was marketed and available until 1984, after which the pump dispenser was introduced. Soon, toothpaste tubes were manufactured by factories and sold widely. In 1882, dental floss was first produced. Later, in 1950, the first fluoride toothpaste was produced.

Surprisingly, most Americans did not adopt good brushing habits until after World War II. Soldiers serving outside the country were required to brush twice a day. As such, they brought the idea of good oral health back to the United States after the war.

In 1883, The National Association of Dental Examiners was founded by the members of the dental boards of several states, establishing uniform standards for dentists. The American Dental Assistants Association was formed in 1924 by Juliette Southard and her female co-workers. The first female dental assistant was hired in New Orleans in 1885.

Dental research took a faster pace in the late 1800s. In 1887, an industrial laboratory was established in Boston called Stowe & Eddy Dental Laboratory. However, the earliest known dental laboratory in the U.S. was Sutton & Raynor, which opened in New York City around 1854. In 1890, Willoughby Miller, an American dentist in Germany, highlighted the basis of dental decay in his book "Micro-Organisms of the Human Mouth". This promoted the movement to brush teeth and use dental floss regularly.

In 1899, Edward Hartley Angle was a leader in making orthodontics a dental specialty, beginning by classifying the various forms of malocclusion. In 1900, he established Angle School of Orthodontia in St. Louis, the first school of orthodontics, along with the first dental specialty journal, *American Orthodontist*, 1907.[9]

In 1869, Henry Bliss Noble, after being rejected from two dental schools, was the first African American to earn a dental degree.[10] Henry Bliss Noble graduated from Harvard University's School of Dentistry in their inaugural class.

In past years, teeth were removed without the use of anesthetics, a procedure that was extremely painful. In the 1790s, a British chemist experimented with the use of nitrous oxide as an analgesic, though the major side effect was laughter.

---

9   American Dental Association, "History of Dentistry," *American Dental Association*, n.d., https://www.ada.org/en/member-center/ada-library/dental-history

10 American Dental Association, "Celebrating Black History Month: Trailblazers in Dentistry," *American Dental Association*, February 24, 2020, https://www.ada.org/en/publications/new-dentist-news/2020-archive/february/celebrating-black-history-month-trailblazers-in-dentistry

He gave nitric oxide a nickname, "laughing gas". In the next fifty years after the discovery of Nitric Oxide, the gas became well known and is still used today. In 1905, a German chemist, Alfred Einhorn, discovered procaine during the period of "painless dentistry". He named this a local anesthetic drug Novocaine.

The drill took hours to finish a filling. With the invention of a high-speed, air-driven handheld dental drill in 1951, the time to prepare a tooth for the filling was decreased to a few minutes. After receiving a patent for the mechanized dental drill in 1871, in the 1880s, James Beall Morrison promoted the drill's use. Dentistry entered the modern age when Novocaine and the high-speed drill were invented. The first dentists made use of chisels and hammers to knock out decayed teeth. In 1896, American dentist, Charles Edmund Kells, incorporated X-ray technology in dentistry, allowing accurate diagnosis of dental diseases.[11]

In 1908, Greene Vardiman Black, the leading reformer and educator of American dentistry, published his monumental two-volume treatise "Operative Dentistry", which remains an essential clinical dental text. He later developed improved methods for filling teeth, standardized operative procedures, and instrumentation. He also developed an enhanced amalgam and pioneered the use of images for teaching dentistry. In 1913, Alfred C. Fones, renowned as the Father of Dental Hygiene, opened Fones Clinic for Dental Hygienists in Bridgeport, Connecticut, the world's first oral hygiene school. In 1937, Alvin Strock inserted the Vitallium dental screw implant, the first successful metal implant.

In 1948, President Harry S. Truman signed a congressional bill that formally established the National Institute of Dental Research (later called the National Institute of Dental and Craniofacial Research), which also initiated federal funding for dental research.

A fully reclining dental chair was initiated in 1958. Lasers were developed in 1960 and approved for soft tissue work, such as the treatment of periodontal disease. The first marketed electric toothbrush was developed in Switzerland after World War II and launched in the United States. This innovation led to a cordless rechargeable model in 1961. In 1997, the erbium YAG laser received approval from the Food and Drug Administration in the treatment of tooth decay. Today, dentists use advanced technology such as Computer-Aided Design and 3D printing to craft dental restorations that look and feel like natural teeth.

---

11   The Editors at Encyclopaedia Britannica, "Dentistry," *Encyclopaedia Britannica*, January 4, 2018. https://www.britannica.com/science/dentistry

PART 3
PREPARATION

CHAPTER 17
PRE-DENT TIMELINE AND PLANNING CALENDAR

DEPENDING UPON WHEN YOU BEGIN

Ideal Plan (Previous Summer DAT)

Summer Before Applying – Study for and take the DAT, research dental schools, volunteer, shadow, research.

Fall Before Applying – Clinical, research, volunteer, coursework, meet with pre-health advisor.

Winter Before Applying – Gather transcripts, request recommendations, prepare personal statement.

Initial Application – June 1 – Complete application; input courses/grades, select dental schools.

Summer After Submission – Register for CASPer, (within two weeks of receipt), classes, volunteer, shadow, research, pre-dent summer program, check application status.

Fall After Submission – Finish remaining supplementals, prep for interview, interview, classes, scribe, check application status.

Winter After Submission – Admission decision December 1st (or 15th COVID-19 delay) or show continued interest, present new information.

Mid-Start Plan (Spring DAT)

Summer Before Applying – Begin preparing for the DAT, volunteer, shadow, research, pre-dent summer program.

Fall Before Applying – Clinical, research, volunteer, coursework, study, meet with pre-health advisor.

Winter Before Applying – Gather transcripts, request recommendations, study and take the DAT.

Initial Application – June 1 – Complete application; input courses/grades, prepare personal statement, research and select dental schools.

Summer After Submission – Register for CASPer, complete supplementals (within two weeks of receipt), classes, volunteer, shadow, research, pre-dent summer program, check application status.

Fall After Submission – Finish remaining supplementals, prep for interview, interview, classes, scribe, check application status.

Winter After Submission – Admission decision December 1st (or 15th COVID-19 delay); show continued interest; present new information.

Late Start Plan (After Application DAT)

Summer Before Applying – Take classes, volunteer, shadow, research, pre-dent summer program.

Fall Before Applying – Clinical, research, volunteer, coursework, meet with pre-health advisor.

Winter Before Applying – Finish classes, get spring transcript, request recommendations, prepare personal statement.

Initial Application – Summer – Complete application; input courses/grades, prepare personal statement, research and select dental schools.

Summer After Submission – Register for CASPer, study and prepare for the DATs, volunteer, shadow, check application status.

Fall After Submission – Complete supplementals (within two weeks of receipt), prep for interview, interview, classes, scribe, check application status.

Winter After Submission – Admission decision December 1st (or 15th COVID-19 delay) through winter/spring; show continued interest; present new information.

FOR DENTAL SCHOOL ENTRY 2022 AND 2023

Prospective applicants for future cycles can expect very similar sequencing.

One year in advance of the application process: prepare for the search beginning as early as your undergraduate sophomore year.

Identify your pre-dental advisor and establish contact.

Most large research institutions provide a pre-dental or pre-medical advisor for their undergraduates who wish to pursue a dental degree.

Research dental schools.

Tend to organization, dates, filing materials, and recordkeeping.

Budget for an expensive process and set the size of your application list accordingly.

- DAT = $495/administration + $45/score report
- First application = $259; additional applications = $112 each
- Interviews: Appropriate clothing and travel expenses

Six months in advance: Plan for DAT and prepare application materials.

Prepare transcript requests to be sent to: ADEA AADSAS, P.O. Box 9110, Watertown, MA 02471

Write Personal Statement (PS)

Solicit 4 letters of Evaluation/Recommendation may be submitted (In 2021, composite letter counts as 1)

Three months in advance: Take the DAT.

One month in advance:

TMDSAS application opens on May 3rd.

ADEA AADSAS application opens on May 11th.

You may establish your account and fill in all parts of your application until the first date of submission May 17th for TMDSAS and June 1st for ADEA AADSAS. You will need to enter personal information, all coursework and grades, personal statement, information about your DAT date(s), and select dental schools to which you will apply.

Apply!

Earliest submit date:
>   May 17 - TMDSAS
>   June 1 - ADEA AADSAS

Deadlines vary by dental school; the last possible submission date is in early February.

Don't wait that long, though, since schools admit on a rolling basis.

After you apply

What happens to your application?

- Transcript Verification and GPA Re-Calculation (ADEA AADSAS combined GPA)
- DAT Scores imported from ADA; CDAT imported from Canadian Dental Association (CDA)
- Specific Program Requirements – Questions Tab (certain programs) – supplemental questions and essays
- ADEA AADSAS Process Completion – Applications are submitted to your designated dental schools
- Dental Schools review applications

Next steps

- Respond to interview invitations as soon as you receive them – confirm and set a date
- Attend interviews – travel arrangements if in person or virtual
- Reply to offers of admission within the required timeframe

"

There is no elevator to success. You have to take the stairs.

– Zig Ziglar

CHAPTER 18

DOCUMENTATION AND ORGANIZATION

You are prepared, you have a checklist, and now you must manage your dates and deadlines. It is hard to overstate the importance of task management. While planner pads, online task management programs, or a system of reminders on your phone are helpful, the tasks included in applying to dental school are only a few you must complete. Planning a year in advance is not too early. Prevent deadlines from sneaking up on you!

THINK AHEAD

Remember that an early application significantly improves your chances of getting an early review and an early interview.

Mindful planning pays dividends. Your life probably already consists of some combination of the following: coursework, assignments, discussions, tutoring/advising, mentoring, research, service, shadowing, athletics, music/art, exercise/meditation, family, friends, social activities, cleaning/organizing, trips, and taking a break. The dental admissions process adds complexity to an already-packed schedule, but careful organization will help you take things one day at a time.

ACADEMIC DOCUMENTATION

Students whose credits have been earned from multiple sources, such as Advanced Placement or a different institution are well-advised to maintain a spreadsheet of their coursework. Having all information in one place will come in very handy when checking and double-checking your progress with the schools to which you will apply. Also, you will have all the necessary information at your fingertips when it is time to complete the application itself. Official transcripts will also need to be requested when you submit your application.

EXTRACURRICULAR DOCUMENTATION

Every meeting, game, and social gathering of your undergraduate experience does not need to be recorded, but you should document the following:

Anything that informed your desire to study dentistry

Document undergraduate research (and graduate, if applicable) relevant to the study of dentistry and healthcare.

Any activity in which you officially represented your institution

Examples of such activities include but are not limited to: Musical groups, art training solar car competitions, robotics competitions, athletics, speech and debate, mock trial, Model United Nations, chess tournaments, college-sponsored service trips, and science contests.

Any activity in which you held a leadership position

Leadership skills are valuable in dentistry. Leadership in social clubs, athletic teams, science teams, or competition groups are valuable experiences. Document your role, along with the goals you set and the objectives you accomplished.

UNPREDICTABLE DATES OF SECONDARIES

Caution: Secondaries occasionally have deadlines. You do not want to get a secondary back and then put it on the back burner. Secondaries do not arrive at the same time. Since each university's process is independent, secondaries come whenever the dental school sends them. Thus, if you apply to 10 – 15 schools, you could have 10 – 15 sets of new assignments at times that are not on your calendar until you get the notice. Be prepared to get them. Look through each secondary you get to determine what they require and when it needs to be returned.

Students often open a secondary weeks later only to find that the deadline to submit is the end of that week. The result is an emergency situation that does not fit nicely into their schedule. Studying, exams, and responsibilities are all on the line. Worst of all, after the tremendous amount of work and significant costs to apply, some students skip a secondary altogether because they simply cannot complete the requirements with the other items on their plate.

INTERVIEW DATES AND PLANNING

You will not know ahead of time if you will get an interview or, if so, when that must be scheduled. You may need to travel to the school for the interview. This opportunity is fantastic because it signifies you are at the top of the pack and you made it through the next round of cuts. You should be excited. However, this puts a burden on your schedule. You also want to squeeze in some time in your schedule to prepare for your interviews.

You want to know enough about that particular dental school to know what is important to them. In speaking with an admissions director from a dental school, she mentioned that she found it disheartening that an interviewee knew little about the school and had no interest in the culture or community of that city and state. Thus, it is essential to get to know the dental school more thoroughly than you did when you selected the school initially and later wrote your secondaries.

WHEN TO EXPECT SECONDARIES

You cannot "expect" to get a secondary because it is up to the school to decide whether to offer this to you. However, if you have grades and scores comparable to the students in the program, there is a high likelihood of getting a secondary.

After you complete, sign, pay, and submit your initial application, the documents and school choices are not automatically sent off to the schools you chose. Your application must undergo a verification process. First, ADEA AADSAS and TMDSAS must ensure that they have received all of your required transcripts. You can submit without the letters of recommendation submitted, though they are still required. You can also submit the application without the DAT. Do not wait to take the DAT first. While schools may not consider you until after they have received your DAT scores, delaying submission puts you farther behind in the process.

Your application will go into a queue for review, though there may be hundreds or thousands ahead of you, so submitting your application early will put you closer to the head of the pack. All applications must be verified before they are sent on to the schools.

ADEA AADSAS and TMDSAS matches each of the colleges, courses, and grades you input with each of the transcripts you submitted. If you make a mistake, the application may be sent back to you for you to fix. Additional verification will take place. Make sure you send in correct information and check for any errors.

While you are waiting, you may think the process is taking a long time. However, it is in the best interest of the processing service to complete the verification in a timely manner. Thus, while it can take as much as six weeks to process and send off your applications to schools, if you submit early and are at the front of the queue, your application will move through faster and you will receive your secondaries sooner.

DIGITAL OR PAPER FILING SYSTEM

You will research schools, collect information from college fairs, and get letters and materials in the mail. Create a system that works for you to file this information away. Organization is vital so that you have a system to keep track of:

- Transcripts
- Letters of Recommendation Requests
- Essays and Supplementals
- Resume Versions
- Separate Folders For Each School on Your List
- Application Copy
- Interviews and Thank You Notes
- Communications with Admissions
- Passwords, Access Numbers, IDs

FLEXIBILITY

Since some assignments, requirements, and responsibilities are known, and some are unknown, you need to be flexible. Map out on a calendar everything you know you need to accomplish. Block out your course, job, and volunteer schedule. Then, predict and plan times to set aside for those upcoming requirements that you do not know. Leave two chunks of time each week for application requirements.

A month after you submit your application, you could start receiving secondaries. Set aside two blocks each week at days and times that work for you. The application opens May 11th and the first time you can press submit is on June 1st. Be prepared!

Preparation for the dental school application process will be made much easier through disciplined recordkeeping and organization.

If a hundred college students were asked to describe their method(s) for documenting and tracking information, one hundred different replies would be solicited. Everyone is wired a little differently and has been exposed to various tools, technological and old-school alike.

FINAL NOTES

It will be handy to include in your records the names and contact information of anyone in admission or at a dental school as well as contact in dentistry and possible recommenders. Simply make a note of such people when you record the relevant activity.

Only very disciplined students recognize and protect personal time for journaling and reflection. If you do keep a journal, consider incorporating it alongside the other application materials you compile. The notes may be invaluable once you begin the writing tasks of your dental school applications.

The best advice? Find what works for you and stick with it.

> *Better is possible. It does not take genius it takes diligence. It takes moral clarity. It takes ingenuity. And above all, it takes a willingness to try.*

– Atul Gawande

CHAPTER 19

ACADEMIC REQUIREMENTS - COURSEWORK, GPA, AND PREREQUISITES

KEEP A CLOSE EYE ON THE DETAILS

When it comes to academic admissions at any level, applicants should check every institution's requirements personally and resolve any ambiguities with admissions personnel.

Err on the side of being too careful and do not assume that the current year's requirements will remain unchanged. All admissions details tend to be moving targets, particularly in the wake of the pandemic.

MINIMUM AMOUNT OF UNDERGRADUATE COURSEWORK

Not all dental schools require the completion of a bachelor's degree. The majority of matriculating students have earned a BA or, more commonly, a BS degree, but exceptions certainly exist.

COURSEWORK

Prospective dental students should think of required coursework categorically; classes are either considered a prerequisite or an elective. As you might expect, dental prerequisites are often heavy in the sciences.

WHAT ABOUT AP COURSEWORK AND COMMUNITY COLLEGE CREDITS?

Again, most schools' policies vary when it comes to requirements completed away from a traditional four-year college setting, and details are provided on each website. The purpose of the provided chart is to give the applicant a general idea of who grants what kind of credit, and under what circumstances.

Once the applicant locates institution-specific policies about AP and community college credits, a few trends become apparent. Most dental schools want applicants to complete as much of their coursework as possible at a four-year college; official policies do not always reflect a student's best interest. Also, COVID-19 related quarantines made it necessary for dental schools to relax requirements for students applying during this time. For example, many institutions modified their policies to allow for Pass/Fail credit. The applicant should be mindful of the possibility that schools may reverse those changes at some point.

Academic policies by dental school: AP/IB courses and community college coursework

Source: AMEA.org, Dental School Explorer

Dental school	Min hrs*	Max at CC*	PRE/AP*	PRE/CC*	ELEC/AP*	ELEC/CC*
Arizona School of Dentistry and Oral Health	90			Yes	No	Yes
Missouri School of Dentistry and Oral Health	90		Yes	Yes	Yes	Yes
Boston University School of Dental Medicine	120	30	Non-sciences only	Non-sciences only	Yes	Yes
California Northstate College of Dental Medicine						

Dental school	Min hrs*	Max at CC*	PRE/AP*	PRE/CC*	ELEC/AP*	ELEC/CC*
Case Western Reserve University School of Dental Medicine	90		Must appear on transcript	Yes	Must appear on transcript	Yes
Columbia University College of Dental Medicine	90		Yes	Yes	Yes	Yes
Creighton University School of Dentistry	64	64				Yes
Dental College of Georgia at Augusta University	90		Yes	Yes	Yes	Yes
East Carolina University School of Dental Medicine		60	Sometimes	Sometimes	Yes	Yes
Harvard School of Dental Medicine	47		Yes	Yes	Yes	Yes
Herman Ostrow School of Dentistry of USC	60	60	No	Yes	No	Yes
	*Min # of undergrad hours req.	*Max # of hours allowed at a comm. college or 2-year institution	*PRE=prequisite courses	*ELEC=elective coursework	*AP=AP or IB coursework credit	*CC=coursework completed at community college or other two-year institution

Dental school	Min hrs*	Max at CC*	PRE/AP*	PRE/CC*	ELEC/AP*	ELEC/CC*
Howard University College of Dentistry	96	48	No	Yes	No	Yes
Indiana University School of Dentistry	90	60	No	No	Yes	Yes
Lake Erie College of Osteopathic Medicine School of Dental Medicine	120	60	Yes	Yes	Yes	Yes
Loma Linda University School of Dentistry	96	64	English only	Yes	Yes	Yes
Louisiana State University Health New Orleans School of Dentistry	90		Yes	Yes	Yes	Yes
Marquette University School of Dentistry	90	45	English only	Yes	Yes	Yes
Medical University of South Carolina College of Dental Medicine	120	60	Yes	Yes	Yes	Yes
Meharry Medical College School of Dentistry	96		No	Yes	No	Yes
Midwestern University College of Dental Medicine--Illinois	120		Yes	Yes	Yes	Yes

Dental school	Min hrs*	Max at CC*	PRE/AP*	PRE/CC*	ELEC/AP*	ELEC/CC*
Midwestern University College of Dental Medicine--Arizona	90		Yes	Yes	Yes	Yes
NYU College of Dentistry	90	60	One per subject	Lower-level courses only	One per subject	Lower-level courses only
Nova Southeastern University College of Dental Medicine	90	60	Yes	Yes	Yes	Yes
Oregon Health & Science University School of Dentistry	90		Yes	Yes	Yes	Yes
Roseman University of Health Sciences College of Dental Medicine	60		Yes	Yes	Yes	Yes
Rutgers, The State University of New Jersey, School of Dental Medicine	8	60	No	Yes		Yes
Southern Illinois University School of Dental Medicine	90	60		Yes	Yes	Yes
Stony Brook University School of Dental Medicine	90	60	Scores of 4 or 5 only	Yes	Scores of 4 or 5 only	Yes
Texas A & M College of Dentistry	90	60	Yes	Yes	Yes	Yes

Dental school	Min hrs*	Max at CC*	PRE/AP*	PRE/CC*	ELEC/AP*	ELEC/CC*
Texas Tech University Health Sciences Center El Paso School of Dental Medicine						
Temple University School of Dentistry	90	6			Yes	Yes
The Ohio State University College of Dentistry	90		Must appear on transcript	Yes	Must appear on transcript	Yes
The University of Iowa College of Dentistry and Dental Clinics	90	60	Yes	Yes	Yes	Yes
Touro College of Dental Medicine at New York Medical College	90		No	Yes	No	Yes
Tufts University School of Dental Medicine	37		No	No	No	Yes
University at Buffalo School of Dental Medicine	90		Must appear on transcript	Yes	Must appear on transcript	Yes
University of Alabama at Birmingham School of Dentistry	90	60	Yes	Yes	Yes	Yes
University of California, San Francisco, School of Dentistry	90	70	Max of 3 semesters	Yes	Max of 3 semesters	Yes

Dental school	Min hrs*	Max at CC*	PRE/AP*	PRE/CC*	ELEC/AP*	ELEC/CC*
University of California, San Francisco, School of Dentistry	93	64	Official score report required	Yes	Official score report required	Yes
University of Colorado School of Dental Medicine	90	60	Yes	Yes	Yes	Yes
University of Connecticut School of Dental Medicine	90		Yes	Yes	Yes	Yes
University of Detroit Mercy School of Dentistry	60	60	Yes	Yes	Yes	Yes
University of Florida College of Dentistry	90		Yes	Yes	Yes	Yes
University of Illinois at Chicago College of Dentistry			No	Yes	No	Yes
University of Kentucky College of Dentistry	120	60	Must earn grade, not P/F	Yes	Must earn grade, not P/F	Yes
University of Louisville School of Dentistry	90	60	Yes	Yes	Yes	Yes
University of Maryland School of Dentistry	90	60	Yes	Yes	Yes	Yes
University of Michigan School of Dentistry	90	60	Must appear on transcript	Yes	Must appear on transcript	Yes

Dental school	Min hrs*	Max at CC*	PRE/AP*	PRE/CC*	ELEC/AP*	ELEC/CC*
University of Minnesota School of Dentistry	87	64	Yes	Yes	Yes	Yes
University of Mississippi Medical Center School of Dentistry	90	65		Yes	Yes	Yes
University of Missouri--Kansas City School of Dentistry	120	60	If additional advanced courses in the subject have also been taken	Contact school		Contact school
University of Nebraska Medical Center College of Dentistry	90		Yes	Yes	Yes	Yes
University of Nevada, Las Vegas, School of Dental Medicine	90	60		Yes	Yes	Yes
University of New England College of Dental Medicine	90			Yes		Yes
University of North Carolina at Chapel Hill Adams School of Dentistry	96	64	Must appear on transcript	Yes	Must appear on transcript	Yes
University of Oklahoma College of Dentistry	90		Yes	Lower-level courses only	Yes	Lower-level courses only

Dental school	Min hrs*	Max at CC*	PRE/AP*	PRE/CC*	ELEC/AP*	ELEC/CC*
University of Pennsylvania School of Dental Medicine		60	Yes	Yes	Yes	Yes
University of Pittsburgh School of Dental Medicine	90	60	Yes	Yes	Yes	Yes
University of Puerto Rico School of Dental Medicine	90	90	Yes	Yes	Yes	Yes
University of Tennessee Health Science Center College of Dentistry	97		Must appear on transcript	Yes	Must appear on transcript	Yes
The University of Texas School of Dentistry at Houston	90	60	Yes	Yes	Yes	Yes
University of the Pacific School of Dentistry	90		Yes	Yes	Yes	Yes
University of Utah School of Dentistry	90	60	Yes	Yes	Yes	Yes
University of Washington School of Dentistry	120		Yes	Yes	Yes	Yes
UT Health San Antonio School of Dentistry	90		If credit awarded by undergrad institution	Yes	If credit awarded by undergrad institution	Yes

Dental school	Min hrs*	Max at CC*	PRE/AP*	PRE/CC*	ELEC/AP*	ELEC/CC*
Virginia Commonwealth University School of Dentistry	90	60	Yes	Yes	Yes	Yes
West Virginia University School of Dentistry	90	64	English only	Yes	Yes	Yes
Western University of Health Sciences College of Dental Medicine	90		English only	Yes	Yes	Yes

All men by nature desire knowledge.

– Aristotle

CHAPTER 20
WHAT IS YOUR MAJOR?

D
ental schools do not restrict admission to applicants from particular undergraduate majors. Students matriculate from all disciplines to begin their dental coursework. Additionally, DMD and DDS programs promote diversity of thought and thus appreciate the insights afforded a student who has studied a subject which is decidedly un-dental. However, as of 2020, **almost two-thirds of new dental students majored in the biological sciences.**[1]

Think about it. Approximately 1500 academic disciplines are available to undergraduates.[2] Even if one considers only the broad categories of majors, a lot are available--business, communications, performing arts, architecture and design, engineering, agriculture, social sciences, languages, and a list of others too long to include. So, why do so many dental students hold degrees in the biological sciences?

All things being equal, there is no preference for one major over another. However, biology coursework requirements accomplish double duty by filling prerequisite requirements for dental school as well as providing necessary preparation for the DAT. Thus, it is reasonable to expect a strong presence of students who have majored in the biological sciences.

Any major can work for you. Keep in mind the element of *opportunity cost*. English majors could be poised to be among the best communicators in their dental cohorts—but they must be accepted to dental school first. A

---

1   American Dental Education Association, U.S. Dental School Applicants and Enrollees, 2020 Entering Class
2   Per the Integrated Postsecondary Education Data System

great deal of planning and hard work would be necessary for an English major to complete his or her own degree qualifications while also satisfying dental schools, prerequisites and mastering DAT material.

The table below shows the distribution of undergraduate majors across all dental school applicants and enrollees. Additionally, you can see the average admit rates for each major.

Undergraduate fields of study			
Field of study	% of applicants	% of enrolling students	Admit rate
Biological and Biomedical Science	62.1%	63.5%	58.3%
Health Professions and Related Programs	8.5%	8.2%	55.0%
Physical Sciences	4.2%	4.2%	57.5%
Psychology	4.0%	3.9%	54.5%
Parks, Recreation, Leisure and Fitness Studies	2.8%	2.7%	54.7%
Multi- or Interdisciplinary Studies	2.5%	2.5%	57.1%
Business, Management, Marketing and Related Support Services	2.3%	2.2%	55.5%
Family and Consumer Sciences or Human Sciences	2.0%	2.2%	62.8%
Engineering and Engineering-related Fields	1.6%	1.8%	65.9%
Social Sciences	1.6%	1.7%	61.6%
All Other Majors	8.4%	7.2%	48.4%

Source: ADEA Guide to Dental Schools, Fall 2021 and 2022

Steps before deciding on an undergraduate major:

1. If you want to go to dental school and have yet to declare an undergraduate major, start by investigating the specific curricular guidelines for each institution within the Dental School Explorer on the ADEA website. First, what courses are required? Then, what is recommended? You may be surprised by some of the requirements. Some DMD/DDS-granting institutions want to see evidence of study outside the sciences and may require English or a certain number of units in social sciences. Art, too, may be required or recommended.

2. Do some preliminary research about the content of the DAT by downloading the most current version of the Dental Admission Test Candidate Guide. You will be able to find it on the website of the American Dental Association (ADA). The scope of the exam is described in detail and should provide clarity about which undergraduate courses will be useful in preparation.

3. Take inventory of your own interests and areas of intellectual curiosity. What major sounds interesting, if not the biological sciences? How about within the biological sciences?

4. Finally, get into the weeds with the way your undergraduate institution works academically. Be conversant about the basics. What courses must all students at your university complete? What courses must a microbiology major complete? How about a student in a different field of study entirely?

5. Connect with your pre-health advisor as you move toward the selection of a major. You are making a big decision and you deserve the support of a faculty member or non-faculty advisor who understands both the terrain at your institution as well as the expectations of those schools to which you will ultimately send your dental application.

FINAL NOTE

For those of you whose majors did not equip you with the content or available time to prepare for dental school, fear not. You may not be able to apply to dental school with your current classmates, but you can take a semester, a year, or two, and then engage in the application process. Participation in a post-baccalaureate program (see Chapter 53) is one of many ways you might choose to spend the time. The average age of entering dental students varies by school but is typically about 24. With careful planning and intentional execution, you may find yourself right on schedule.

"

Part of being successful is about asking questions and listening to the answers.

—Anne Burrell

CHAPTER 21

ACADEMIC ACTIVITIES AND PRE-DENT ADVISING

PRE-DENT ADVISING

Most research institutions have individual and group pre-dental advisory sessions for prospective dental students. On smaller campuses, that advisor may serve a broader set of students within multiple pre-health disciplines.

It is advisable to meet with your pre-dental advisor as early as possible, first to establish a connection and then to ask questions and get advice about proceeding on your academic pathway. Not only will your advisor have college-specific knowledge about your professors, courses, or trajectory, they might also know a lot about individual dental schools. Your advisor may be able to steer you in the right direction, given your unique circumstances.

Ideally, you will build a team of supporters around you while preparing to apply to dental school. No matter how large or small the team, your pre-dental advisor will be an essential player. That individual is also likely to have the most up-to-date information about changes from year to year regarding the admissions process.

ACADEMIC CLUBS

Academic clubs are popular and often serve as both a social network and academic community for students with similar interests. Students seeking intellectual stimulation and collegial groups are more likely to suffer from an abundance of choices rather than a dearth of opportunities. As your 'free time' becomes infrequent, it also becomes more valuable. How many activities can you do well without sacrificing other responsibilities?

Students planning to apply to dental school have to hold priorities in a delicate balance. They must take time away from schoolwork (in the interest of staying healthy) without letting too much of that time go to waste (in the interest of staying competitive). Ideally, they can plug into a couple of organizations that offer camaraderie and fun while also scaffolding their futures.

Pre-Dent/Pre-Med Clubs are especially popular because they are the pathway clubs to healthcare professional programs. Not only do these groups often bring in speakers, but they also connect students with summer programs and mentorship opportunities. They can help you network while giving you the crucial information you need to plan your application process and future career.

Health professions clubs provide an academic society away from your coursework to collaborate and communicate with students who are traveling along your same journey. You may see these same students in the future. Through these groups, you can establish a bond that could last for life. However, you will also develop shared academic and personal interests aside from dentistry.

Honorary societies such as Omicron Delta Kappa and Mortar Board are not healthcare-specific. They are accessible to students from a variety of majors and might round out your organizational involvement.

Some schools have living-learning communities (LLCs) where you can participate in activities with students outside of your major set of interests. These LLCs often provide social outlets within the context of intellectual curiosity.

Take a deep breath, make thoughtful decisions, and have a responsible amount of fun!

Pre -Dental Societies have been established on many college campuses and deserve a look from all people considering careers in dentistry. In the absence of a Pre-Dental Society, you might find a Pre-Med Society in which prospective dentists also participate. Another option would be to start a chapter of one of the dental fraternities below. This option offers you the chance to demonstrate leadership and provide a valuable forum on your college campus.

Delta Delta Sigma or Delta Sigma Delta Dental Fraternity

Established in 1882, $\Delta\Sigma\Delta$ or $\Delta\Delta\Sigma$ is the oldest and largest international dental fraternity. The letters were transposed years ago (DDS DSD); there are chapters of both.

Xi Psi Phi Dental Fraternity

The second oldest dental fraternity, $\mathrm{X}\Psi\Phi$, was established in 1889 to stimulate intellectual and social interaction, primarily at medical schools.

Psi Omega Dental Fraternity

The third oldest dental fraternity, $\Psi\mathrm{O}$, was established in 1892 to maintain professional standards and encourage both scientific investigation and literary culture. Its spring 2021 online 'newspaper', *Frater*, features opportunities to submit original dental comics, community service award opportunities, and grants for publishing student articles. Updates on dental club activities during COVID-19 are interesting, including activities during the pandemic, transitioning dental school online, and seminars on debt reduction.

Alpha Omega Dental Fraternity

Established in 1907, AO was established to fight discrimination in dental schools. A group of Jewish dental students created Alpha Omega, the fourth dental fraternity. Activities included donating dental ambulances to the Royal Canadian Dental Corps and the U.S. Army, incorporating chapters in Israel, and a Holocaust Survivors Oral Health Program. Its journal, *Alpha Omegan*, combined with the journal Compendium to provide information regarding dental practice and patient care.

"

Learning is a treasure that will follow its owner everywhere.

— *Chinese Proverb*

CHAPTER 22
RESEARCH AND PUBLICATIONS

S tudents often enter college believing they are a vessel to be filled with knowledge. Yet, knowledge continues to expand.

EXPANDING KNOWLEDGE AND BREAKTHROUGH SCIENCE

For example, the Fermilab, a joint venture of the University of Chicago, and the Universities Research Association (URA) have discovered information about particle physics, published in April 2021, that may change the way we understand the 'Standard Model' in the biggest finding in subatomic particles in a decade.[1] In May 2021, researchers at Duke University developed fully recyclable, printable electronics using graphene that could be used to create next-generation technology.[2] In September 2020, researchers at Harvard University and the Medical University of Vienna deciphered the cell layer process in regenerative dentistry, showing the pathways of stem cells as they form into odontoblasts, dentin, and tooth enamel to determine the impact on tooth sensitivity.[3]

---

1   UChicago News, "First Results from Fermilab's Muon G-2 Experiment Strengthen Evidence of New Physics," *UChicago News*, April 7, 2021, https://news.uchicago.edu/story/first-results-fermilabs-muon-g-2-experiment-strengthen-evidence-new-physics

2   Graphene-Info, "Graphene Applications: What is Graphene Used For?," *Graphene Info*, Updated July 12, 2020, https://www.graphene-info.com/graphene-applications

3   Jan Krivanek et al., "Dental Cell Type Atlas Reveals Stem and Differentiated Cell Types in Mouse and Human Teeth," *Nature Communications* 11, no. 4816 (2020), https://www.nature.com/articles/s41467-020-18512-7

RESEARCH ADVANCES SCIENCE

Advancements in oral health and dentistry are constantly being made. Across all of medicine, research in immunology, cancer biology, and biochemistry continue to make strides because researchers seek greater understanding. University faculty could not do this without student research support. In college, I researched the regeneration of nerves in the extremities of mice in late stages of diabetes. Years later, scientists are now able to regenerate nerves. Whatever research projects you choose will take science one step farther.

Understanding disease and decay is the first step toward prevention and treatment. If you are serious about dentistry, medicine, and the care of patients, you should consider research. Progressing the field you plan to enter, you gain a firmer foundation in what science means on a broader basis.

Research is not required to get accepted to medical school. However, if you do pursue this avenue, take it seriously and participate actively. Being a paramedic is just as valuable and takes about the same amount of time. Choose whatever fits your interests, abilities, and passions. Your knowledge of science and the scientific method in alternative forms is what is truly important rather than the name of an important researcher on the laboratory's door.

EVERY STEP YOU TAKE IS PROGRESS

Even in a small lab working on a small project, science takes a step forward. Understanding how this process works is valuable and contributes to your ability to succeed. There is much we do not know. By working in a lab, you take ownership of a larger project. Even if you inject a hundred mice a week, you are still part of a big picture and can better understand connections.

Progress begins with the scientific process and discovery. Often your research qualifies for college credit. Most colleges offer independent study credits whereby you write up a plan, get signatures, and complete the project.

WORKING WITH A PRINCIPAL INVESTIGATOR (PI)

The first step is to find a lab where you can do substantive work and ultimately develop your own research project. At first, though, you will be at the bottom of the totem pole. Start looking during your first or second year so that you can progress. Many labs have funding available. If not, there are usually university research scholarships. Summer research often comes with fellowship funds.

Typically, you begin a project by surveying the literature on topics surrounding the lab's investigation and understanding the research goals. Most of the work you do will be technical or procedural work with cells, solutions, animals, or data entry. Whatever you do is valuable. You will work at the discretion of your principal investigator (PI), a post-doc, or a graduate student. While you will typically work under their supervision and complete tasks as required, you may be invited to lab meetings or colloquia where you can expand your knowledge.

Part of the training in dentistry and medicine is to master the terminology. There are thousands of terms. Through research, meetings, mentorship, data entry, analysis, and writing you will learn more about the instrumentation, tests, and implications that will also help you in your classes. Do not be afraid to ask a question. PIs and post-docs have many more years of training and were once in your position. Everyone needs to learn from scratch. You are no different. Do not be afraid if you do not know everything.

WORK IN AREAS OF YOUR INTEREST

You should be interested in the work you are doing. Often, you will work on this research project for years. You should find it truly fascinating and not just because there is an opening. When you apply to dental school, you are likely to use this experience as one of the experiences on your application. You may discuss it in your interview. If you are enthusiastic, interviewers can tell from your expressions. If you just did it to 'look good', that will be apparent as well. Sincerity is important.

PUBLICATIONS

If you have worked in a lab, supporting the research process throughout, you are likely to be listed as one of the contributors to the project as an author. The first author on a paper is typically the PI. The second might be a post-doc or graduate assistant. You may not be one of the first two. Nevertheless, having your name on a publication means that you were a significant enough part of the process to be named at all. However, being one of the last authors on a paper is fine. Look for chances to conduct your own independent research project and publish your findings or present them in a poster session.

"

Be fearless in the
pursuit of what
sets your soul on
fire.

— Jennifer Lee

CHAPTER 23

CLUBS: YOUR INTERESTS & INVOLVEMENT IN SCHOOL

Needless to say, most college students enjoy extracurricular activities. Most pre-dent students do too, though time limitations, along with a variety of tasks and responsibilities, can be constraining. Nonetheless, the college experience should be fun and interesting so prioritize some extracurricular involvement.

COMMUNITY SERVICE

Most students applying to dental school in the 2020s have grown up on a steady diet of the importance of community service with messaging and school requirements. There is no question that some high school students approach service opportunities as boxes to check and tasks to be done. In college, however, your future as a dentist is closer, and you are in a better position to consider how volunteer experiences might inform, or even directly affect, your future.

If you want to make a difference on campus, in the community or the world, there are opportunities to help, from day care to nursing homes. Environmental causes like trash removal, recycling, and advocacy are popular, as well as nature, animals, birds, and marine life. However, you might enjoy clubs like Campus Relay for Life, College Mentors for Kids, and Habitat for Humanity.

Service is also a great way to enhance your sense of well-being. You are making a contribution. All work and no play can make pre-dent students unhappy. There are no right or wrong choices. Some of these can fit in different categories. However, the point is for you to find outlets for social interaction.

Social Clubs

Fraternities and Sororities
Spirit Committees
Arts Clubs
Political Groups
School Pride Club
Music Clubs
Social Action Committees
Chess Club
Language Clubs

Intercultural Organizations
Model United Nations
Cultural Student Union
LGBTQ+ Groups
Speech and Debate
Veterans Associations
Gay-Straight Alliance
Feminists Club

Community Service Organizations

Campus Relay for Life
College Mentors for Kids
Alpha Phi Omega
Muscular Dystrophy Association
Habitat for Humanity
Peace Organizations
United Cerebral Palsy
Democratizing Education
American Heart Association

Autism Speaks
Circle K International
International Medical Corps
Doctors without Borders
Fellowship of Christian Athletes UNICEF
American Cancer Society
Oral Health Foundation
Missions of Mercy (ADCFMOM)
National Children's Oral Health Foundation (NCOHF)

Science Clubs/Activities/Competitions

Research Club
Pre-Dent Club
Robotics Club
Journal Review Team
Health Advisory Group
Advanced Vehicle Technology Competition

Biology/Chemistry Club
Archeological Dig
STEMtors
Global Medical Brigades
MEDLIFE
EcoCar Mobility Challenge
Baja SAE Competition

Medtronic Student Design

BMEidea

ADHA Research Poster Competition

EFP Undergrad Essay Competition

DEBUT challenge

Amgen Scholars Prog at NIH

Touch of Genius Prize

(CCR) Cancer Research Intern

DiabetesMine Design Challenge

Cleantech UP

IADR Hatton Competition

American Student Dental Assn

Service to the College/Faculty/Student Body

Student Government

Student Newspaper Journalist

Research Assistant

Health Center Volunteer

Admissions Ambassador

Band/Marching Band

College Radio Show Host

Orientation Day Leader

Speaker Coordinator

Teaching Assistant

Athletic Event Organizer

Orchestra

School Television Station

Science Fair Volunteer

Museum Tour Guide

Green Campus Program

Mentorship

Choir/Vocal Group

Library Assistant

First-Gen Ambassador

Theater Docent

Campus Gardens

Academic Tutor

Dance/Performance Group

Personal Growth

Religion

Tai Chi

Association

Hillel

Yoga Clubs

Outdoors Club

Youth Ministries

Martial Arts

Spiritual Groups

Young Life

Mindful Meditation Groups

Ski/Triathlon /Ping Pong, etc.

Bible Study

Therapy Dog Group

Recreations Clubs

Stress Relief Week

LEADERSHIP

You will need to demonstrate leadership. Find one or two areas where you can serve by leading and lead by serving. However, meaningful leadership does not have to take the form of the highest office in a group. You can demonstrate leadership influence or initiative through your efforts to make your organization better.

RELAXATION AND REFUELING

Allow yourself some social outlets as well as some activities which cultivate time for reflection or physical fitness. You will need a full tank of gas, so to speak, when you begin dental school. Such reserves of energy and spirit must be cultivated intentionally.

SUSTAINED INVOLVEMENT

Whatever you choose to do, dental schools are looking for your passions and interests, as evidenced by your sustained involvement. A small handful of initiatives is always more attractive to the application reader than something completed in a scattershot manner, an hour or two every year.

Dental admissions readers are looking for commitment. Tenacity will be necessary for the completion of your dental degree and for delivering the best services possible day in and day out. Your involvement demonstrates that you find meaning in service and have connected your skills and objectives with your desire to help others.

However, the most important objective when writing about volunteer service in your essay is demonstrating commitment. Compassion is a necessary ingredient to collaborate with classmates, work with future patients, and even for self-care. Dentistry is a tough profession, even once a critical mass of knowledge and expertise has been acquired. In an environment that is often characterized by anxious patients, tired staff members, and complex treatment plans, daily motivation must come from the heart.

AMERICAN DENTAL ASSOCIATION NOTE

The American Student Dental Association distinguishes community service from community outreach as follows:

> Community outreach involves providing professional services, or services of a specific expertise, to a group of people who may not otherwise have access to those services. It is performed where those in need are located.

> Community service is work done for the benefit of the local community overall. Community service can be completed remotely.[1]

---

1   American Student Dental Association, "Community Outreach and Community Service," *American Student Dental Association*, n.d., https://www.asdanet.org/index/programs-events/community-outreach

In short, community outreach means offering one's professional services at no charge; community service is more general and less specific to one's vocation. The comparison is a helpful framework for building one's volunteer experiences.

Community Outreach: You are not a dentist just yet, but you can still help in a dental setting. Possible resources for brainstorming such opportunities include but are not limited to your pre-dental advisor, the dentists you shadow, the Pre-Dental Society at your college, and the ASDA website.

Community Service: Pathways to more general community service can be found everywhere. Most college student groups work with charitable organizations, and college-sponsored service trips are not unusual. Websites like dosomething. org present a wide array of choices. The point is, get out there and serve, keeping in mind the potential for longer-term involvement if you find a great fit.

A FINAL WORD

Make good decisions. Do not engage in any disreputable activity. It is tempting for students to adopt an "everybody does it" attitude when it comes to behaviors commonly associated with college. Yet, for better or worse, you inhabit a world in which one bad mistake can be captured and shared digitally; that single moment can damage your chances for admission, possibly forever.

Think of it this way; many elements of the admissions process are out of your control. Your conduct, though, is an exception.

Tell me and I forget. Teach me and I remember. Involve me and I learn.

– Benjamin Franklin

CHAPTER 24
CLINICAL EXPERIENCES AND SHADOWING

SHADOWING AND CLINICAL EXPERIENCES IN DENTISTRY

Shadowing a dentist and gaining experience in the field of dentistry is an essential component of dental school preparation. First, the experiences teach important skills regarding terminology, dental office practices, and routine procedures. Second, shadowing gives you a better idea of whether or not you want to pursue this field and commit your life to the practice of dentistry. Third, by shadowing and completing other clinical experiences in dentistry, you are demonstrating to the admissions committee that you know what is expected and that you have made an informed choice to pursue dental school.

During COVID-19, shadowing experiences were difficult to find. Many practitioners did not let additional people into their practices. Even patients with appointments were not allowed to wait in a lobby or be accompanied by family members. Nevertheless, some people were able to shadow a family friend, parent, or someone close to them in the dental field. The pursuit of dentistry without having some sense of the day-to-day dentist-patient experience at multiple practices misses a component that had previously been available to applicants.

When you do shadow, ask questions, and learn as much as you can. Practitioners who welcome prospective students into their offices typically want to share their insights, and your questions will allow them to do that.

Contact your dentist, or perhaps a dentist your parents know. Even if it is just a phone interview, ask what they enjoy most and inquire about any concerns they have about the future. How do they see their commitment to the field, responsibility to patients, and ethical practices? More than one interview is helpful and provides a broader perspective to understand the field of dentistry and how you may run your practice in the future. Shadowing can also be an excellent way to gain exposure to the dental specialties.

Later, during your interviews, you may be asked to describe your shadowing experiences and explain what intrigued you or surprised you about dentistry. Prepare in advance for these sessions, because they provide a chance for your curiosity and genuine interest to shine. Here are some questions to consider:

1. What experiences left an impression on you?
2. What did you learn from the dentists you shadowed?
3. What are the challenges and opportunities in the field of dentistry?
4. What formative experiences led you to be sure dentistry is your future?

All dental schools in the United States recommend or require at least some shadowing prior to the application process. Needless to say, the complexities surrounding the COVID-19 pandemic may impact expectations for the 2021-22 cycle—and possibly beyond.

Dental admissions committees consider the amount of shadowing experience in the context of the student's circumstances. Students who were unable to complete a satisfactory number of hours, or who could not meet dental school shadowing requirements in some other way should use available space in their personal statement to describe particular obstacles which kept them out of offices and clinics.

Shadowing tips:

More is not always better. You want to experience as much shadowing as possible, but quality can shine as much as quantity. Fulfill the various schools' expectations, but also be mindful about which opportunities to pursue.

Even if your schools of choice do not restrict the types of dental shadowing you complete, take some tips from those institutions which do. Often, their requirements represent good rules of thumb.

Do

- Shadow multiple dentists in multiple offices.

- Shadow at least one general dentist and a pediatric dentist, if possible. Both kinds of professionals will likely address the kinds of cases you will encounter early in your dental school career.

- Shadow a dentist in different specialty areas if they are of interest.

- Make yourself helpful as you are able without interfering in the work at hand.

Do not

- Restrict your shadowing experiences to a parent who is a dentist. (Obviously, this caution applies only to students with at least one parent who practices dentistry.)

- Spend the majority of your shadowing hours in the offices of a specialist. A student who shadows exclusively with an orthodontist, for example, is less likely to draw on diverse experiences when writing the dental school application than a student who spent time in multiple practices. It is great to have a specialty in mind, but not to the extent that it overshadows your immediate pursuit, which is a general dentistry degree.

- Talk too much, get in the way, ask too many questions, talk down to the dental staff or otherwise make yourself an unwanted visitor in the future. (Use common sense and you will do fine.)

Dental School	Number of hours, if provided	Level of importance	Other Notes
Arizona School of Dentistry & Oral Health	50	Required	
Missouri School of Dentistry & Oral Health	50	Recommended	
Boston University School of Dental Medicine		Recommended	
California Northstate College of Dental Medicine		(No information available)	
Case Western Reserve University School of Dental Medicine	50	Strongly recommended	
Columbia University College of Dental Medicine		Required	
Creighton University School of Dentistry	65	Recommended	
Dental College of Georgia at Augusta University		Strongly recommended	
East Carolina University School of Dental Medicine		Required	
Harvard School of Dental Medicine		Strongly recommended	
Herman Ostrow School of Dentistry of USC	10-20	Recommended	
Howard University College of Dentistry	30	Strongly recommended	
Indiana University School of Dentistry	100	Recommended	
Lake Erie College of Osteopathic Medicine School of Dental Medicine	100	Required	

Dental School	Number of hours, if provided	Level of importance	Other Notes
Loma Linda University School of Dentistry	50	Required	100 recommended
Louisiana State University Health New Orleans School of Dentistry	25	Required	25 required
Marquette University School of Dentistry		Strongly recommended	
Medical University of South Carolina James B. Edwards College of Dental Medicine	100	Strongly recommended	
Meharry Medical College School of Dentistry	50	Required	
Midwestern University College of Dental Medicine-Illinois		Strongly recommended	
Midwestern University College of Dental Medicine-Arizona	100	Recommended	
NYU College of Dentistry	100	Strongly recommended	
Nova Southeastern University College of Dental Medicine		Strongly recommended	
Oregon Health & Science University School of Dentistry	50	Required	At least 25 hrs must be in general practice
Roseman University of Health Sciences College of Dental Medicine	50	Required	50 required

Dental School	Number of hours, if provided	Level of importance	Other Notes
Rutgers, The State University of New Jersey, School of Dental Medicine	50	Required	
Southern Illinois University School of Dental Medicine	30	Strongly recommended	
Stony Brook University School of Dental Medicine	100	Strongly recommended	
Texas A&M College of Dentistry		Recommended	
Texas Tech University Health Sciences Center El Paso School of Dental Medicine		(No information yet available)	
Temple University School of Dentistry		Strongly recommended	
The Ohio State University College of Dentistry	40	Required	
The University of Iowa College of Dentistry & Dental Clinics		Strongly recommended	
Touro College of Dental Medicine at New York Medical College	30	Strongly recommended	
Tufts University School of Dental Medicine	50	Required	
University at Buffalo School of Dental Medicine	100	Recommended	
University of Alabama at Birmingham School of Dentistry	100	Required	

Dental School	Number of hours, if provided	Level of importance	Other Notes
University of California, Los Angeles, School of Dentistry		Strongly recommended	
University of California, San Francisco, School of Dentistry	100	Strongly recommended	
University of Colorado School of Dental Medicine	50	Required	
University of Connecticut School of Dental Medicine	40	Required	
University of Detroit Mercy School of Dentistry	60	Required	
University of Florida College of Dentistry		Strongly recommended	
University of Illinois at Chicago College of Dentistry	50	Strongly recommended	
University of Kentucky College of Dentistry	20	Required	50 recommended
University of Louisville School of Dentistry	40	Required	Must be in general dentistry
University of Maryland School of Dentistry	100	Recommended	
University of Michigan School of Dentistry	50	Required	
University of Minnesota School of Dentistry	50	Required	

Dental School	Number of hours, if provided	Level of importance	Other Notes
University of Mississippi Medical Center School of Dentistry	70	Required	70 required
University of Missouri-Kansas City School of Dentistry	100	Required	
University of Nebraska Medical Center College of Dentistry		Required	
University of Nevada, Las Vegas, School of Dental Medicine	100	Required	
University of New England College of Dental Medicine	30	Required	
University of North Carolina at Chapel Hill Adams School of Dentistry		Required	Recommended minimum of 50 hrs
University of Oklahoma College of Dentistry	100	Required	
University of Pennsylvania School of Dental Medicine		Required	
University of Pittsburgh School of Dental Medicine	50	Required	
University of Puerto Rico School of Dental Medicine		Recommended	Shadowing is recommended; no specific number of hours provided
University of Tennessee Health Science Center College of Dentistry	50	Strongly recommended	

Dental School	Number of hours, if provided	Level of importance	Other Notes
The University of Texas School of Dentistry at Houston		Required	
University of the Pacific Arthur A. Dugoni School of Dentistry	40	Required	
University of Utah School of Dentistry	40	Required	40 required
University of Washington School of Dentistry	50	Required	50 required
UT Health San Antonio School of Dentistry		Required	
Virginia Commonwealth University School of Dentistry	100	Required	At least 50 must be spent in general practice
West Virginia University School of Dentistry		Required	
Western University of Health Sciences College of Dental Medicine	30	Required	

"Be fearless in the pursuit of what sets your soul on fire."

– Jennifer Lee

CHAPTER 25
SUMMER DENTAL OPPORTUNITIES

SUMMER HEALTH PROFESSIONS EDUCATION PROGRAM

Another opportunity for additional learning is the Summer Health Professions Education Program (SHPEP), which is a free program offered at twelve universities. The program provides enrichment, access, and information for students interested in the health professions. These two-to-five week programs assist with science, math, clinical, and professional experiences. These programs include:[1]

Columbia University Irving Medical Center offers students interested in the health professions the opportunity to focus on core science learning to prepare for medical, dental, nursing, physical therapy, and other programs. Clinical experiences include simulation-based learning with virtual patients, realistic scenarios, and checking vital signs and symptoms. Students receive a stipend and meal subsidy. *Program dates: are June 18, 2021 – July 30, 2021*

Howard University offers an enrichment program to support students toward building a culture of health and promoting diversity in healthcare. The goal is to provide access to those from underrepresented minorities and disadvantaged families who are interested in pursuing careers in the health sciences. Training includes General Chemistry, Genetics, Organic Chemistry,

---

1   Summer Health Professions Education Program, "Program Sites," *Summer Health Professions Education Program*, n.d., https://www.shpep.org/sites/

Biochemistry, Physics, Communications, Writing, and Mathematics. Students receive a stipend and meal subsidy. *Program Dates: June 6, 2021- July 16, 2021*

Rutgers, The State University of New Jersey serves Rutgers New Jersey Medical School, School of Dental Medicine, School of Nursing and Ernest Mario School of Pharmacy. This program is not lecture-driven. Learning primarily revolves around exposure to healthcare teams and the importance of each member to achieve positive patient outcomes. Students receive a stipend and meal subsidy. *Program Dates: June 7, 2021- July 16, 2021*

The University of Alabama at Birmingham works in partnership with University of Alabama at Birmingham (UAB) School of Medicine (SOM), School of Dentistry (SOD), School of Optometry (SOO), and School of Health Professions (SHP)'s Physician Assistant program. The program goal is to increase diversity in health professions by recruiting and preparing underrepresented minorities. Students observe real-time clinical encounters and debriefings with physicians. Students access Kaplan iHuman simulation interactive program (https://www.i-human.com/), participate in self-guided weekly preceptorship pairings, and observe clinical experiences through telehealth shadowing. Students receive a stipend and meal subsidy. *Program Dates: June 7, 2021 – July 16, 2021*

University of California Los Angeles Schools of Medicine, Dentistry, and Nursing are committed to developing future leaders in medicine, dentistry, and nursing and improve healthcare delivery, policy, and research in underserved communities. With a rigorous academic enrichment program, scholars participate in weekly problem-based learning with clinical cases and simulation experiences. Social hours and movie nights are included. Students receive a stipend and meal subsidy. *Program Dates: July 6, 2021 – August 13, 2021*

University of Florida offers an immersive program for scholars to engage in case-based learning and clinical experiences in Dentistry, Medicine, Nursing, Pharmacy, Public Health, and Veterinary Medicine. Students prepare for professional school through academic training, workshops, and study strategies. In addition to clinical simulation opportunities, students examine the U.S. healthcare industry, public policy, health disparity, and issues concerning access. Students receive a stipend and meal subsidy. *Program Dates: May 10, 2021 - June 18, 2021*

University of Iowa exposes students from underrepresented groups to Carver College of Medicine, College of Dentistry, College of Pharmacy, and College of Public Health. Students study Anatomy/Physiology, Physics, and Organic Chemistry to prepare for these courses. Scholars learn to work in healthcare teams. Scholars gain hands-on lessons with suturing kits, molecular modeling kits, dental molds, and pharmacy compounding kits. Students receive a stipend and meal subsidy. *Program Dates: June 7, 2021-July 16, 2021*

The University of Louisville includes the University of Louisville Schools of Medicine, Nursing, and Dentistry, and the Sullivan University College of Pharmacy, Louisville, KY. Scholars explore the impact of diabetes and cardiovascular disease. Academic training includes organic chemistry, biochemistry, and physiology. Virtual "meet-ups" will occur with practicing clinicians. Virtual patient scenarios will take place at the Standardized Patient Center and Simulation Labs. Students receive a stipend and meal subsidy. *Program Dates: May 31, 2021 – July 9, 2021*

The University of Nebraska program is led by faculty and staff from the UNMC Colleges of Medicine, Dentistry, Nursing, and Public Health. The program is guided by Virtual Learning Community Leads (VLCLs), who assist scholars in connecting with healthcare mentors in their professional area. VLCLs link scholars with shadowing opportunities in their local community. Students receive a stipend and meal subsidy. *Program Dates: June 13, 2021 -July 23, 2021*

University of Texas Health Sciences Center at Houston, which educates more than 5,000 professionals, supports UTHealth McGovern Medical School, School of Dentistry, and Cizik School of Nursing. Students engage in wellness activities like yoga, Tai Chi, Zumba, and other physical and mental activities. Scholars engage in hands-on health-related activities. Participants will attend a suturing workshop. Stethoscopes are sent for heart listening activity and blood pressure readings. Surgical gloves and gowns are sent to simulate infection control. Students receive a stipend. *Program Dates: June 1, 2021- July 9, 2021*

University of Washington's program will be virtual in 2021 with no clinical activities. Teaching assistants will work with participants to develop online community-building activities. Students receive a stipend. *Program Dates: June 21, 2021-July 30, 2021*

The Western University School of Health Sciences program is designed to provide diverse medical experiences for scholars planning to go into one of the healthcare professions. Some clinical tracks may have telemedicine clinical shadowing. Students receive a stipend and meal subsidy. *Program Dates: June 21, 2021 – July 30, 2021*

"

A ship is safe in a harbor, but that's not what ships are for.

–William Shedd

CHAPTER 26
INTERNATIONAL STUDY/ EXPERIENCE

PLANNING A DENTAL EXPERIENCE ABROAD

The need is great. In many countries, half of the residents have never seen a dentist, and few of the rest have had regular dental care. According to the World Health Organization, 3.58 billion have oral health conditions worldwide.[1] Severe health conditions could result without access to treatment. Even in the United States, many have untreated dental caries (tooth decay). According to the Center for Disease Control,[2]

- Percent of **children** aged 5-19 years with untreated dental caries: 13.2% (2015-2018)
- Percent of **adults** aged 20-44 with untreated dental caries: 25.9% (2015-2018)

Whether you are in college, dental school, or a practicing dentist, there are numerous possibilities to serve in a foreign country. The experience will be novel no matter where you go or what service you provide. Most trips abroad expose volunteers to unique opportunities to see the world through a new lens.

---

1   World Health Organization, "Oral Health," *World Health Organization*, March 25, 2020, https://www.who.int/news-room/fact-sheets/detail/oral-health?utm_source=volunteerforever.com&utm_medium=referral&utm_campaign=dental-volunteer-abroad-medical-mission-trips-dentists-students
2   CDC, "Oral and Dental Health," *Centers for Disease Control and Prevention (CDC)*, n.d., https://www.cdc.gov/nchs/fastats/dental.htm

Volunteering in support of oral health could encompass everything from teaching proper oral hygiene and providing toothbrushes to extracting teeth and performing root canals. Whatever skills you have, they will be properly utilized.

WHO CAN VOLUNTEER?

Some programs allow students from high school to dental school to volunteer. Dentists with all specialties are encouraged to serve. Dental hygienists are also desperately needed in some regions. Internships offer a wide range of possibilities for volunteers. As long as a person is healthy and willing to support a community abroad, they can be students, graduate students, or adults in any profession.

EXPERIENCES

Dental shadowing offers clinical opportunities to provide insight into your future dental career. Some experiences are more rustic with only basic tents and equipment, while others are in clinics, hospitals, or other medical facilities. In developing countries, dentists face the challenges of limited facilities, resources, and equipment. Furthermore, experiences in impoverished areas span oral health and dental conditions since few people have access to dental care. Many patients enter with extreme pain, extensive tooth decay, and the need for complex surgeries.

EXPECTATIONS, GUIDELINES, AND RESPONSIBILITIES

With any program you choose, you are expected to follow the rules, have a positive mindset, and be willing to perform any tasks required. Volunteers are expected to follow personal sanitary and cleanliness practices. Professionalism is essential in these workplaces. Not that this needs to be said, but volunteers are expected to work.

Note that some rural settings do not have creature comforts like running water or electricity or running water. You will need to make do. Occasionally, dental volunteers are untrained, and dentists perform procedures in which they do not have the skills. Some volunteer organizations are not reputable, so do your due diligence.

Your clinical responsibilities should be focused on observation, shadowing, and support. You should not be asked to assist in actual dental procedures. Your priority must be on the patient's support, comfort, and welfare. All decisions regarding how to treat a patient must be left to the dentists or responsible officers. It is possible that the only interaction you will have with a patient is helping them fill out the intake forms and taking their temperature.

LOCATION

Dental students in their clinical period of study may be allowed to perform hands-on skills care, while pre-dental students typically assist.

Projects Abroad have locations open in Africa (Ghana, Tanzania), Asia (India, Nepal, Sri Lanka, and Vietnam), and Latin America & the Caribbean (Argentina, Jamaica, Mexico). For example, Projects Abroad offers students the chance to shadow dentists in Guadalajara, Mexico, where disadvantaged communities lack access to basic medical and dental services.[3] The dates are flexible, and students must have a basic knowledge of Spanish.

Plan My Gap Year has medical support programs in Bali, Ecuador, Ghana, India, Peru, Sri Lanka, Tanzania, and Vietnam.[4] The experience in Bali's 500-patient Tabanan General Hospital includes shadowing in all departments. Participants also gain experiences with holistic healers, birth clinics, and homes for the elderly.

---

3   Projects Abroad, "Dentistry Internship in Mexico," *Projects Abroad*, n.d., https://www.projects-abroad.org/projects/dentistry-internship-mexico/?utm_source=volunteerforever.com&utm_medium=referral&utm_campaign=dental-volunteer-abroad-medical-mission-trips-dentists-students

4   Plan My Gap Year, "Medical Missions Overseas," *Plan My Gap Year*, n.d., https://www.planmygapyear.co.uk/medical-mission-trips

Maximo Nivel offers healthcare opportunities in Costa Rica, Guatemala, and Peru. For example, since Peru provides universal healthcare, it might be expected that all citizens have access. However, some have limited access, no resources, and little training. Opportunities in Peru are available in rural clinics where there are no facilities to provide check-ups, take vitals, assist with medical records, and clean and prepare equipment.[5] Maximo Nivel requires participants to be 18, commit to at least a week, be hardworking, positive, and prepared to do whatever tasks are required.

DURATION

Programs can last for as short as a week to as long as a semester. Most programs prefer that you remain in the host country for at least a week, and longer is preferred if that option is available.

TRAVEL COSTS

The flight and other transportation costs can be expensive, even if the local community or mission has provided a tent or cabin for the dental team. There are a few ways to fund your trip. One is purchasing cheap student plane tickets with StudentUniverse, church mission funding through a church, GoFundMe, or some other fundraising option.

A handy guide with a list of programs may be found at Volunteer Forever: Dental Volunteer Abroad & Medical Mission Trips – updated in 2020 and written by Nick Callos.

5   Máximo Nivel, "Medical & Healthcare Volunteer," *Máximo Nivel*, n.d., https://maximonivel.com/volunteers/medical-healthcare/?utm_source=volunteerforever.com&utm_medium=article&utm_campaign=dental-volunteer-abroad-medical-mission-trips-dentists-students

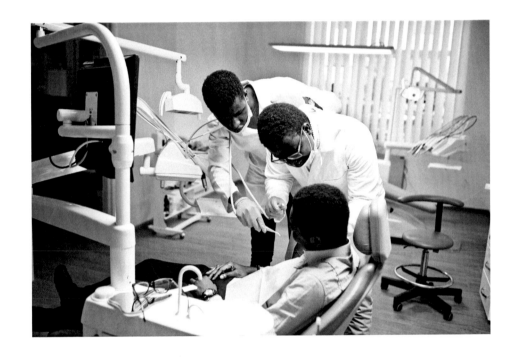

> " "
>
> *Always make a total effort, even when the odds are against you.*
>
> – Arnold Palmer

CHAPTER 27
TRAINING AND CERTIFICATIONS

I s there specialized training that might set you apart from other applicants when you apply to dental school? More importantly, what can you learn or do which will actually help you be a strong dental student and, eventually, a great practitioner? The answers to those questions are one and the same. Training and certification in the medical field, especially in the dental field, will prepare you for dental school.

To clarify, in this context, "training and certification" refers to the successful completion of a formalized curriculum rather than casual mentorship or oversight in a job. Shadowing, while beneficial and, indeed, required of most dental school candidates, is not considered training or certification.

CERTIFICATIONS ACCESSIBLE TO YOU

Bright students working intently toward goals six or seven years down the road may overlook their eligibility to seek more immediate certification in a medical or dental area. In other words, your work toward establishing a career at the highest levels of a profession does not disqualify you from experience in a supportive or auxiliary role in the meantime.

Do you wonder what kinds of certifications are accessible to you, a busy young adult with a rigorous academic schedule and, no doubt, leadership responsibilities, too? Depending on the amount of time you are willing and able to sacrifice in the interest of real-world credentialing and experience, consider these options.

The most obvious and quickest training is a **CPR** certification course. You will be required to become CPR-certified once you begin dental school, anyway. **Lifeguard training** and certification (e.g., Red Cross) is another option. What about going a little deeper, though? You might be surprised to know that high school graduates can be certified as **EMT**s (emergency medical technicians) in a matter of weeks, depending on a given state's requirements. Phlebotomy training is an excellent skill as well, and certification can take as little as four weeks.

BUT IS A CERTIFICATION NECESSARY?

No.

The subject of certification is raised for two reasons: 1) You will encounter people in dental school who entered with certifications, but usually, those credentials were earned irrespective of their eventual plans to go to dental school. Some dental hygienists decide to go on to earn a DDS or DMD. Or, you may meet someone who has worked as a licensed dental laboratory technician but only recently realized a desire to be, say, a prosthodontist. 2) Students who want exposure to a particular body of knowledge or experience often like the structure and sense of accomplishment which comes through certification.

Formal training is absolutely not required of a dental school applicant, though. So, what kind of experience or training is most likely to strengthen your candidacy?

Orthodontist Dr. Paul Tran, longtime practitioner and clinical instructor, suggests going a step further than shadowing:

> "Personally, I think working part-time for a dentist--not just shadowing a few hours here and there-- is a great way to differentiate yourself. Many applicants shadow a few hours with a dentist prior to applying to dental school, but I worked about 3 hrs a day for a dentist while in college. That taught me a lot about the field of dentistry, but also helped me tremendously when in dental school. I was familiar with lots of dental procedures and felt comfortable working on patients."

You must be the decision-maker when it comes to any unique training or credentialing. Students probably tire of advice like this, but it stands: you have to determine your own best course. If there were a formula, everyone would follow it and be deprived of their individuality.

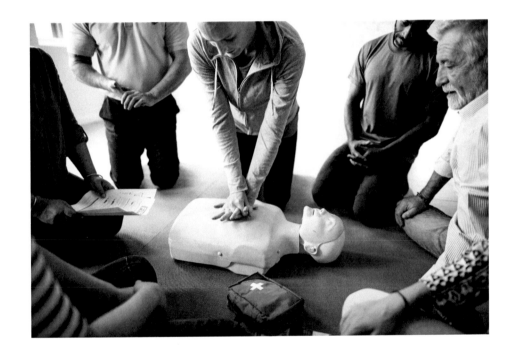

PART 4

PRE-APPLICATION: TESTING AND RECS

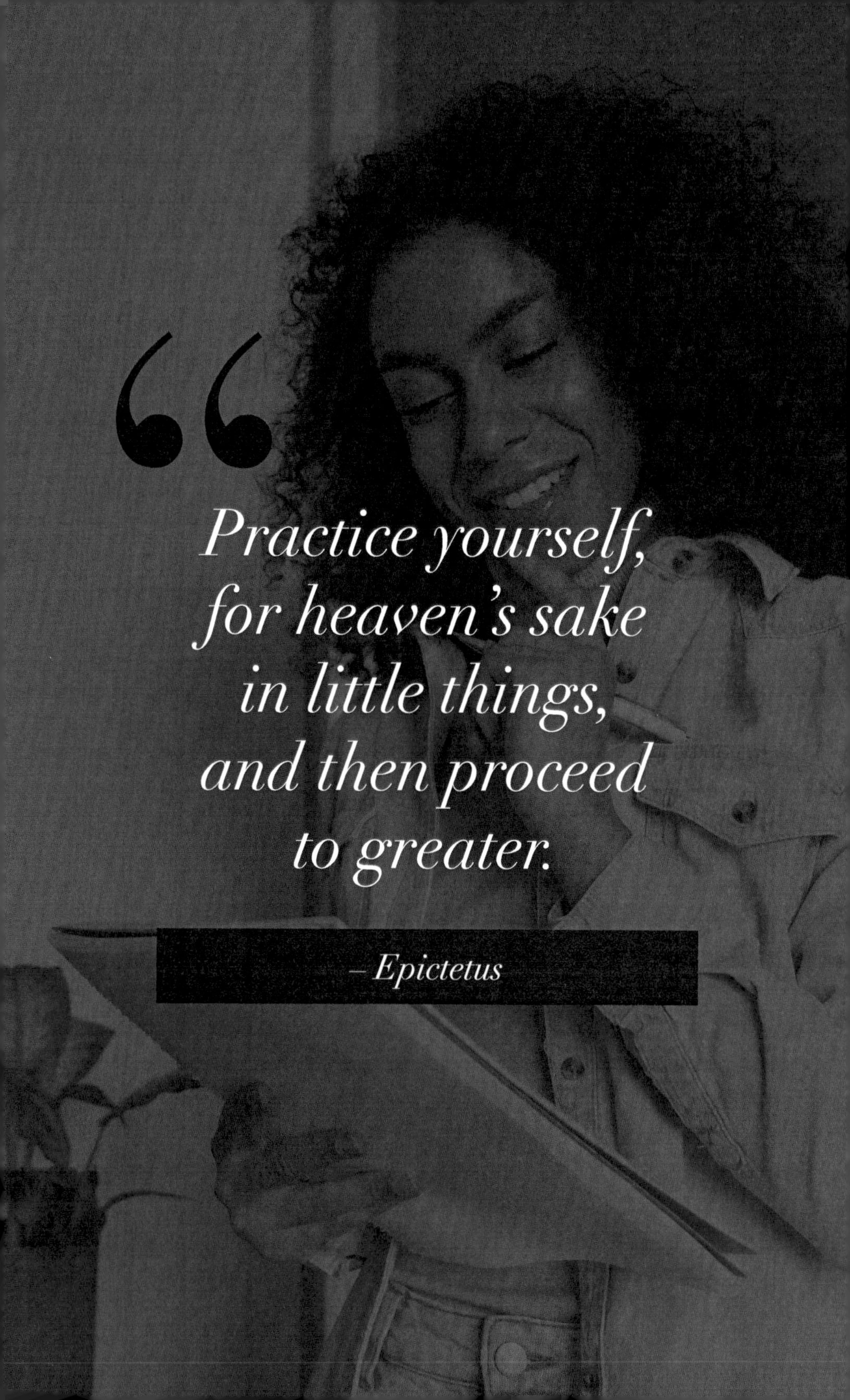

> "Practice yourself,
> for heaven's sake
> in little things,
> and then proceed
> to greater.

— *Epictetus*

CHAPTER 28
CHECKLISTS

- ✔ DAT
- ✔ Letters of Recommendation
- ✔ Personal Statement
- ✔ Shadowing/Volunteer Activities
- ✔ Application
- ✔ Secondaries
- ✔ CASPer
- ✔ Interviews
- ✔ Updates
- ✔ Admission

When You Start

☐ Choose an online/reminders/planner pad task management calendar system

☐ Write down requirements and responsibilities

- Coursework, assignments, discussions, tutoring/advising, mentoring, research, service, shadowing, athletics, music/art, exercise/meditation, family, friends, social activities, cleaning/organizing, trips, and breaks
- Application requirements like dates applications open/close, testing, letters of recommendation, etc. (see timeline)

☐ Create file folders to organize information from schools

Summer/Fall

- ☐ Pre-health advisor meeting
- ☐ Pre-health committee letter
- ☐ Pre-requisite classes
- ☐ Connect with ADA, ADEA, AADSAS, TMDSAS
- ☐ Research dental schools
- ☐ Purchase DAT preparation book
- ☐ DAT tutoring, test prep class, or independent study
- ☐ Register for DENTPIN (ADA website)
- ☐ Register for the DAT
- ☐ Prepare for DAT
- ☐ Download previous year's ADEA AADSAS to review

Winter/Spring Before Applying

- ☐ Pre-health advisor meeting
- ☐ Take the DAT
- ☐ Outline your personal statement
- ☐ Request letters of recommendation
- ☐ Follow up with the committee letter of recommendation
- ☐ Follow up with individual recommenders
- ☐ Write your personal statement
- ☐ Request transcripts.
- ☐ Send transcripts to application services

May/June Application

- ☐ Complete AADSAS
- ☐ Complete TMDSAS
- ☐ Input personal statement and school-specific questions (see "program materials")

- ☐ Fill in courses and grades section
- ☐ Select colleges
- ☐ Check formatting and spelling
- ☐ Certify, pay, and submit on June 1
- ☐ Review/error check on AADSAS and TMDSAS total/science GPA

Summer/Fall

- ☐ Check application status
- ☐ Register for CASPer
- ☐ Take/retake DAT if necessary
- ☐ Secondaries (complete within two weeks of receipt)
- ☐ Prep for Interviews
- ☐ Interview
- ☐ Follow up with schools
- ☐ December 1st – First Decisions

Winter/Spring

- ☐ ADEA AADSAS application closes February 3rd
- ☐ Interviews continue through March
- ☐ Update schools on new accomplishments
- ☐ Show expressed interest in waitlist schools

> There is no boundary or limit in your brain. The only hindrance is your emotions! Study! Don't give up! Aim high! And you'll see the fruits of your success!

— Unknown

CHAPTER 29
DAT PLAN AND PREPARATION

The American Dental Association (ADA) offers the Dental Admission Test (DAT) each year to candidates interested in attending dental school. The DAT is required for admission. However, some schools may have waived the requirement due to COVID-19. Therefore, we suggest checking for updates. Also, there may be changes to the test questions/types for 2021 and 2022 that may alter a candidates' test preparation.

Time Required: 5 hours and 15 minutes (with optional sections)

DAT Breakdown and Timing	
Tutorial (Optional)	15 minutes
Survey of Natural Sciences	90 minutes
Perceptual Ability Test	60 minutes
Scheduled Break (Optional)	30 minutes
Reading Comprehension	60 minutes
Quantitative Reasoning Test	45 minutes
Post Test Survey (Optional)	15 minutes
Total Time (actual testing = 4 hrs, 15 min)	5 hours 15 min

An unofficial score report is generated upon completion of the test.

PURPOSE

The DAT is a multiple-choice test designed to assess the academic background of dental school applicants. Performance on the exam is taken into consideration in the dental school admissions process. However, admission to most dental schools is holistic, which means that other factors are used, including GPA, clinical experiences, research, and volunteer service. Each school considers the DAT according to their institutional data science, needs, and priorities.

SCORING

Scores are disaggregated into three science scores which are averaged with reading comprehension and quantitative reasoning to give a composite academic average. Spatial ability is a separately reported score.

Total Score: 1 to 30 (national average 19)

Sample Score Report

	Date	July 31, 2021
Dental Admission Testing Program Examinee's Report of Scores	American Dental Association Department of Testing Services 211 East Chicago Avenue Chicago Illinois 60611-2637	
Area Tested	**Standard Score**	
Perceptual Ability	19	
Quantitative Reasoning	21	
Reading Comprehension	22	
Biology	20	
General Chemistry	23	
Organic Chemistry	25	
Total Science	22	
Academic Average	22	
Standard scores used in the testing program range from 1 to 30. Only the standard scores are reported to the dental schools. Through the use of standard scores, it is possible to compare the performance of examinees taking different editions of the Dental Admission Test.		
The Academic Average is the average of five scores rounded to the nearest whole number. Quantitative Reasoning, Reading Comprehension, Biology, General Chemistry, and Organic Chemistry.		
The Total Science score is a standard score based on all 100 questions in the Biology, Chemistry, and Organic Chemistry tests. It is not the average of the three science scores.		

CONTENT

Four Sections: Survey of Natural Sciences, Perceptual Ability, Reading Comprehension, and Quantitative Reasoning.

Each question is independent. There is no penalty for guessing; do not leave a question unanswered. Answer questions you know quickly, marking others so you can return and spend more time.

SNS - Survey of Natural Sciences (100 questions; 90 minutes; separate scores given for each section)

Biology (40 questions)

- Cell & Molecular Biology
- Diversity of Life
- Structure & Function of Systems
- Developmental Biology
- Genetics
- Evolution, Ecology, & Behavior

Chemistry (30 questions)

- Stoichiometry
- Gases
- Liquids & Solids
- Solutions
- Acids & Bases
- Chemical Equilibria
- Thermodynamics & Thermochemistry
- Chemical Kinetics
- Oxidation-Reduction Reactions
- Atomic & Molecular Structure
- Periodic Properties
- Nuclear Reactions
- Laboratory

Organic Chemistry (30 questions)

- Mechanisms
- Chemical & Physical Properties of Molecules
- Stereochemistry
- Nomenclature
- Reactions & Compound Synthesis
- Acid Base Chemistry
- Aromatics & Bonding

PAT - Perceptual Ability Test (90 questions; 60 minutes; spatial ability & reasoning)

Preparation on this section significantly improves performance.

- Apertures
- View Recognition
- Angle Discrimination
- Paper Folding
- Cube Counting
- 3D Form Development

RCT – Reading Comprehension Test (50 questions; 60 minutes; spatial ability & reasoning)

The reading comprehension test consists of three reading passages. Knowledge of the specific scientific or social science principles is not necessary as the information is contained in the passage. Your job is to read and analyze the content. Prepare for this using practice exams and techniques to learn how to give a cursory read and manage your time.

QRT – Quantitative Reasoning Test (40 questions; 40 minutes; on-screen four-function calculator provided)

- Mathematics – algebra, data analysis, comparisons, and probability and statistics
- Word Problems – applied mathematics

EXAM PREPARATION

Prepare for the DAT as if this is the only time the test will be taken. Repeated testing is not advisable, but you may. Do not take the DAT as a "practice run". Not only do you have to wait 90 days to repeat the test, but some schools will average your scores. Three test takes are allowable before a special request must be submitted.

Determine whether you will get tutoring, test prep class, or study independently. Preparation options include:

DAT Study Guides	Guidebook Practice Tests
DAT Practice Tests	Test Preparation Services
DAT Website Purchase	Tutor Services

SCORING AND SCORE REPORTS

Score Range: 1 to 30   National Average: approximately 19

Scores on the DAT are scaled to compare each score with the scores of the other candidates. Scores are based upon the correct responses with no penalty for guessing. Some unidentified questions are experimental with information used to create future tests.

Note: Scores cannot be voided once testing has begun.

Official scores must be submitted directly from the testing agency. Candidates authorize DTS permission to release official scores. If a test is retaken, all scores are reported. Scores are transmitted three to four weeks after the test date.

Note: Designated recipients cannot be edited or canceled after submission.

Additional score reports may be requested. An additional fee is required with the new score report request.

FEES

$495 – *Initial Application* - This charge includes the administration and official score reporting to every school listed on the application to take the test.

$45 – *Score Report* - This cost is charged for every school to which an additional score report must be sent.

$65 – *Audit Fee* - This charge is to review the test and check the results (within 30 days) if they do not appear to be correct.

$125 – *Extension Fee* – If a test cannot be taken on the specified date, a test taker can extend the test up to 45 days. Only one extension must be made per test application. The extension cannot be made until the original date is canceled.

At the time of application to take the exam, all schools selected are included in the application fee, regardless of the number of schools selected. Thus, candidates should send official scores to every school they are considering for admission.

Fees are nonrefundable and nontransferable.

Fee Waiver – Check with the DAT testing agency to determine how to get a partial fee waiver. These are granted on a first-come, first-served basis.

CANCELATION AND RETESTING

Scores cannot be voided once the candidate has been seated by test center staff at a computer and agrees to start the test. From that moment, that test counts as one of the three allowable takes before a petition to permit must be requested. A retake cannot take place for 90 days.

A student who takes part of the DAT will be assigned the lowest possible score for any sections not completed. Thus, if a test taker only completes one section, all four sections will be scored based upon what was submitted at the time of leaving the test and a new application and fee is required for retaking. When candidates authorize scores to be sent, the official scores are submitted directly from the testing agency. If retaken, scores from all sittings are reported. When retesting, a new application must be created, and associated fees processed.

Perseverance is not a long race; it is many short races one after another.

–Walter Elliott

CHAPTER 30
TOEFL AND INTERNATIONAL TESTS

International students can apply for nearly all U.S. and Canadian dental schools. The first step for all non-native English-speaking students is to demonstrate English proficiency. To do this, you will need to take the Test of English as a Foreign Language (TOEFL) or the International English Language Testing System (IELTS). Many schools require a 100 on the Internet-Based (iBT) test, though some have lower minimum scores. For example, UNLV set its minimum at 80, and Creighton University is set at 88 or above (no section below 20) for the TOEFL and an overall score of 6.5 (no section below 6.0) for IELTS.

Next, on the ADEA website, two terms seem very similar – International Student and Foreign-Trained Dentist. These are very different, and the process for applying is different as well. An international student is considered to attend dental school as a first-year student and attend for the duration of the program. A foreign-educated dentist is a student who completed dental school in another country and wants to attend dental school in the U.S. to become certified as a dentist in the United States. A foreign-educated dentist is already a dentist but not schooled the way U.S. dentists are trained. According to the ADEA, the official definitions are:[1]

---

1   ADEA, "International Students," *ADEA*, n.d., https://www.adea.org/GoDental/Non-traditional_Applicants/International_students.aspx

International Student: A native of a foreign country that is in the process of completing or has completed their undergraduate education in the United States. Alternatively, a student from another country that wishes to attend dental school in the United States or Canada on a student visa.

Foreign-Educated Dentist: An individual who has attended, graduated, and earned a dental degree from a dental school in a country other than the U.S. or Canada.

Since the processes for each of the two designations above are different, you must follow the pathway depending upon your situation. Also, if you are already a dentist but trained abroad, you can earn advanced standing and thus do not have the same length of time to complete dental school or the application process.

FOREIGN-EDUCATED DENTIST PROCESS

Use the ADEA Centralized Application for Advanced Placement for International Dentists (ADEA CAAPID). Typically, the programs offer advanced standing and thus are shorter in length. The application process is simplified with a single application process without the need to complete supplemental applications to each program.

INTERNATIONAL STUDENT APPLICANT TO DENTAL SCHOOL

To apply, you will complete all parts of the AADSAS application in English, inputting undergraduate schools, coursework, and grades in the same way as other applicants. There are no differences in the required essays and supplemental applications. You will need to check the websites to determine if the schools you have chosen accept international students.

FINANCIAL AID AND SCHOLARSHIPS

International students will have to look harder for financial aid and scholarships since most of the available assistance is through the U.S. federal government for citizens and permanent residents. Scholarships have varied requirements. However, some of these are strictly merit-based. You may qualify for one of these options. Check to see if any apply. For example, Creighton University has the Matteo Ricci Scholarships for International Students, offered to students with "excellent academic records and F-1 visa status".

You will also need to show the ability to pay using a form you can get from the financial aid office online or in person. The form is not complicated, though the part that is difficult is getting your family (if necessary) and bank at home to sign the form confirming funds available. The U.S. government requires international student applicants to certify that they can provide adequate funding to cover the cost of a U.S. education. Admission cannot be finalized, and an I-20 issued until the Office of Admissions verifies the applicant's complete Graduate Student Certification of Available Finances Form.

Check with the dental school financial aid office to see what they suggest. Some financial aid offices are excellent with helpful staff who truly want to help you find the money you need. These staff members believe that if their admissions offices accepted you, they picked you from a long list of excellent candidates and truly want you to attend. They will help.

However, there are a few financial aid offices where the staff cannot be bothered and brush you off by sending you down a rabbit hole with no cheese on the other side. Do not get discouraged or think the whole school is like that. Particularly during the pandemic, some staff members responded once a week and only vaguely answered questions, while others went over and above the call of duty even if they were in isolation. Customer service was hit or miss.

For Canada, you can apply for the Express Entry – Federal Skilled Worker Program. Canada wants skilled workers and welcomes trained dentists for immigration. This avenue is popular with people who want to live in Canada. You must demonstrate that you have funds. There is a form that must be signed by the banking representative showing that you have the necessary balance in the bank to pay.

LOANS

Private loans are available through banking institutions as well. If you have a U.S. co-signer, you can often get a loan for the full cost of attendance, depending on the co-signer's creditworthiness. If you choose the loan option, just make sure you have read through the requirements, as there will be provisions regarding interest, repayment, and postponement. Focus on the interest rate and repayment because you might want to try a second or third bank.

Don't settle for the first one until you do your research. There is a huge difference between Full Deferral, Interest Only, and Immediate Repayment. The interest, terms, and conditions could make a difference of $100,000. Also, remember, you may choose a residency program in oral surgery, orthodontics, or other specialty and thus remain in school for much longer.

ADEA suggests that you consider using the private company, eduPASS, for assistance.

> " Don't be afraid to ask questions. Don't be afraid to ask for help when you need it. I do that every day. Asking for help isn't a sign of weakness, it's a sign of strength. It shows you have the courage to admit when you don't know something, and to learn something new.

— *Barack Obama*

CHAPTER 31
RECOMMENDATION PLAN

etters of recommendation, letters of evaluation, and/or committee letters are a required part of the application process. The ADEA AADSAS is incomplete without letters of evaluation, although they do not need to be submitted by the time you send your application. However, to ensure that you will get these on time, you should request these early. Recommenders typically need time to formulate what to write. Since recommenders find it useful to have information available to them about your interests, progress, and goals, providing them with your current resume and personal statement is valuable.

On the AADSAS site, you may submit a maximum of four individuals who will provide letters of evaluation. While you do not need to provide all four, you should provide at least three letters. Science teachers are the best because they can assess your ability in classes closest to the field of dentistry. You might also choose the leader of your research team, volunteer effort, dentist, or someone who knows your academic and professional performance. Your application will be verified as complete, even if the recommendations come in after your application is submitted.

The letters you submit provide a fuller picture of who you are as an applicant and how you will perform as a professional. The individual might offer insights into your commitment to dentistry and ability to perform under pressure. These individuals have observed your work and are the eyes and ears of the admissions committee. Since many of the schools consider a student holistically, they rely on those who can attest to your abilities, personality traits, and work ethic. In the supplementals, a dental school might request an additional letter of recommendation from a source that offers them further information.

COMPOSITE OR COMMITTEE LETTER

Your undergraduate institution may offer the opportunity to request a committee letter. For example, at the University of Chicago, the health professions committee writes a "Health and Medicine Committee Letter" to support dental school applicants. This letter is designed to further explain a student's academic and college experience as well as additional unique qualities.

Undergraduate institutions that have committee letters identify their letter of support using different names. Each has a unique process. Many times there are a set of steps, submissions, and time requirements. As early as you know you want to go to dental school, find out from your advisor or someone else at your institution what system your school uses. You want to make sure you have the requirements met by their established timeline. They need transcripts, essays, and recommendations. Start early! You will need to build relationships with a few people who will become your recommenders.

INDIVIDUAL LETTERS OF EVALUATION

These letters will come from your professors, advisors, lab supervisors, volunteer supervisors, dentists, clinical practitioners, or others who have worked with you in a professional capacity. Planning ahead of time is helpful. At some schools, where class sizes in the sciences are large, faculty may not know the students well and cannot evaluate their academic performance or professionalism in clinical settings.

The only thing they may know about a student is that they earned an A in the class, which does not say much about the student and amounts to a very weak recommendation. This situation makes it awkward for students to ask a professor. Furthermore, that professor may not be willing to write the recommendation because they do not feel comfortable doing so. Finding a recommender who will write a good letter necessitates that you get to know your professors well enough so that they can provide a strong assessment of your personal qualifications as well as your academic ability.

Often principal investigators (PIs) on a research project also know their assistants well since they spend most of their time mentoring their doctoral candidates. Typically, if you are on one of these teams, the only person you communicate with is the doctoral student. Thus, students often ask if they can use the doctoral student as their recommender. The answer is yes. Why? They are, in effect, your supervisor and the one you work with on a day-to-day basis in the lab. They know you best and have a good sense of how to assess your abilities.

Getting good letters of evaluation is a function of getting to know the recommender and determining their ability to write a good recommendation. They can do this best if you communicate well and provide them with the information they need to write the best evaluation for your application.

Letter of Recommendation

it May Concern:

pose of this letter is to recommend

manager or related position.

excellent office and administr

project, while gaining the acce

work she produces is on-time an

valuable part of our management

we have acquired a larger perce

skills and pleasant personal

e for employ

d her w

*Ask what makes
you come alive
and go do it.
Because what the
world needs is
people who have
come alive.*

— Howard Thurman

CHAPTER 32

COMMITTEES – APPLICATION/LETTER

HEALTH PROFESSIONS COMMITTEE PROCESS

Some colleges have an extensive committee review process to obtain a committee letter of recommendation, letter of evaluation, or 'introduction to the applicant', depending upon the university. For example, at Johns Hopkins University, students receive an 'introduction' to the dental school after completing their process, which is done on Blackboard. Dental school applicants must complete the online Health Professions Committee Application (HPCA).

A 'packet' of personal and academic information, demographic information, extracurricular activities, and health and science pursuits is collected to formulate the committee letter. The good news is that by ordering your transcripts, listing your activities, writing essays, and organizing your personal information, you have done much of the legwork for the AADSAS. The bad news is that the process tends to be laborious at a time in the semester when you have zero time.

The committee deadlines often come right at midterms. Committees are likely to say that the process is easy, but students beg to differ. Besides, it is stressful. You do not know what they will say, and your future is on the line. Often students' parents insist that everything be done promptly while you feverishly manage responsibilities, leadership, lab projects, coursework, shadowing, and volunteer service at the same time.

To get a committee letter or packet at some schools, you must satisfy a set of conditions. The first is that an advisor needs to 'advise' whether you should take a year off to improve your skills before attempting to proceed through the process. Some will caution that the committee letter may not look great given the competitive applicants.

They may point you to PowerPoints, articles, data, and tracking mechanisms to help you make the 'right' decision about post-bacc programs, graduate school options, or a clinical/research position. You must also be on track to complete your degree and dental school upper-division science requirements.

While your advisor may be right that another year would improve your chances, parents are not always forgiving and challenge their kids to apply anyway against their advisor's wishes. This tug and pull creates tension and uncertainty. Meanwhile, challenging classes pose quite a different and immediate problem, sometimes with lab partners who are also attempting to manage the committee process with school work and do not pull their weight.

Your designated pre-professional advisor can assist with the process. The advisor makes the first assessment as to whether you are a likely candidate based upon your profile, GPA, DAT, personal statement, and activities. The challenge at any competitive school is that they can dissuade you from applying. The next group that can discourage you from applying is the committee.

This group also evaluates your readiness as an applicant or likelihood of acceptance. They significantly influence whether you are accepted. The committee writes a composite letter that can support your admission or provide a lukewarm acknowledgment of your application. They might also tell you that they will not write a letter on your behalf. On the positive side, the advisor and the committee have significant experience and can tell whether students a likely to be accepted with a 5% or so error. On the negative side, they can suggest you wait a year and take steps to improve your chances without giving you a chance.

DEADLINES, DEADLINES, DEADLINES

Calendars are your friend. If you did not need one for your studies because you 'remember everything', you will soon find that there are simply too many dates. The committee process demands strict adherence to deadlines, or else you will not get the letter. Missing a deadline means waiting an entire year or dodging the committee packet process altogether.

A question I am always asked is, "Can students circumvent the committee process?" Well, you should go through the school process. Particularly, if you are a good candidate, it is advisable and extremely helpful. However, there is no button on the AADSAS that throws out your application if you use individual recommendations rather than the committee letter. After all, some people decide to apply to dental school late, after the deadline. These students missed the committee process.

Note:

Most schools that use committee letters allow their graduates to utilize their services for a few years after graduation.

"

A goal is not always meant to be reached, it often serves simply as something to aim at.

– Bruce Lee

CHAPTER 33
CASPER TEST

C ASPer is the Computer-Based Assessment for Sampling Personal Characteristics administered by Altus Assessments to determine the non-academic qualities that may determine if you would make a good dentist.

CASPer is a situational judgment test that is designed to assess decision-making in specific scenarios. The test takers are asked to judge a situation. Using their on-the-spot judgment, they respond to a dilemma in a medical/dental setting. After reviewing the choices provided, they respond with the appropriate alternative they believe best fits the vignette.

The questions vary from capabilities to thinking skills and give medical and dental schools a clearer picture of the applicant's decision-making, problem-solving, and situational management abilities. Both in dental school and in the practice of dentistry, individuals must be able to manage and resolve difficult problems quickly and appropriately. While these behavioral skills were once not considered, dental schools have increasingly sought to gain a deeper insight into applicants' actions and reactions when put under pressure. Relationship-building and communication are valued skills that dental schools consider essential to becoming a good practitioner.

THE CASPER TEST ASSESSES:

- Collaboration
- Communication
- Empathy
- Equity
- Ethics
- Motivation

- Problem Solving
- Professionalism

- Resilience
- Self-Awareness

THE TEST

60 – 90 Minute Test

Questions progress to the next automatically.

There is an optional 10-15-minute break halfway through.

12 Scenarios (8 Video-Based & 4 Word-Based)

Each is followed by 3 open-ended questions (5 minutes).

Not Computer Scored

Each test is individually scored by more than one specially-trained evaluator.

Test Scores Forwarded Automatically

After scoring is completed, tests are forwarded to the designated schools

NOTE: Spelling Mistakes Do Not Impact Your Score

Since you can take the test from your choice of appropriate locations, you can create an environment that works for you. Eliminate distractions. If you believe headphones will help you, most test centers will let you use them.

Read the prompt fully. Reflect and think through what you want to write in response to the three open-ended questions. You only have five minutes, and you want to be broad but clear. Since you have five minutes to complete each response, use your time wisely. Focus on what you are trying to relay rather than the spelling or format.

Since a different reader will rate the next section, they will not be prejudiced on what you might have done wrong in a previous section. Also, there are 12 sections, so you may do better on another if you make a mistake on one. You also have a short break to relax, collect your thoughts, and get some refreshing water. Draw upon your life experiences as you respond and explain how you would act based on your life situations. Research shows that test-takers who use the full amount of time score higher.

Cheating can be detected by the trained eye and violates the agreement test takers sign. If cheating is determined, scores are withheld, and information is sent to each of the programs. Furthermore, cheating takes time and sophistication.

Since the consequences are high, it is not worth the time or risk. Preparing for the test is enough. Relax and be yourself.

TEST FOR DENTAL SCHOOL - CSP-10101 – U.S. PROFESSIONAL HEALTH SCIENCES

Dates & Fees (CASPer: $25, plus $12/school)

Specific information about dates and fees is typically released in April before the application cycle and varies by program and country. Fees are nonrefundable, so make sure you have the test date and location you desire ahead of time.

Ten considerations before taking the test:

1. Check your account to confirm your test date and time
2. Disable VPNs, Firewalls, and Plug-ins
3. Ensure that your webcam is working and that you have up-to-date Chrome or Firefox browsers
4. Complete the System Requirements Check
5. Familiarize yourself with the test question types and format
6. Practice with the sample scenarios at https://takecasper.com/test-prep/
7. Prepare with additional situational scenarios
8. Find a quiet place where you will not be disturbed and remove noises and other distractions
9. Take the full time to respond and review your answers
10. Relax and be yourself

Note: Applicants are not permitted to take the CASPer test more than once per admissions cycle.

These dental schools require the CASPer (subject to change):

- Boston University
- California Northstate University
- Case Western University
- Indiana University
- Temple University, Kornberg School of Dentistry
- The University of Louisville School of Dentistry
- University of California, San Francisco
- University of Missouri, Kansas City
- University of Utah

PART 5

WHERE AND HOW TO APPLY

> " *What lies behind us, and what lies before us are small matters compared to what lies within us.*
>
> – *Ralph Waldo Emerson*

CHAPTER 34
ADEA AND AADSAS

ADEA AADSAS – Application for *all U.S. dental schools* – Opens May 11th - First Submit June 1st.

TMDSAS – Application for *Texas residents* applying to Texas dental schools – Opens May 3rd – First Submit May 17th

CAAPID – Dental school application for *foreign-educated dental graduates* applying for advanced standing in U.S. dental schools. Application Cycle - March 4th – February 22nd

1. Apply Early
2. Applications cannot be verified, and the process cannot continue unless ALL official undergraduate transcripts are received.
3. AADSAS verification takes 4 – 6 weeks; TMDSAS verification takes 2 – 4 weeks
4. Attend the GoDental Virtual Fair
5. AADSAS Academic Updates: Aug. 13 – Sept. 30 or Dec. 2 – Feb. 2
6. AADSAS "Decision Day" – December 1st

Official transcripts should be sent to:
ADEA AADSAS Transcript Processing Center
P.O. Box 9110
Watertown, MA 02471

If using express mail, send to:
ADEA AADSAS Transcript Processing Center c/o Liaison International
311 Arsenal Street, Suite 15
Watertown, MA 02472

> *Asking for other's guidance helps you see what you may not be able to see. It's always important to check your ego and ask for help.*

— Ken Blanchard

CHAPTER 35

WHAT TO LOOK FOR IN A DENTAL SCHOOL

There are many factors to consider when applying to dental school. You want to apply to enough schools so that you have choices, but the cost of applying can be alarming. For the 2021-2022 application season, applicants pay $259 for the first dental school and $112 for each additional school and that is before you pay for the supplemental application fee. For 16 schools, that cost is $259 + 15 x 112 = $1,939 + 16 x supplemental fee. If the supplemental fee averages $50/school, the cost is $1,929 + 16 x $50 = $2,729. With this kind of expense just to submit applications, you want to look carefully at what you want in a dental school.

DENTAL SCHOOL RANKINGS

Comparing one dental school to another is complicated. The factors that are most important to some – cost, location, job prospects, and income potential – may be very different than the factors for another – prestige, state-of-the-art technology, and the likelihood of a top-notch residency. People are different. Their needs and preferences are different as well.

Wanting to pick the 'best' school, people rely on rankings. However, how do you factor in debt burden, scholarship opportunities, weather, collegiality, and patient interaction when some cannot be quantified? Would you get more, better, or diverse experiences in a rural area, big city, or specialty clinic? Thus, your ranking based on your needs could be very different than another applicant's ranking.

CONSIDERATIONS

Cost	Collegiality/Competitiveness
Equipment	GPA Range
Alumni Support	Weather
Location	State Where There is Growth
Technology/Internet	DAT Range
Endowment	Political Viewpoint
Acceptance Rate	International Students
In-State/Out-of-State Apps	Coursework Required
Length of the Program/Summers	Average Age of Admits
Debt Burden of Graduates	Rankings
Religious Foundation	Due Date
Clinical or Research Focus	% of Nontraditional Admits
Income After 10 Years	Difficulty of Classes
Number Who Get Residencies	Student Feedback
Types of Clinical Experiences	Difficulty to Apply
Job Prospects	Friend/Family of Alumnus
Prestige	Student-Faculty Ratio
Patient Interaction	Specialty Subjects
Scholarship Possibilities	Student Life
Demographic Make Up	

The American Dental Association (ADA) and American Dental Education Association (ADEA) do not rank and do not sanction any rating system or publication that ranks dental schools. They implore "view these rankings with caution." However, many applicants are eager to find quantifiable ways to evaluate or assess one school versus another. Servant-leadership-oriented students are typically in school working, leading, shadowing, and taking tests. They are challenged by the many tasks associated with the dental school admissions process.

While the ADA and ADEA shun rankings, many colleges highlight their rank on their website. The University of Michigan is quick to say that they are the number one dental school in the United States based on world rankings and the University of Washington promotes its fourth-place status. Meanwhile, Harvard is the most difficult to enter in terms of grades and scores, and the University of Puerto Rico is the least expensive for the four-year total price. The University of Mississippi has the highest acceptance rate, while Boston University is best for Oral Surgery. Which school is best depends on your criteria.

The 2020 Shanghai Rankings, based upon a survey of 1,500 educational leaders worldwide, orders U.S. schools are as follows:

#1. University of Michigan School of Dentistry

#2. University of North Carolina at Chapel Hill Adams School of Dentistry

#4. University of Washington School of Dentistry

#5. Harvard School of Dental Medicine

#6. The University of California Los Angeles School of Dentistry

#7. Penn Dental Medicine at the University of Pennsylvania

#8. The University of California San Francisco School of Dentistry

#11. University of Buffalo School of Dental Medicine

#19. University of Southern California Herman Ostrow School of Dentistry

#21. New York University College of Dentistry

#22. University of Pittsburgh School of Dental Medicine

#25. University of Iowa College of Dentistry

2021 Quacquarelli Symonds (QS) is also a worldwide ranking. The top U.S. dental schools on this list are:

#2. University of Michigan School of Dentistry

#7. The University of California San Francisco School of Dentistry

#8. Harvard School of Dental Medicine

#15. University of Washington School of Dentistry

#16. Penn Dental Medicine at the University of Pennsylvania

#17. New York University College of Dentistry

#21. University of North Carolina at Chapel Hill Adams School of Dentistry

#22. University of Iowa College of Dentistry

#25. The University of California Los Angeles School of Dentistry

These rankings certainly do not mean that other dental schools are not good or do not have excellent faculty. Take these rankings as somewhat subjective. Ultimately, you should base your decision on the factors that are most important to you.

> " Being 'brave' only when it's safe doesn't count. Be brave when it's difficult. That's when it matters most.

— Unknown

CHAPTER 36

WHERE TO APPLY

PRIORITIES AND LIMITATIONS

The decision about where to apply is a function of your priorities. You may not have the grades and scores to get accepted into a university like Harvard. However, if you are close but out of range, you may have a good shot for many of the other schools. This limitation should inform your decision. You can still apply if you are not in the middle 50th percentile, but your chances are just decreased.

Your best bet is to create a chart of schools and put the most important factors to you. Each chart would be unique, though there are a few versions in this book.

With the cost of some dental schools skyrocketing at over $500,000 for four years, many students prioritize costs and access to scholarships in their decision-making process. The debt burden of dental school graduates is extraordinary.

HOW MANY APPLICATIONS?

The next question you will want to ask yourself is how many dental schools will you put on your final list. More sounds better until you have to complete the secondary applications, and there are a few essays and more research. You might be better off applying to fewer schools and completing those applications well. A good target is to research 20 schools and narrow the list down to between 14-16 schools. This number is still a lot of work, but it is more reasonable than 30.

DENTAL SCHOOL SPECIFIC DEADLINES (2021-2022)

September 1, 2021
> LSU Health New Orleans School of Dentistry

September 30, 2021
> Dental College of Georgia at Augusta University
> University of Oklahoma College of Dentistry
> University of Tennessee College of Dentistry

October 1, 2021
> The University of Iowa College of Dentistry
> University of Missouri-Kansas City School of Dentistry
> University of Mississippi School of Dentistry
> University of Nebraska College of Dentistry
> The Ohio State University College of Dentistry

October 9, 2021
> University of British Columbia Faculty of Dentistry

October 15, 2021
> University of Colorado School of Dental Medicine
> University of Michigan School of Dentistry
> University of Utah School of Dentistry
> McGill University Faculty of Dentistry

October 30, 2021
> Texas A&M University College of Dentistry
> The University of Texas School of Dentistry at Houston

October 31, 2021
> UCSF School of Dentistry

November 1, 2021
> Loma Linda University School of Dentistry
> University of Florida College of Dentistry
> University of New England College of Dental Medicine
> UNC at Chapel Hill School of Dentistry
> Oregon Health & Science University School of Dentistry
> Dalhousie University Faculty of Dentistry
> University of Pittsburgh School of Dental Medicine
> University of Washington School of Dentistry
> West Virginia University School of Dentistry

University of Toronto Faculty of Dentistry

November 15, 2021
University of Alabama at Birmingham School of Dentistry
Arizona School of Dentistry & Oral Health
Roseman University College of Dental Medicine, Utah

November 21, 2021
Southern Illinois University School of Dental Medicine

December 1, 2021
Western University College of Dental Medicine
University of Connecticut School of Dental Medicine
Nova Southeastern University College of Dental Medicine
University of Illinois at Chicago College of Dentistry
Indiana University School of Dentistry
Missouri School of Dentistry & Oral Health
East Carolina University School of Dental Medicine
Stony Brook University School of Dental Medicine
University of Pennsylvania School of Dental Medicine
University of Puerto Rico School of Dental Medicine
University of Saskatchewan College of Dentistry

December 15, 2021
University of South Carolina College of Dental Medicine
Meharry Medical College School of Dentistry

December 16, 2021
Boston University School of Dental Medicine

December 31, 2021
University of Maryland School of Dentistry
University of Detroit Mercy School of Dentistry
Columbia University College of Dental Medicine

January 1, 2022
Midwestern University College of Dental Medicine – AZ
UCLA School of Dentistry
Midwestern University College of Dental Medicine – IL
University of Kentucky College of Dentistry
Harvard School of Dental Medicine
UNLV School of Dental Medicine

Case Western Reserve School of Dental Medicine
Virginia Commonwealth University School of Dentistry
Marquette University School of Dentistry

January 15, 2022
Temple University School of Dentistry

January 24, 2022
University of Buffalo School of Dental Medicine

January 31, 2022
Rutgers University School of Dental Medicine

February 1, 2022
Herman Ostrow School of Dentistry of USC
University of the Pacific School of Dentistry
Howard University College of Dentistry
Lake Erie College School of Dental Medicine
Tufts University School of Dental Medicine
Creighton University School of Dentistry
New York University College of Dentistry
Touro College of Dental Medicine, NY Medical College

February 3, 2022
University of Minnesota School of Dentistry

> **Keep your face always toward the sunshine— and shadows will fall behind you.**
>
> —Walt Whitman

CHAPTER 37
APPLICATION TIMELINE AND CHECKLIST

DETAILED TIMELINE

Whenever You Start

- Make a calendar of requirements and responsibilities.
- Be proactive! This is your future.
- Applying early gives you the greatest chance for an early interview.
- Organize yourself to take full advantage of the rolling admissions process.

Summer/Fall

- Meet with pre-health advisor.
- Determine if your university requires a pre-health committee letter.
- List the steps of the process to obtain this letter (transcripts, personal statement, interviews).
- Check off all prerequisite classes required for admission.
- Get to know the terms associated with dental school admissions and professional organizations (ADA, ADEA, CODA, AADSAS, TMDSAS, etc.).
- Research dental schools - *The ADEA Official Guide to Dental Schools*.
- Determine whether you will get tutoring, test prep class, or study independently.
- Get a DENTPIN on the ADA website: https://www.ada.org/en/education-careers/dentpin/dentpin-registration.

- Register for the DAT.
- Purchase DAT study materials and/or register for a review class.
- Prepare for DAT. Put study times in your calendar.
- Open ADEA AADSAS to look ahead to review application questions (you are not obligated to submit) at ADEA AADSAS | Applicant Login Page Section (liaisoncas.com).
- Print out the application in a Word or PDF file.
- Fill in information that you can transfer onto your application next spring.

Winter/Spring Before Applying
- Meet again with pre-health advisor before applying.
- If you haven't yet, take the DAT. Do so by the beginning of August
- Outline your personal statement.
- Request letters of recommendation.
- Follow up with the committee letter of recommendation.
- Follow up with individual recommenders.
- Write your personal statement.
- Request copies of all of your transcripts to fill in the application.
- Send copies of all of your transcripts to the application services.

May/June Application
- AADSAS and TMDSAS applications open May 11 (rolling admissions, apply early, submit June 1).
- Note: You can submit without DAT scores or all letters of recommendation. However, these must be forwarded ASAP.
- Fill in personal information into AADSAS and TMDSAS applications
- Input your personal statement.
- Fill in every post-secondary school you attended along with the courses and grades you earned.
- Select the colleges to which you will apply.
- Note: Check the "Program Materials" section and complete additional questions to colleges you have selected.
- Check for formatting and spelling errors before you finish; make sure you follow all instructions.
- Certify, pay, and submit on June 1. while you can submit after June 1, the queue can get long. The earlier you submit the better.

- Your application goes into a queue.
- AADSAS verification process (4 - 6 weeks); TMDSAS (2 – 4 weeks).
- Inputted classes and grades are matched to corresponding transcripts.
- Check for errors; look at the AADSAS and TMDSAS total GPA and science GPA.

Summer/Fall

- Check your application status.
- Register for the CASPer test in June or July.
- Take/retake the DAT if necessary. Remember that you must wait 90 days to retake the test.
- Complete the secondary/supplemental application (within two weeks of receipt).
- Interviews are offered beginning July/August.
- Note: Some schools will not extend an interview offer until all recommendations and test scores have been submitted.
- Prep for Interview
- Interview
- Follow up with schools if you have not heard back from them to confirm they have everything. Sometimes they are missing a letter of recommendation or DAT score.
- December 1st 15th COVID-19 delay)– First decisions are announced.

Winter/Spring

- ADEA AADSAS application closes February 3rd.
- Interviews continue through March.
- Update schools about your new accomplishments.
- Connect expressed interest in schools where you are waitlisted.

"Waste no more time arguing about what a good person should be. Be one."

– Marcus Aurelius

CHAPTER 38
CODA-ACCREDITED CANADIAN DENTAL SCHOOLS

Prospective dentists should know that several North American dental schools outside the United States offer potential options for their training. While countries all over the world train dentists, only graduates of those in Canada and Puerto Rico enjoy acceptance by the American Dental Association and recognition of their institution's accreditation.

APPLYING TO CANADIAN DENTAL SCHOOLS

Not all Canadian dental schools accept applications from U.S. residents. Likewise, not all Canadian schools accept the ADEA AADSAS application or the U.S. version of the DAT. As with other dental schools, detailed information can be found either on the institutional websites or within the Dental School Explorer utility on the American Dental Education Association website.

An overview of basic information about North American dental schools outside the US is provided in the following table.

CANADIAN DENTAL SCHOOL POLICIES			
DENTAL SCHOOL	Applications open to US citizens	Accepts US DAT	Participates in ADEA AADSAS
DALHOUSIE UNIVERSITY FACULTY OF DENTISTRY (NOVA SCOTIA)	Yes	Yes	Yes
MCGILL UNIVERSITY FACULTY OF DENTISTRY	Yes	Yes	Yes
THE UNIVERSITY OF BRITISH COLUMBIA FACULTY OF DENTISTRY	Yes	Yes	Yes
UNIVERSITE DE MONTREAL FACULTE DE MEDECINE DENTAIRE	No	No	No
UNIVERSITE LAVAL FACULTE DE MEDECINE DENTAIRE	No	No	No
UNIVERSITY OF ALBERTA SCHOOL OF DENTISTRY	Yes	No	No
UNIVERSITY OF MANITOBA DR. GERALD NIZNICK COLLEGE OF DENTISTRY	No	No	No
UNIVERSITY OF SASKATCHEWAN COLLEGE OF DENTISTRY	No	No	Yes
UNIVERSITY OF TORONTO FACULTY OF DENTISTRY	Yes	Yes	Yes
WESTERN UNIVERSITY SCHULICH SCHOOL OF MEDICINE & DENTISTRY	Yes	No	Yes

Like their American counterparts, Canadian dental schools often require interviews before extending an offer of admissions. There is little difference, if any, between the two countries when it comes to their interview objectives and processes.

Anyone from the U.S. who is considering a Canadian dental school should know that they are statistically more likely to be admitted to a U.S. institution. According to the American Dental Education Association's *Official Guide to Dental Schools for Students Entering Fall 2021 or Fall 2022*, only 1 in 7 dental school applicants gained admission to a Canadian dental program. The rate for U.S. students is significantly higher. Additionally, most Canadian programs give preference to Canadian residents who live in-province.

Do not overlook the obvious challenges inherent in attending a program in another country.

Keep in mind that the adventures gained through international study come with their own unique set of challenges.

The crossing of international borders is regulated. Differences in policies, teaching styles and methodologies can be fraught with hassles. Also, world affairs can cause disruptions depending on the geopolitical context and—as evidenced by the COVID-19 pandemic—the state of public health. A passport does not constitute sufficient documentation for a U.S. resident attending dental school in Canada. A study permit must be acquired once you have accepted an offer. Background checks are often required as well.

For students who are not proficient speakers and readers of French, living in parts of Canada may stretch the comfort zone. Obviously, the extent to which French is employed, both in the public square as well as the classroom, will depend on the province in which the school is located.

When the time comes for you to look ahead to your dental employment, licensure and its requisite testing will become common threads of conversation. As implied earlier in this passage, a U.S. student at a Canadian dental school should have no trouble acquiring a license to practice in either country, but the student should understand that their path to licensure might vary from that of other classmates.

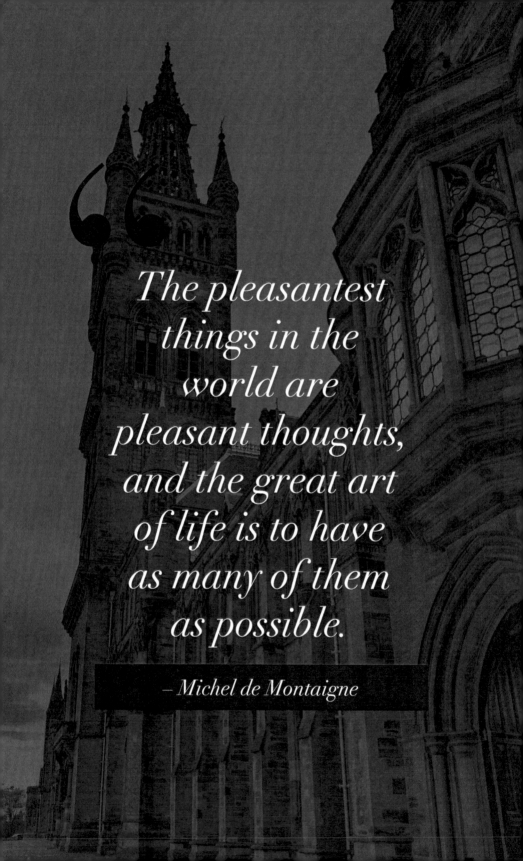

The pleasantest things in the world are pleasant thoughts, and the great art of life is to have as many of them as possible.

— *Michel de Montaigne*

CHAPTER 39

INTERNATIONAL DENTAL EDUCATION

INTRODUCTION

The United Kingdom (U.K.) is made up of England, Scotland, Wales, and Northern Ireland, with capitals in London, Edinburgh, Cardiff, and Belfast, respectively.[1] The British Commonwealth includes 54 countries, among those are Australia and Canada.

DENTISTRY IN THE UNITED KINGDOM

To earn a B.D.S. (Bachelor of Dental Surgery) or BChD degree in the United Kingdom, you must complete 5 years (6 years with a foundation year) of undergraduate study. There are sixteen dental schools in the U.K.; two of them are graduate entry, and two are postgraduate entry dental institutes. Note that since the B.D.S. or BChD degrees are undergraduate degrees, to practice dentistry in the U.S., you will need an additional three years of dental school while earning a DDS or DMD are required.

To become a dentist in the U.K., an additional vocational training (V.T.) program is required that usually takes one to two years after graduation. After these clinical experiences, students obtain the full National Health Service registration. However, graduates must register with the G.D.C. (General Dental Council) to meet the governing body's professional requirements before being allowed to practice.

---

1   The Commonwealth, "United Kingdom," *The Commonwealth,* n.d., https://thecommonwealth.org/our-member-countries/united-kingdom

Dentistry in the U.K. is comprehensive, competitive, and arduous. Academically and technically, the material is challenging, involving the study of the cause, prevention, management, and treatment of oral and dental diseases. The first year of study takes a fundamental approach to medical and clinical knowledge in the areas of oral biology, biochemistry, physiology, and anatomy. As dental study progresses, technical course work is carried out, later requiring supervision with state-of-the-art dummies for practical application.[2]

ADMISSIONS REQUIREMENTS/PROCESSES IN THE U.K.

To study dentistry in the United Kingdom, the following requirements must be met:[3]

1. English language proficiency
2. Written test for dental education in the U.K.
3. International Baccalaureate level fulfillment
4. Medical test

The English language is a core subject. Every student should be well-trained in grammar and writing before starting the admission process in the U.K. Consequently, any of the following are acceptable for proof of mastery:

- IELTS (International English Language Test) - passing score of 7.0 and 6.5 per section
- P.T.E. (Pearson Test of English) - average score of 70 & no score less than 65 in each skill domain (one sitting). Some schools are higher.
- C.A.E. (Advanced Cambridge English) or (C.P.E.) Proficiency in Cambridge English (C.P.E.) - average score of 185 and at least 185 in each scoring domains (one sitting)
- International Baccalaureate (IB) - A score of 5 or higher in Standard (SL) or Higher level (HL) English

Typically, the English language test is valid for two years.[4]

Several dentistry programs in the U.K. require written tests in subjects, referred

2   Study In U.K. , "UK Dentistry Courses," *Study in U.K.* , n.d., https://www.studyin-uk.com/popular-courses/dentistry/

3   University of Liverpool, "Dental Surgery BDS," *University of Liverpool,* n.d., https://www.liverpool.ac.uk/study/undergraduate/courses/dental-surgery-bds/entry-requirements/

4   University of Manchester, "English Language Requirements," *University of Manchester,* n.d., https://www.manchester.ac.uk/study/international/admissions/language-requirements/

to as A-Levels, like Chemistry and Biology. Three A-Levels are typically required with scores from AAA to ABB. A student can enter dental school in the U.S. without A-Levels grades by completing a "Gateway to Dentistry" or "Pre-Dental" year.

However, some universities also use written tests in GCSE (General Certificate of Secondary Education) subjects with grades of AAABBB or 777666; including biology, chemistry, English language, mathematics, art, history, geography, including linguistic sciences. Still, other universities in the U.K. may include a U.K. CAT (U.K. Clinical Aptitude Test) admission test. This test is designed to test students' cognitive abilities as well as attitudes, logical reasoning, and critical thinking. These include:[5]

i.   Verbal Reasoning - Evaluates students' abilities to think logically and reach a reasoned conclusion. This section usually involves 11 passages to read 44 questions in 21 minutes.

ii.   Quantitative Reasoning - Numerical problem solving with 36 questions in 24 minutes, including information in tables, charts, and graphs

iii. Abstract Reasoning – Tests convergent and divergent thinking with 55 questions in 13 minutes

iv.   Decision Analysis - Assesses problem-solving that infer relationships, making informed judgments, and interpreting the response with 1 scenario and 28 questions to be answered in 32 minutes

v.   Situational Judgment – Provides situations regarding medical ethics and measuring responses

A minimum of 37 points is usually set as International Baccalaureate (IB) requirements in the U.K. The score varies from year to year, depending on the points set by individual universities.

Candidates must undergo medical testing to show evidence of vaccination against COVID-19, hepatitis B and C, and other infections.

LIST OF DENTAL SCHOOLS IN THE UNITED KINGDOM

The General Dental Council recognizes 18 dental schools in the U.K. offering programs that lead to a British University dental degree. They comprise 12 in England, 4 in Scotland, 1 in Wales, and 1 in Northern Ireland.

5   Study in U.K. , "UK Dentistry Courses," *Study inU.K.* , n.d., https://www.studyin-uk.com/popular-courses/dentistry/

ENGLAND

	University Name	University/City	Year Established
1.	Barts and The London School of Medicine and Dentistry	Queen Mary University of London	1995
2.	School of Dentistry	Birmingham	1828
3.	Bristol Dental School	Bristol	1833
4.	School of Dentistry	University of Central Lancashire	1842
5.	Guy's King's & St. Thomas's Dental Institute	King's College London	1799
6.	Leeds Dental Institute	Leeds	1904
7.	Liverpool Dental School	Liverpool	1834
8.	Manchester University Dental School	Manchester	1874
9.	Newcastle University Dental School	Newcastle	1834
10.	Peninsula College of Medicine and Dentistry	Exeter Plymouth	2000
11.	Sheffield School of Clinical Dentistry	Sheffield	1828
12.	U.C.L. Eastman Dental Institute	University College London	1948

SCOTLAND

	University Name	University/City	Year Established
1.	University of Aberdeen School of Dentistry	Aberdeen	1947
2	University of Dundee Dental School	Dundee	1967
3.	Edinburgh Dental Institute	Edinburgh	1860
4.	Glasgow Dental School	Glasgow	1451

WHALES

	University Name	University/City	Year Established
1.	Cardiff University Dental School	Cardiff	1931

NORTHERN ISLAND

	University Name	University/City	Year Established
1.	Queen's University Belfast School of Dentistry	Queen's University Belfast	1821

DENTISTRY IN CANADA

Canada's capital city is Ottawa, with incorporated cities including Alberta, British Columbia, Manitoba, New Brunswick, Newfoundland, and Labrador, Nova Scotia, Ontario, Prince Edward Island, Quebec, Saskatchewan, Northwest Territories, Nunavut, and Yukon, with their capital as Edmonton, Victoria, Winnipeg, Fredericton, St. John's, Halifax, Toronto, Charlottetown, Quebec City, Regina, Yellowknife, Iqaluit, and Whitehorse respectively.[6]

The National Dental Examining Board (NDEB) of Canada, in conjunction with agencies such as the Commission on Dental Accreditation of Canada and the Royal College of Dentists of Canada, oversees the practice of dentistry.

To successfully complete an application for dental schools in Canada, candidates must finish a two-part[7] examination administered by the National Dental Board of Canada (NDEB).[8] The examination is taken by dental students at accredited Canadian and American dental schools no earlier than three months before graduation. Typically, this is during March of a student's graduating year. After successful completion of the examination, NDEB grants certification to the candidates.[9]

LIST OF DENTAL SCHOOLS IN CANADA

- Dalhousie University Faculty of Dentistry
- McGill University Faculty of Dentistry
- University of Alberta Faculty of Dentistry
- University of British Columbia Faculty of Dentistry
- University of Laval Faculty of Dentistry
- University of Manitoba Faculty of Dentistry
- University of Montreal Faculty of Dentistry
- University of Saskatchewan College of Dentistry[10]

---

6   Statistics Canada, "Population and Dwelling Count Highlight Tables, 2011 Census," *Statistics Canada,* n.d., https://www12.statcan.gc.ca/census-recensement/2011/dp-pd/hlt-fst/pd-pl/Table-Tableau.cfm

7   The National Dental Examining Board of Canada, "How to Apply," *The National Dental Examining Board of Canada,* n.d., https://ndeb-bned.ca/en/non-accredited/application

8   Sarah Hua, "Practicing Dentistry in Canada as an Internationally Trained Professional," *World Education Services,* December 7, 2018, https://www.wes.org/advisor-blog/practicing-dentistry-in-canada/

9   The National Dental Examining Board of Canada, "How to Apply," *The National Dental Examining Board of Canada,* n.d., https://ndeb-bned.ca/en/non-accredited/application

10 University of Toronto Faculty of Dentistry, "The International Dentist Advanced Placement Program (IDAPP)," *University of Toronto Faculty of Dentistry,* n.d., https://www.dentistry.utoronto.ca/prospective-

- University of Toronto Faculty of Dentistry
- University of Western Ontario Faculty of Dentistry

ADMISSIONS PROCESS/REQUIREMENTS IN CANADA

Admission into Canadian dental schools requires the Dental Aptitude Test (DAT) given by Canadian Dental Association (CDA). This test evaluates students' academic ability, comprehension of scientific information, two and three-dimensional visual perception, and manual dexterity.[11]

University admissions processes vary by school.

A. University of Toronto Dental School Requirements

- Three years completion of full-time undergraduate study
- Courses listed on the school's website completion are required
- A minimum of 3.0 GPA is required
- Completion of DAT with application deadline within two years
- Proficiency in written and spoken English

B. University of Western Ontario Dental Schools Requirements

- Physiology. Plus, at least one semester of laboratory courses in Biochemistry and Organic Chemistry completion of an undergraduate/ graduate degree at any accredited university
- Laboratory courses in Organic Chemistry, Biochemistry, and Human or Mammalian Physiology

C. Western University Dental School Requirements

- Applicants must complete a 4-year undergraduate degree.
- Applicants must complete required courses with a minimum grade of 74.5%.
- Completion of DAT.

D. University of Manitoba Dental School Requirements

- One year of Biology, the origin of life, cell theory, genetics, micro-organisms, metabolism, animals and plants classification, the relation between structure and function, ecology, and evolution.
- One year of Organic Chemistry, Biochemistry, Microbiology, Physics,

---

students/international-dentists/join-DDS-IDAPP

11 College Learners, "Dental Schools in Canada Requirements," *College Learners*, n.d., https://collegelearners.com/dental-schools-in-canada-requirements/

and first-year English. All science courses must include laboratory components with minimum GPA of 2.5.

In conclusion, the conditions and requirements for studying dentistry vary from one university to another. However, they may be divided into four groups:

- Eligibility criteria
- Testing – some dental universities use the DAT, CASPer, and/or the Medical College Admission Test (MCAT).
- Biography or short text
- Recommendation Letters
- International candidates are required to take either TOEFL, CAEL, IELTS, or other recognized English test.

DENTISTRY IN AUSTRALIA

There are nine dental schools in Australia in the states of New South Wales, Victoria, Queensland, Western Australia, and South Australia.

The table below provides a guide to the ATAR (Australian Tertiary Admission Rank) scores for entry into every dentistry program in Australia in 2020.[12]

AUSTRALIA					
States	University	Undergraduate Course or Undergraduate Plus Masters	ATAR-2020 Entry	UCAT Required for 2021 Entry	Interview Required for 2021 Entry
NEW SOUTH WALES	University of Sydney	3-year Bachelor of science followed by 4-year Doctor of Dental Medicine- 7years in total	Minimum 99.6 for general entry Indigenous pathway applies	No	Written assessment and panel discussion
	Charles Sturt University- Orange Campus	Bachelor of Dental Science – 5 years	Check with university Rural and Indigenous pathways apply	Yes	Yes

VICTORIA	University of Melbourne	See Chancellor's Scholars Program (ATAR 99.90) or Guaranteed entry pathway – 3years undergraduate degree with prerequisites followed by a four-year Doctor of Dental Surgery – at least seven years in total	99.90 (ATAR) 90.00 (ATAR) for students of Indigenous descent	No	No
	La Trobe University – Bendigo	Bachelor of Dental Science (Honors) – 5 years	99.00 (Selection Rank with adjustment factors) 87.30 (lowest ATAR to receive an offer in 2020)	Depends on your entry pathway	Check with university
QUEENSLAND	Griffith University – Gold Coast Campus	Bachelor of Oral Health in Dental Science / Master of Dentistry – 5 years	99.8 (ATAR) Priority will be given to students from a rural background	No (but will be required for 2022 entry)	No (but a multiple mini interview will be required for 2022 entry)
	James Cook University – Cairns	Bachelor of Dental Surgery – 5 years	Check with university	No	Written application form required. No interview.
	University of Queensland	Bachelor of Dental Science (Honours) – 5 years	99 (lowest adjusted to receive an offer in 2020) 94 (lowest score without adjustments to receive an offer in 2020)	No	No

| WALES | University of Western Australia [13] | U.W.A. has a High Academic Achievement, Rural and Broadway School Leaver pathway – each of which involves a 3-year undergraduate science degree followed by the 4-year Doctor of Dental Medicine – 7 years in total | 99 (High Academic Achievers) 96 (Rural or Broadway) | Yes | Yes |

Besides the ATAR, other entry requirements for dentistry may include:[14]

- UCAT score
- Interview
- Predicted ATAR form
- Manual dexterity & spatial awareness test
- Eyesight requirements
- Written application
- Questionnaire completion
- A police check
- First aid training completion
- Health checks and immunization

13 University of Western Australia, "Courses," *University of Western Australia*, n.d., https://www.uwa.edu.au/schools/dentistry#anchor-Courses-021B556D-9887-4F7C-B495-33ABBC67B737

14 My Health Career, "ATAR for Dentistry – Your Guide to the ATAR for Every Dentistry Course in Australia in 2020," *My Health Career*, July 20, 2020, https://www.myhealthcareer.com.au/career-and-university/atar-for-dentistry-2020/

PART 6

INITIAL
APPLICATION

"

*Magic is believing
in yourself, if
you can do that,
you can make
anything happen.*

– Johann Wolfgang von Goethe

CHAPTER 40
INTAKE FORM AND ACTIVITIES

Finally! It's May of the year before you hope to matriculate as a new dental student. Now is the time to get started on your actual, official dental school application. Hopefully, you have prepared in advance and are armed with all the information you need to complete your application in short order. You will not be able to submit the AADSAS until June 1, but you want to have it ready to submit as soon as possible once the application is "live."

I.   Which platform to use?

Prospective DMD/DDS candidates do not apply directly to dental schools. Instead, a shared application platform is used by multiple schools. In theory, these platforms function like the Common Application or Coalition Application, in that they streamline the details and provide administrative support. Also, like the undergraduate Common App, they simplify the process so applications are submitted to multiple schools.

This book focuses almost exclusively on the AADSAS (American Association of Dental Schools Application Service) application. However, it bears mentioning that some students will need to complete a different application, instead of or in addition to the AADSAS.

Two dental school application platforms are available:

1. AADSAS (American Association of Dental Schools Application Service)

2. TMDSAS (Texas Medical and Dental Schools Application Services)

Four dental schools will admit students to begin their studies through TMDSAS.[1]

Texas A & M College of Dentistry *

Texas Tech University Health Sciences Center El Paso Woody L. Hunt School of Dental Medicine

The University of Texas School of Dentistry at Houston*

UT Health San Antonio School of Dentistry

* Schools with an asterisk will accept the AADSAS from non-Texas applicants.

Let's break this down:

Applicants who will use the AADSAS only: Non-residents of Texas not applying to Texas Tech or to the UT Health San Antonio School of Dentistry

Applicants who will use the TMDSAS only: Texas residents only applying to the four Texas-based dental schools

Applicants who must use both the AADSAS and the TMDSAS: Texas residents applying to at least one dental school outside of Texas

II. When to Apply

First things first: You will apply to dental school during the calendar year before you begin dental school--probably over a year in advance of your first day as a student dentist.

If you hope to begin dental school in the Fall of 2023, work ahead, gather materials, and write your personal statement.

Dental applications open in May, giving you several weeks of a "work" period, during which you can complete the application, check and double-check all inputs, and be ready to hit "submit" on June 1 (mid-May for TMDSAS). Once the application is available, you will have a place to compile all of the work you have been doing.

---

1 Two dental schools will welcome their first entering classes in the Fall of 2022--California Northstate College of Dental Medicine and Texas Tech's Woody L. Hunt School of Dental Medicine. As of May 2021, Texas Tech mentions only the TMDSAS app.

The earlier you submit your application, the better.

III. Application Basics

The AADSAS consists of four primary sections

The section names, as well as examples of contents, are below.

Personal Information
- Demographics
- Family background
- Environmental factors
- Citizenship

Academic History
- Transcript
- Coursework entry
- High school information
- DAT

Supporting Information
- Letters of recommendation (more on this in Chapter 41)
- Documentation of your experiences

Program Materials

School-specific information for each institution such as:
- Documentation of particular prerequisite courses, and
- Additional essay questions

Once everything has been completed, your application is ready for submission!

Tip: As of this writing (May 2021), an outstanding resource uploaded at the University of Georgia is available to view and download at the following address: https://ppao.uga.edu/_resources/documents/adea_aadsas_application_ walkthrough_2020_2021.pdf

The document is a highly detailed walk-through of every step required during application completion and submission.

A couple of notes:

Once you have submitted your application, it is queued up for a process called verification. One of the tasks accomplished during verification is the recalculation of your grade point average. By using the same formula for all students, the AADSAS presents each applicant using similar measurements.

You can track the progress of your application within your applicant's portal. Also, you will be able to see the status of all documentation relevant to your candidacy.

Pay attention to details. No one can monitor the quality, timing, and specific contents of your application as well as you can. What has been outlined here is intentionally a broad-stroke illustration of the application and its attendant tasks. Carefully read all the instructions, and ask questions from your specific schools when necessary. You have worked hard to compile all components of the application, so be mindful of the fine print, too.

" Live neither in the past nor in the future, but let each day's work absorb your entire energies and satisfy your widest ambition.

— Sir William Osler, FRS, FRCP

CHAPTER 41
LETTERS OF RECOMMENDATION

As noted in Chapter 40, key components of the Supporting Information section within the AADSAS application are your letters of evaluation. **You are allowed four evaluations in support of your candidacy.**

Note: Throughout the dental admissions process, you will find that *evaluate*, along with its various derivatives (evaluator, evaluation), is used interchangeably with *recommend* and its derivatives.

SELECTING YOUR EVALUATORS

Carefully scrutinize all requirements and guidelines about references as provided by your dental schools of choice before asking anyone to serve as a recommender. After you familiarize yourself with each institution's specifications, you can get started with your requests.

Evaluator #1: The committee or composite letter (if applicable)

If your undergraduate institution is organized to support pre-professional applicants through a committee review process, you should embrace that process and do so sooner rather than later. Dental schools know which colleges utilize committees, so they will expect your application to reflect support from that body.

If you attend either a very large university or a college with a large and competitive pool of talent, be forewarned that securing a committee evaluation adds a separate application process on the front end of your dental applications. For an example of how a university systematically recommends students for professional schools, check out the document provided by The University of Pennsylvania's Health Professions Advisory Board: https://cdn.uconnectlabs.com/wp-content/uploads/sites/74/2020/12/DentalSchoolManual2022.pdf

At smaller colleges, the support of a health advisory committee may still be required, but because relatively few students are involved and most of them already enjoy relationships with faculty members, it may be easier to garner a committee letter. At the very least, the process is simpler to navigate.

If your school does not offer committee letters of support, that is fine. It just means you will be able to choose all four of your recommenders. In place of a committee letter, consider asking a professor, a research mentor, or a volunteer coordinator to write a recommendation for you.

Evaluators #2, #3, and #4

You should secure two evaluations from science faculty as well as an evaluation from a dentist. If you have the latitude to ask any faculty members you wish for letters of support, then reflect on your many science classes and think about who has the most to say about you. Who can offer the most positive, academically-relevant insights? Who knows you best?

When it comes to your professional letter of evaluation, here too, you should choose the dentist who can say the most about you. Did any of them seem particularly enthusiastic about your affinity for a dental career? Were you able to be particularly useful in someone's office? The only dentist(s) you should not ask to write for you are parents or other relatives in the field.

Interactions with your evaluators

Everything in this section can be boiled down to preparation and the golden rule. Your willingness and ability to prepare, anticipate, and troubleshoot will go a long way with those who are advocating for your candidacy.

Work Ahead Seek out your recommenders of choice as soon as possible. You are basically dropping a writing assignment on them, so you want to give them plenty of notice and touch base regularly as warranted. Also, many faculty members will be writing multiple letters of evaluation. Be at the head of the line. TIP: Be sure to ask each recommender for their preferred email address.

Details, Details Do your homework by reading the guidelines for letters of evaluation and conveying them to your recommenders accordingly.

Talk Tech Depending on a recommender's age and amount of experience with this type of recommendation, you may need to explain how they will submit their letter electronically. Fortunately, the recommender platform, Interfolio, streamlines the whole process via email.

Follow Up Make a point to let your recommenders know your progress. They have invested time in you! Spend five or ten minutes to make a call or e-mail to fill them in about your future plans.

A Bit Later Once the whole admissions process is behind you, thank your evaluators. A gift card or small present is nice but not necessary. Handwritten, thoughtful notes are the gold standard for expressing gratitude.

Our final note circles back to the AADSAS itself. On your portal, you will be able to track the status of your letters of evaluation. Do not expect the AADSAS system to alert you if your evaluators have yet to engage the system. Instead, decide how often you need to check your portal and set reminders accordingly.

If a recommender seems to be running late with the submission, drop them a quick email, asking how things are going and if they need any further information from you. If the task has slipped their mind, your note will jog their memory without any hint of awkwardness or accusation.

The problem is, we glorify the wrong things and take the right things for granted.

– Unknown

CHAPTER 42
RESUME

Dental school applicants probably have some experience with creating a resume--also called a CV, or *curriculum vitae*. It's time to draw on that skill set once again. Whether or not a dental school application requires the submission of a resume, you should compile or update yours.

THE "WHY"

1. An updated resume that has been tweaked to demonstrate your excellence as a dental school candidate will come in handy when you complete your applications. The hardest part of resume creation is memory jogging, which is often necessary to recall important jobs, research, activities, etc. Almost no one can, in one sitting create a resume that fairly and thoroughly represents key accomplishments and personal attributes. "Sleeping on it" is helpful. You may recall significant pieces of information initially omitted when given a little time. And once the dental school application is online and ready for your entries, the clock will be ticking. Prepare your resume well in advance.

2. Unless instructed otherwise, you should have your resume with you during dental school interviews. Depending on the format of your interview, your resume can serve you well. Faculty members or admissions officers may reference it during your time with them. They may also be more likely to ask you about topics you enjoy discussing and arenas where you most easily shine.

   Word to the wise: Be careful not to include fluff on your resume--activities or accomplishments about which you are *not* particularly enthusiastic. Examples of fluff, or filler, material are one-and-done community service experiences, clubs for which you did not provide meaningful service, or anything that could invite a negative line of questioning.

3. Resume maintenance is a best-practice skill

Consider your resume one of your indispensable tools of success. Even thriving dentists with no plans to make a professional move will benefit from regular updates to their resumes.

Milestones and continuing education components of a career are tough to remember if not recorded frequently. You do not need to update your resume every time you complete a class, but you should make a note about any developments or additions to your body of knowledge. Keep those events in a folder--digital or otherwise. Then wait until a convenient time to assess the value of your entries and decide whether or not each deserves a portion of your valuable CV real estate.

THE "WHAT"

Aside from your name, address, contact information, and the basics of your undergraduate institution, your resume should illustrate where and how you spend your time. For this reason, no particular layout or specific sections are recommended. The organization of the resume is a function of your life and experiences.

A strong pre-dental resume includes evidence of the following:

- Dental school is a tough academic journey. Dental schools cannot afford to lose any more students to attrition than necessary. They look very closely at your projected ability to stick with the program and do well. Less than half a percent - specifically 0.3 percent - of entering dental school students ultimately drop out of their programs for academic reasons.[1] Be mindful to include any honors earned--academic or otherwise--as well as any details which underscore your strong academic ability and persistence.

- **Experience:** you have spent enough time around dentists and dental offices to be sure of your decision to pursue a DMD/DDS. Reflect this on your resume.

---

1   Commission on Dental Accreditation Survey of Dental Education Series (2019-2020), Report 2, Table 20

- **Interest:** your application to their institution must make sense. Most dental schools only want to extend offers of admission to students who will accept those offers and attend. They need to fill their classes with dedicated students in a timely manner.

- **Diversity:** Demonstrate that your uniqueness offers diversity to the entering class.

THE "HOW"

Now, how do you commit all this information to the written word? Thank you, technology! As you may know, almost all word processing software provides free resume templates. Also, websites like Canva offer hundreds of formatting options, including many at no charge to the user.

Rule of Thumb: Try to focus on substance, but do so without forsaking style. Your brainpower needs to be spent articulating and clarifying the content of your resume. However, all that work should be easily digestible from the document itself. It should be well-organized and easy to read and understand. If word processing or document creation isn't your thing, find a friend who has a knack for resume design and ask them to give you a hand. It's time for you to get back to the application itself!

In this digital age, you may choose not to include your address. Many people take that address and put the information into Google to get details about your home that may prejudice the process. Demographic territories, socioeconomic background, and other information are readily available from an address. That is a note of caution from admissions, faculty, and students who have gleaned their own impressions about students.

"

Rock bottom has built more heroes than privilege.

– Unknown

CHAPTER 43

TELLING YOUR STORY: THE PERSONAL STATEMENT

AVOIDING PARALYSIS BY ANALYSIS

When the time comes to apply to DMD/DDS programs, much of your candidacy profile has already been determined. Your coursework choices have been made and your grades are a matter of record. The essay, however, is the part of the application over which you still have 100% control. Instead of relishing the opportunity to take advantage of that, many hopeful dentists are intimidated by the task. And therein lies the same paradox you probably faced as a college applicant: the ability to write anything makes the task more intimidating than inspiring.

Consider the blank space on your laptop. Do you find yourself threatened or overwhelmed by writing your personal statement? If so, you are not alone. Obviously, there are the 4500 characters you need to generate (approximately 600-800 words, or a couple of double-spaced pages). However, the source of anxiety around personal statements usually lies in decisions to make about your topic. It can turn into paralysis by analysis, but it doesn't have to.

Ultimately, you will submit an outstanding personal statement, but the best way to fight off writer's block is to set a more humble intention. Invoking a sports metaphor, start with a solid base hit rather than attempting a home run.

Just think of the essay as a job to be done. Give yourself a time frame in which you will write a first draft and stick to it. Even if that first attempt is lousy, you will benefit from having written something. You now have a narrative edit and revise. That assurance can give you the confidence necessary for later effective choices about style, metaphor, and anecdotes.

The job to be done:

What the personal statement has in common with your undergrad application essay

No matter which application platform you used to apply to your undergraduate program, you probably wrote a personal statement. Your essay was written to meet the same three objectives you have before now:

1. Articulate your rationale for attending dental school;
2. Demonstrate that you can write clearly;
3. Provide evidence of personal qualities which are sought by the dental admissions committee.

The rational

You absolutely must write an essay that convinces the reader that you know what you are getting into, you are certain you want to be a dentist, and that you are willing and able to stay the course and succeed.

Applicants are understandably most concerned about their admissibility. It is the burden of the application reader, though, to look beyond the matter of "getting in," focusing instead on the likelihood of graduating from their institution if they do admit you.

The same personal statement will be read by admissions personnel at each school to which you apply. Therefore, you should not write anything in your essay which refers to a specific school, e.g., "I have been captivated by the research conducted by Dr. Smith at Big State U."

Your job is more general. You need to make the case that your logical next step is the pursuit of a DDS/DMD--and here's the most important part--as a natural consequence of who you are and the experiences which led you to this juncture. The personal statement can be a place to elaborate on information found elsewhere in your application. You tell your story while demonstrating your personality and character.

There is no formula or outline for communicating your "why." However, we will include some questions at the end of this chapter to consider as you decide how to tackle the job.

Effective Communication

You must write a clear, grammatically correct, concise, and focused essay. Period.

Getting Help

If you lack confidence in your writing ability, by all means, seek assistance throughout the writing process. If you are in college, there are plenty of places where you might find help. Officially, the college's writing center is a traditional go-to, but you can also check with your pre-dental advisor or even seek out a fellow student.

If you are not currently in college and need help writing you can go online to find what you need. Tutoring services abound. If you wish to engage an online writing tutor, be judicious as you browse and make sure the company is reputable. We both assist students in fleshing out ideas and editing.

Unfortunately, the internet is home to lots of writers-for-hire, that is, people willing to write your personal statement for a fee. If you find yourself on one of those sites, move along. Frankly, authenticity is one of the primary objectives of your writing. Hiring someone to do it is a very bad idea. Your essay will suffer for it, to say the least. More importantly, it's the wrong thing to do.

Awesomeness

How do you accomplish the task of selling yourself as a great person?

The awkward task of addressing your virtues is difficult for most. "Everyone says I am the nicest person they have ever met." Ick. Instead, adopt the "show, don't tell" approach.

How "you do you" can take many forms. It may be conveyed through anecdotes. You can also influence the reader to pull for you simply by writing from an authentic perspective and sharing your vision or your unique personality traits.

All About Teeth: How does this dental school personal statement differ from your previous college application essays?

Despite accomplishing the same objectives as a college admissions essay, your personal statement for dental school will differ in the following ways:

1. Your personal statement must be dental, dental, and more dental. To

be sure, your personality should shine through your statement, but not at the loss of focus. Your undergraduate college application essay did not have to be "about" any specific topic. For dental school applicants, though, the personal statement provides your best opportunity for making your case, for articulating the reasons you will be a successful dental student and positive member of their community.

2. Needless to say, your personal statement should reflect the maturity of someone your age and be written with the technical expertise one expects of a college graduate.

3. Explanations of any aberrations, suspensions, or details which might weaken your candidacy should be included in the personal statement.

Two Final Tips:

First, limit the number of people from whom you seek feedback on your writing. Experience has proven to us that, if you show your personal statement to 100 people, 97 will suggest a substantive edit. Adjustments must be considered carefully. If someone suggests, for example, that you include a story for which there simply is no space, you may begin to doubt your own content. Whatever the case, we suggest you share your writing with a maximum of three people.

Even with just a small number of readers, if you are happy with your statement as it is, let it go. If you got help, Instead of, "Would you please read this and tell me how to improve it?" say, "Finally! I feel great about my personal statement! Would you mind proofreading it for me? Let me know if you have any significant concerns about the content, but I think I just need a grammar and spelling check." Or, "I have the word count right and included the important points, but if you see an error, I would appreciate it if you pointed that out."

Second, save every draft you write, making a copy of it before opening and renaming another copy for edits or revisions. Just do it. You will appreciate accessing the various drafts when you think your revision may not have been an improvement.

And now, write on!

Ten Brainstorming Ideas

1. Do you consider yourself compassionate? If so, which experiences have developed that quality in you?

2. If you had to identify one moment when you knew you wanted to be a dentist, what would it be?

3. Would your fifteen-year-old self be surprised that you are applying to dental school? Why or why not?

4. What was the most valuable day of your shadowing experiences?

5. Which two or three people outside of your family do you consider your dental role models?

6. Has anything unique in your background led you to study dentistry?

7. When was a smile worth a thousand words?

8. If you witnessed extreme tooth pain, what difference did a dentist make?

9. What difference did false teeth make to a person?

10. What would life be like if you couldn't chew? Have you ever met someone whose teeth were gone, knocked out, or whose mouth was wired shut?

The soul is the same in all living creatures, although the body of each is different.

—*Hippocrates*

CHAPTER 44

DIVERSITY STATEMENT: SHOWING YOUR TRUE COLORS

Almost all institutions of higher learning value and prioritize diversity. From promotional materials to admissions practices, from the racial distribution of the faculty to the religious organizations on campus, colleges aim to be melting pots, welcoming communities in which students and professors from all walks of life can learn from one another. Dental schools are no exception.

TYPES OF DIVERSITY

Gender

Student dentists, as a group, look much different than they did fifty years ago. So do dental faculty members. Most notable has been the increased presence of women and LGBTQ within dental school classes. DMD/DDS faculties are slower to change, of course, but are moving in the same direction nonetheless.

Racial/ethnic

Racial and ethnic diversity tracks more slowly than gender diversity, but dental admissions personnel see pluralism as a critically important institutional objective. Along with the traditional dental school admissions metrics, like average DATs and GPAs, annual results are broken down by ethnic and racial groups. Not only is it important to a university to draw more applicants from diverse backgrounds, it is also a matter of progress to see how those groups fare in admissions and dental school studies.

Age

Another kind of diversity is age. Chapter 63 expands on the range of ages that might be found in a dental class. It is not unusual for someone to discover a passion for dentistry only after earning their bachelor's degree.

Citizenship

Many U.S. dental schools include a percentage of international students from across the world. People from other countries introduce differences to the cohort. Language, religion, foods, traditions add variety to the group.

Socioeconomic

A very tough kind of diversity to add is socioeconomic diversity. Because of the costs associated with a dental degree, DMD/DDS-granting institutions face an uphill climb when it comes to diversifying their classes along socioeconomic lines. That said, the dental community understands the importance of considering an applicant in the context of their environment and associated challenges. The AADSAS incorporates opportunities for students to tell their stories. These narratives are appreciated and considered during the evaluation process.

The categories above do not cover every kind of diversity among either the public in general or even among dental students. Rather, they are provided to give the applicant a broad lens through which to view the idea.

WHAT DO YOU HAVE TO SAY ABOUT DIVERSITY?

Efforts to diversity higher education are more noticeable on some college campuses than on others. However, it is safe to say that all accredited colleges and universities articulate a commitment to students of all colors, beliefs, and backgrounds.

As a part of that shared mission, most prospective dental students will have addressed diversity multiple times during their academic careers. At some point during the dental admissions process, the topic will arise. You will either write about it within your secondary essays or you will be asked about it during your individual interviews.

You should consider how you will talk or write about diversity as an applicant to dental school. Here are a few topics to get you started.

- Consider the "why." What is it about diversity-of any type- which makes it inherently valuable within a community? Give this question some deep thought if you have not encountered it previously. Of course, diversity is beneficial, and you should be able to demonstrate your "why".

- Think about how the experiences of the past few years have shaped your thoughts about or appreciation of diversity. What did you think or write about diversity as a high school student applying to college? How have your ideas evolved or matured?

- What makes *you* diverse? Of course, you are special and wonderful. However, in this context, we mean something different. What about you makes you feel uncomfortably different from your peers, either sometimes or always?

- Have you ever been marginalized by others? When? How? How did you cope with it? How does this part of your story inform your beliefs today?

- List anything tangible you have done to welcome diversity into your community. Were any clubs or groups more "in tune" with diversity?

- Why is diversity important within the field of dentistry?

- Have you participated in any diversity initiatives related to dentistry? If so, list them.

Grab a pen and paper or a Word doc. Write your thoughts about each of the above. Then, sleep on it and return to the questions on a different day, adding more thoughts which have come to mind in the meantime.

What you have to say about diversity depends on the specific question(s) you encounter along the way and the format in which you can express yourself. In preparation, do the significant work of self-reflection, of contemplating the hardest questions faced by society, of seeing yourself within the community and having some ideas about how you might improve your environment. Your thoughts about diversity will be valuable to the reader or interviewer.

If today were the last day of your life, would you want to do what you are about to do today?

— Steve Jobs

CHAPTER 45
THE COVID-19 INTERRUPTION

In a perfect world, every dental school applicant applies the moment the application can be submitted. All steps on the AADSAS are completed according to the directions and no one encounters an error message associated with their account. Everyone's documents are quickly moved through the verification process, and dental schools have plenty of time to evaluate their applicants thoroughly. The playing field is reasonably flat, at least in terms of admissions-side inputs. In a perfect world, dental schools would not have to worry about inequities or special circumstances surrounding anyone's applications.

Also, in a perfect world, there are no pandemics.

Enter 2020. Everything changed as chaos ensued. For most of us in the United States, the wheels came off of our life's vehicles during the second week in March. Not one of you needs a lecture about the deep, wide, and ongoing impact of the COVID-19 emergency, least of all prospective dental students.

First, we recognize the value of human life and do not conflate any admissions process with the tragic loss of loved ones. But you bought this book about dental school admissions, so we owe it to you to talk about the impact of COVID-19 as it relates to your dental school application.

NOT OPTIONAL!

Every dental applicant was affected by COVID-19, and it is the right of each applicant to tell their story. The AADSAS will provide an "optional" opportunity to contextualize your application in light of the pandemic. In our opinion, it would be a big mistake to skip this opportunity to provide more information about pitfalls along with the good preparation you have planned and/or executed.

Will a lot of applicants tell similar stories? Sure. But the objective here is not so much being different as it is to make your case and show the reader even more about yourself. You faced and overcame challenges.

You have tales to recount. We promise. Get started!

Begin by brainstorming all the ways your dental school plans were threatened by the many changes of 2020.

Think **categorically,** first about **the challenges you encountered**:

Academic

- How and when did your coursework resume once you were off-campus?
- Has your planned coursework been affected? How about labs?
- Were your grades affected adversely? How did remote learning affect the way teaching and learning happened for you?
- Was your class standing weakened as a function of Pass/Fail policies?
- How did your relationships with faculty mentors change?
- Were you able to prep for the DAT as planned? Was/is your exam date unchanged from that which you had anticipated?
- Were you able to study efficiently from your home (or other lodging during the pandemic)?
- Was your research project canceled?

Dental

- Which dental shadowing or work opportunities were impacted?
- Were any other dentistry-related hands-on experiences postponed or canceled?
- What was telemedicine or teledental like?

Environmental

- What were your stressors?
- Did anyone in your life die of COVID-19?

- Did you or your family lose a job or a significant amount of expected income?
- Were your professors unable to keep a stable internet connection, or did Zoom cut out?
- Did you face internet problems at home?
- Were your books on campus while you went home?
- Is your family's long-term financial security at risk as a result of Covid?
- Did you have trouble traveling home or returning back to school due to financial or other complications?
- Were any family responsibilities at home delegated to you, e.g. care of younger siblings? Cooking? Cleaning?
- Was there a quiet place to study?

Now, reflect on all you have done to prevail, to recover lost time or experiences.

Organize your notes into the narrative you want to tell, being mindful to write about your challenges in a matter-of-fact way. More bluntly: don't whine.

Over and Above

If you were able to provide any kind of solution or service for your friends, family, community, or neighborhood amidst the COVID-19 quarantines, be sure to include some notes about your efforts and any outcomes.

PART 7

APPLICATION PROCESS CONTINUES

There are in fact two things, science and opinion; the former begets knowledge, the latter ignorance.

– Hippocrates

CHAPTER 46
SECONDARIES

Dental school secondary applications are different for each school. Furthermore, not all dental schools have secondaries.

1. Check the AADSAS Program Specific area to search each school to which you plan to apply and see if the 'secondary' or 'supplemental' is available in the primary application.

2. Wait for dental schools to request secondaries from you. However, check your e-mail and junk mail frequently since you do not want to miss the message or the deadline to submit if there is one. Some schools may request an additional set of transcripts, verification of good standing, essays, explanations, or an additional recommendation.

3. Take time on your secondary essays. If an essay is "optional", interpret that word. Only if it absolutely does not apply is it optional. It is just a way for schools to tell whether or not you are thorough and committed. Besides, this is one more chance to tell them more about you. However, some questions do not apply, like your experience as a veteran. If you were not a veteran, do not feel obligated to write something.

4. Understand the school and unique aspects of the program. Look through the website for information.

5. Edit and proofread your work. Look back at what you wrote after a few hours to see if what you wrote is really what you wanted to say.

6. Time Sensitive: Some schools give you two weeks to return your essays. You need to read through the secondary when you receive

the e-mail and check the date of receipt. Read the instructions and respond promptly.

Be specific in your essays. Generic answers are those that any applicant could write and do not reveal anything about you. For example, if the school asks why you applied to that school, respond with specific reasons that are unique to that school. Do your research. Look up information about the dental school to demonstrate why the dental school is a perfect fit for you and why you are a perfect fit for them.

Using college buzzwords is not enough. Not only that, but every other busy pre-dent student hones in on the same buzzwords without doing adequate research. Imagine if the tables were turned and you were to read a dozen essays from students who BSed their way through the question. Remember that you need to stand out from thousands of other applicants. Writing what you think the school wants to hear or some mash of buzzwords will not get you to your goal.

How you respond is a determining factor as to whether you get an interview. Keep your eye on the prize. Your goal is to get the interview, receive an acceptance letter, and complete dental school.

In the meantime, you need to be highly organized. One way of managing the time crunch between school, activities, and essays piling up during the secondary application process is to research the dental schools ahead of time and make a chart of specific institutional philosophy, programs, classes, lectures, examinations, dental boards, clinical opportunities, organizations, and community-building activities.

Beware that online forums may be biased or even untrue. Read information from the dental school and talk to students who attend if that is possible. Especially now, with the changes in dental student education during the pandemic, a current representative's take on education is better than five-year-old forum responses. If you cannot find a current student or cannot visit in person to meet students, the next best option is through the alumni network. Some of these are even published online or you can locate people through LinkedIn.

You would be surprised to find out that people in dental school admissions offices often answer the phones and will help you locate someone with whom you can speak directly about their program. You might even find graduates from annual reports, like the one at UCLA (https://dentistry.ucla.edu/give-section/give/annual-report).

QUESTIONS YOU SHOULD BE PREPARED TO ANSWER

1. How do you foresee interacting with students and faculty in your DDS program and how do you think this program will help you achieve your career goals?

2. Please choose one experience that you had in the dental or healthcare field listed on your application. Describe what you learned from this experience and how it influenced and/or reinforced your career choice?

3. Describe your most difficult leadership experience and tell us how it was resolved. Why was it difficult? What did you learn about yourself?

4. What did you learn from your community service work that you were surprised by or did not expect? What influenced you to be involved in community work?

5. What accomplishments do you feel set you apart from other applicants?

6. Tell us something about your undergraduate experience that you would change and why.

7. Explain how the COVID-19 pandemic changed your pursuit of dentistry.

8. What unique circumstances or life experiences are relevant to your application that you have not previously presented.

If it were easy, everyone would be a doctor. This is the best job in the world. Despite everything. Because of everything!

— Unknown

CHAPTER 47
INTERVIEW TYPES

Y ou followed all of the steps, completed the coursework, took your tests, received glowing recommendations, wrote your essays, and applied. Now, it is time to finish off the process with a demonstration of who you are and why you would be a good candidate for that dental school. To be prepared for your interviews, you should practice. This is a big step, and it is just around the corner. What do you want dental schools to know about you? What situations are the most relevant?

Admissions committees want to get to know you in person. Even so, you may have a virtual 'Zoom' interview. While the essay portion of the application process is very helpful to determine what you choose to write to a school, an 'in-person' meeting is very different in assessing a student's interest in dentistry, experiences that led them to this juncture, and commitment to attend and persist. In the university's professional environment, you will not only represent the school, but you will eventually work with their patients. Experienced interviewers use this time to determine your communication style and effectiveness in a professional setting.

WHAT IS THE PROCESS?

You will receive a letter or a call from the dental school letting you know that they think you were worthy enough to get one of their few interviews. This moment is both exciting and uncertain at the same time. Remember, they must have been impressed by something they read or saw in your application. Now they just want to learn a little bit more. They are inviting you to their campus or possibly to attend a virtual interview.

Respond to the interview request as soon as you have a calendar in front of you and can schedule a time. Do not wait. There are often limited openings.

You might feel nervous. You know why you want to attend dental school, and the interview gives you the chance to explain your reasons to the committee. Reduce your anxiety by reviewing questions, practicing with someone, and considering what you want to say. Mock interviews are very helpful.

WHO INTERVIEWS YOU?

Your interviewers are either admissions team members or professors in the department who have agreed to participate in the interview process. Dental school professors have a vested interest in ensuring that the class is composed of a collegial body of students who will work well with the other students and, of course, the faculty.

Often alumni or current dental students are available to answer your questions as well. They may also be asked of their impression of candidates, which may or may not be used in the decision-making process.

TYPE OF INTERVIEWS

Each school has a different process. Interviews used to be on the campus so that the college could see you, greet you, and get to know you more personally. For you, it was the chance to walk around the campus as well so that you could take in the environment, meet students more personally, and see the facilities. However, during COVID-19, few schools had on-campus interviews. Thus, most of the interviews were in a virtual format. Here are some of the different types of interviews.

Open File Format

As the name implies, your file is open, and the interviewer knows what you submitted in your AADSAS. Often the grades and DAT scores are omitted so that the interviewer is not prejudiced by knowing your admissibility based on the school's quantitative assessment. The interviewer, in this case, is likely to ask questions that are based upon your application, clarifying what you wrote, and getting to know your story in your words.

Closed File Format

In this case, your file is closed. The interviewer does not know what you put on your initial application or your secondaries. You are a blank slate to them. They are likely to explore your interest by asking you general questions and leading to those that are more specific. Occasionally, the interviewer will be able to see your file after the interview.

Traditional Interview

In this interview, a fixed set of questions are asked. The questions are decided upon ahead of time. All interviewers ask the same questions. In this way, there is a standardization of the process. Thus, while the interviewers might change, the answers can be, in some way, compared to other candidates.

Panel Interview

This type of interview is a typical format whereby a committee of two or three people interview you simultaneously. In this way, they can meet afterward to confer about each candidate and score, rank, or evaluate the interview in some substantive way to provide a recommendation to move forward with the candidacy. One or more interviewers may have seen your file, but the questions are typically from a set of questions defined before the process starts and will not be unique to your application.

Multiple Mini Interviews

More colleges are going to the Multiple Mini Interview (MMI) style, though not all schools use this format. In this process, you will proceed from station to station. You will be asked a short format question for that station, or you will be given a scenario, photo, or a case to evaluate and provide a response. Occasionally, you will be asked a follow-up question.

A FINAL NOTE

Be yourself. Relax. Enjoy the experience. They chose you over other candidates. It's yours if you exude confidence, commitment, and desire. Know why you want that school. Go for it!

A strong, positive self-image is the best possible preparation for success.

— Joyce Brothers

CHAPTER 48

THE INTERVIEW

Since the application can be submitted on June 1st, you can get your secondaries as early as late June. Thus, you may be offered an interview as early as the end of July. Many colleges offer mock interviews both with the pre-health advisor and through the Career Services department.

Be prepared to ask questions about the school so that you learn more as well. If you have multiple offers, you will want to make sure you are 100% committed to that school and that program. The following four years of dental school are academically as rigorous as any experience you have had thus far. It would be best if you found a place where you believe you will thrive. If you are not invited to ask questions during the interview, talk to students on campus to learn more about the environment.

VIRTUAL INTERVIEW – 20 POINTS TO CONSIDER

ADEA AADSAS has, an excellent PDF document called "Virtual Dental School Interviews: Dos and Don'ts". They recommend the following:

1. *Be Prepared* – Be prompt and seated in front of your webcam 15 minutes before the scheduled interview.

2. *Learn* – Know the dental school's mission.

3. *Quiet and Isolated* – You do not want to be interrupted during your interview, so it is best to find a quiet and private place free from distractions.

4. *Clean Environment and Well-Lit* – Construct your environment so that it is clean, neat, and well-lit. A neutral background without distractions is best.

5. **Re-Read the Interview Invitation** – Information in the interview invitation may prove to be helpful. You want to prepare for the right type of interview (traditional, panel, MMI) and follow the instructions they provide.

6. **Research the School** – Prepare for the interview by researching the school, understanding their philosophy, and knowing what they published regarding their academic environment.

7. **Check Your Equipment** – Make sure that your computer, webcam, and Wi-fi are operational.

8. **Be Professional** – Your attire should be fitting for a professional job interview- simple, tasteful, and modest. Similarly, if you choose a background, test how it looks. Ensure that your screen name is your first and last name.

9. **Time Zone Check** – Since dental schools exist in multiple time zones, one error students make is not matching the appointment time to the correct time zone.

10. **Get Enough Sleep** – You are expected to be clear-headed, quick-minded, and at the top of your game. Make sure you have a good night's sleep before the interview.

11. **Tell Roommates or Family** – Share your interview schedule with your roommates or family to avoid issues of someone coming into the room or overloading the Wi-fi.

12. **Mock Interview Practice** – Schedule and participate in a mock interview with your pre-dent advisor or career center. Use the feedback to adapt your body language and get suggestions on improving your responses.

13. **Cell Phone Turned off** – Make sure your cell phone is off or on silent.

14. **Photo ID** – You may be asked to show a photo ID at the interview. Put it next to your computer before you begin.

15. **Smile and Relax** – Sit up straight in the center of the camera's frame and smile. Be calm and speak slowly while making eye contact.

16. **Listen Carefully and Speak Genuinely** – Listen to the interviewer's questions and take your time to answer with an honest, genuine response.

17. **Note Taking and Questions** – If you take notes, take them on a pad next to your computer. The noise of the keyboard and the distraction of typing can be disruptive. Prepare thoughtful questions ahead of time and put them on the pad.

18. ***Be Humble, Courteous, and Polite*** – Both during the interview and with any communications afterward, be respectful, thoughtful, and responsible. If you promised to follow up, do so shortly after the interview.

19. ***Thank You E-Mail*** – After the interview, send a thank-you note telling the interviewer(s) that you appreciated their time and are welcome to ask any other questions. If possible, reference something from the interview to jog their memory. With hundreds of interviews, it is hard for the interviewer to remember you. You might put your picture in the signature section of your e-mail.

20. ***Patience*** – Be patient. You have done your job and sent a thank you. You now have to wait. However, it is not disrespectful for you to reach out to admissions representatives in a couple of weeks if you have not heard anything.

You know what you put on your application. However, review what you wrote anyway. Also, while you are aware of your beliefs, commitments, and accomplishments, write down a few ideas to remember to communicate. With these steps, you are better prepared to answer questions for the Open File Format, Closed File Format, Traditional Interview, and Panel Interview. You should practice, for sure, but the Multiple Mini Interview (MMI) is different.

MULTIPLE MINI INTERVIEW

In this format, you will be sent to stations whether your interview is in person or virtual. The stations are not long, usually 7 – 10 minutes. Each station will be different.

In one station, the interviewer may ask you why you want to become a dentist. This question is fairly typical, and you should be very clear why you have chosen dentistry. You might also be asked what skills you have that will make you an excellent dentist or what skills are you missing that you believe you need to have to be a great dentist? Time yourself as you prepare to answer the question with time to spare for the interviewer to ask a follow-up question.

In the next station, you might be asked how COVID-19 impacted your education. You know some reasons, but you want to be succinct. Prepare by picking out a few examples that you can explain in a couple of sentences.

Next, you might be asked an ethical question, like, "If your classmate cheated on an exam and you knew about it, what would you do?" Brainstorm four or five scenarios. Like, what if you were asked to perform a procedure in an emergency that you studied but never practiced? What if you knew that the medicine a patient needed was unavailable, and your mentor gave the patient a placebo to reassure them? What would you say and do if you were treating a patient and you accidentally broke their tooth?

At the next station, you might be given a photo of a dentist, climbers on a rugged mountainside, skiers in an avalanche, friends at a beach campfire, or students in a university lecture. You may be asked what you see, what people are experiencing, or what you think happens next. The answer you give tells quite a bit about how you see the world and its people.

The next station might present you with a video. This station is much like the picture type. You will watch the short video and then be asked by the interviewer to discuss what you saw and what the situation means. The situation may relate to dentistry or not.

Next, you might be given a card or be shown a slide with a scenario or vignette with one to two minutes to formulate how you would handle the situation presented before entering the room and sitting down or having the interviewer show up on the screen to hear your answer.

In a similar role evaluation station, you will be asked to play a role. A person will enter the room acting out a part. The person may be confrontational or attitudinal. You must interact with the individual while the 'interviewer' watches your actions and reactions. This exercise aims to see if you can be calm in your communication and handle the situation with a professional demeanor.

MUCH CAN BE LEARNED

The interview process reveals much about the applicant's personality, humility, and ability to communicate effectively. You will be evaluated based upon your poise, confidence, communication, reactions, arguments, and suitability for dentistry. Be yourself. You got to this point, and you need to demonstrate why you would be a good candidate. Good Luck!

The life so short,
the craft so long
to learn.

— *Hippocrates*

CHAPTER 49
THE HOME STRETCH: UPDATING YOUR APPLICATION

After you submit your dental school application, you earn grades from courses completed after submission in the spring or you may decide to take additional classes in the summer. On the other hand, you might accept a position as a scribe or work in a dental office. An international service organization might contact you with a chance to work in a foreign country for part of the summer, or you might work with Operation Smile helping children with cleft palates. Either way, your life will continue, and you will have new and meaningful experiences to add to your application.

There are three update opportunities. One is your academic update that you will do through the ADEA AADSAS application. Another includes activities, service, and clinical work that you pursued after you submitted your secondaries and possibly even after your interviews. The third type is showing your continued interest.

ACADEMIC UPDATE (AU) OF YOUR ADEA AADSAS APPLICATION

While you cannot change your personal statement or the colleges on your initial application, you can update your coursework, grades, and academic information. After submission and after your application has been verified, you may have completed courses or enrolled in new classes and want to show your work in progress. This update is optional, but it may have some value to one or more of the colleges to which you applied.

Academic Update Window

August 13th to September 30th

December 2nd to February 2nd

During these periods, you are allowed to enter in-progress and planned coursework. Provided that you have at least one program in "verified status" by the official deadline, February 2nd, you can input an academic update. Look for the "Check Status" tab to determine your application status.

You want to ensure that your application is up-to-date with the correct information about how you are progressing academically and what you are taking. Frequently, classes you expected to take are canceled, changed, overlapped, or you chose new courses due to your new interests. Either way, it is helpful to update your application.

If you have new grades to add, your ADEA AADSAS GPA may change. This addition could improve your chances or not, depending upon the grades you receive. Your newly calculated GPA is sent to your programs. Note: You can add any new grades from terms that ended after submission or courses you plan to take. You may not update coursework or grades from past terms that were verified in the initial process.

However, just inputting new courses and/or new grades is not enough. You must also send official transcripts from each of the schools directly to ADEA AADSAS after the application service sends you an e-mail with a confirmation that your academic update was successful. ADEA AADSAS requests that you do not send transcripts before you receive confirmation. If so, your transcripts will need to be resubmitted.

Your request for an academic update will go into the queue for verification. Expect this process to take approximately two weeks. When complete, you will be notified via e-mail that your academic update has been verified. You may only update your grades one time during the academic update period so ensure that you are inputting the most current courses and grades.

To Update Coursework

1. In the Academic History section, click on Transcript Entry and Edit. Add grades from 'in progress' coursework and click Completed.
2. If you are adding a new term, click Add Term and input classes you plan to take and any grades you might have earned.

3. When you are done, click Save All and then Submit My Updates.

4. When you receive your e-mail from ADEA AADSAS confirming your submission, send your official transcripts.

To Update Your Profile, Contact Information, or Programs

1. *Contact* - Enter your new contact information – e-mail, address, phone.

2. *Profile* - For profile changes, you can change your username, password, or security questions if your information has been compromised.

3. *Letters of Recommendation* – You may edit information, delete incomplete evaluations, or add new evaluations provided you have not exceeded your limit.

4. *Programs* – Provided a program deadline has not passed, you may add a program.

5. *Scores and Achievements* – While you may not edit or delete what has already been inputted and verified, you may add new test scores, activities, awards, and recognition.

6. *"Update My Application"* – When you are done making your updates, click on Update My Application.

Two other updates are also valuable. One is updating your individual schools with information that is pertinent to your application for admission. The other is updating your schools with a note of your continued interest.

An important note of caution.

Many students are anxious about this process. Dental school admissions officers could be annoyed by aggressive students when they are doing their best to evaluate candidates. Use your communications sparingly. You want to make sure your schools are aware of anything new and that you are highly interested in their program, but you do not want to contact them every time you start a new activity, win a new award, or get a new certification. Thus, you want to hold off until you have your fall or spring activities set.

"

He who is not everyday conquering some fear has not learned the secret of life.

— Ralph Waldo Emerson

CHAPTER 50

APPLYING FOR FINANCIAL AID

The good news is that dentistry is a growing profession, and there are positions available. The U.S. Bureau of Labor Statistics data anticipates growth in this field over the next ten years. Data as of spring 2021 shows that the increase in dentists needed is over 10% while the salaries are good,[1] averaging,[2]

Owners of Dental Practices: $232,980

Oral Surgeons: $234,990

Orthodontists: $237,990

The average salary for salaried general dentists is about $50,000 lower.

At the same time, dental school is expensive. The estimated expenses at some schools are a half-million dollars, leaving new dentists with significant debt. The May 2021 published figures for four dental schools are.

Dental School	Costs of Attendance (4 year total)
UC San Francisco	$250,000 (CA-res); $300,000 (non-res)
UPenn	$507,826
Tufts	$511,960
USC (California)	$545,876

COST OF ATTENDANCE

This total cost of dental school includes tuition, room, board, books, equipment, fees, transportation, and miscellaneous costs. However, this four-year commitment pays off with numerous benefits and a rewarding career.

With these kinds of costs, for four years of dental school plus another $350,000 or more for a residency in orthodontics or oral surgery, your post-graduate education costs are significant. Thus, it is essential to consider some of your options.

All students can apply for money via the Free Application for Federal Student Aid (FAFSA). Even if you do not qualify for a grant, you should apply through the FAFSA so that you will have loan options. You may receive loans that do not accrue interest until after you finish your program.

FEDERAL DIRECT STUDENT LOANS

If you are enrolled in a dental school program, you may qualify for a Direct Unsubsidized or Direct Grad PLUS student loan. To be eligible, you must:

- Be a U.S. citizen or an eligible non-citizen
- Possess a valid social security number
- Comply with selective service registration requirements (males must register between the ages of 18 and 25)
- Enroll or be accepted as a degree-seeking student in an eligible degree or certificate program
- Be enrolled at least half-time
- Maintain satisfactory academic progress
- Not have a record of default on a federal student loan

COMPLETE THE FAFSA
(FREE APPLICATION FOR FEDERAL STUDENT AID)

The FAFSA opens October 1st annually for the following school year. This form must be completed prior to the start of each academic year.

YOUR FINANCIAL AID OFFER

While you are not obligated to accept any award, you will receive an acknowledgment that you applied and an offer from the university.

Typically, in the spring of each year, the university will contact students with instructions as to how to access their offer, or you will find the award information in the university's portal under financial aid. If you receive an e-mail, you will be given information on the next steps in the financial aid process, including entrance counseling, completing loan applications, consent forms, and master promissory notes. Your financial aid offer will include educational expenses for the loan period.

SCHOLARSHIPS

Some organizations charge students for looking up scholarships. You should not have to pay for help. You can get information from the financial aid offices at the dental schools you plan to attend. On the websites of most dental schools, there are lists of outside scholarships or school/private sponsored scholarships. The amounts may not be huge, but they are a start. Some dental schools offer scholarships for $500 or $1,000 or sometimes $2,500 for students from various minority groups. Some are larger, like the University of Pennsylvania's scholarship program, which offers a $40,000/year non-need-based scholarship for select candidates.

You may also apply for scholarships through outside sources like the following:

American Dental Association
American Dental Education Association
American Student Dental Association
Alpha Kappa Alpha Scholarship
Black Excel; The College Help Network
Colgate-Palmolive and National Medical Fellowship (NMF)
Graduate Fellowships and Post Doctoral Awards for Minorities
Hispanic Dental Association Foundation
Proctor & Gamble Scholarship Program
Hispanic Scholarship Fund
Indian Health Professions Scholarship Program
NAMME: National Association of Medical Minority Educators, Inc.
NDA: National Dental Association Foundation
Scholarships for African Americans
Special Higher Education Grant Program
United Negro College Fund

DEBT FREE OPTIONS

National Health Service Corps (NHSC)

This is a government-funded program that seeks to provide primary healthcare to those with limited access in "Health Professional Shortage Areas". This program started in 1972 and has helped thousands of dental students pay for dental school. With the high cost of dental school, you should apply for this program for the chance that you can be free from school debt.

Choose between the loan repayment program[3] or the scholarship program.[4] Read through the current eligibility requirements.

Students applying to the scholarship program have a service commitment of one year of service commitment per scholarship year or partial scholarship year with a two-year minimum and four-year maximum. The funding offered includes:

- Tuition
- Required Fees
- Reasonable Educational Costs
- Monthly Support Stipend

The locations where you will serve upon graduation include sites in all fifty states and U.S. territories, including:

- Federally Qualified Health Center (FQHC)
- Rural Health Clinic
- Hospital-affiliated Primary Care Outpatient Clinic
- Indian Health Service, Tribal Clinic
- State or Federal Correctional Facility
- Community Facilities
- Free Clinics
- Mobile Units
- Immigration and Customs Enforcement
- Health Service Corps

Military Dentist Loan Repayment Program

Army – If you are enrolled in an ADA-accredited dental school program, you may be eligible for a full-tuition scholarship for up to four years. Some dental

---

3   Health Resources and Services Administration, "Loan Repayment," *Health Resources and Services Administration*, n.d., https://nhsc.hrsa.gov/loan-repayment/index.html

4   Health Resources and Services Administration, "National Health Service Corps Scholarship Program," *Health Resources and Services Administration*, April 2019, https://nhsc.hrsa.gov/sites/default/files/NHSC/scholarships/nhsc-scholarship-fact-sheet.pdf

students will receive a $20,000 signing bonus. This package also comes with books, academic fees, and a monthly stipend. You are required to serve after you finish dental school. Your training will commence during your academic breaks as you ramp up to your military commitment after graduation.

Navy – The U.S. Navy also offers the opportunity to emerge from dental school debt-free. The Navy Health Professions Scholarship Program (HPSP) offers 100% tuition during dental school, plus a $20,000 signing bonus and a monthly stipend of $2,200 for four years. You will also be reimbursed for equipment, insurance, books, and supplies. Another option is the Navy Health Services Collegiate Program (HSCP) which provides you between $157,000 to $269,000 while attending dental school. The Navy also offers funding of more than $275,000 for your dental residency. Practicing dentists can receive a signing bonus of $150,000 to $300,000.

PART 8

DECISIONS, DECISIONS

Attitude is a little thing that makes a big difference.

—Winston Churchill

CHAPTER 51

"DECISION DAY" – DECEMBER 1

If the 2020s were like the 2010s, then 'Decision Day' would be December 1. However, students applying for Fall 2021, learned that 'Decision Day' was moved back to December 15. The date is still before the holidays so you will either celebrate or wait.

Remember that most dental schools have rolling admissions, so the December 1st or 15th dates are rather arbitrary. Whichever date it will be for 2022 or 2023 admissions, this is just the first date when colleges respond with acceptances. There is plenty of time during the next few months in which you could be accepted. If you are not accepted in December, there is still January, February, March, and April.

Rolling admissions means that colleges continue to admit students during the process. Thus, the application review, interview, and admissions process continues until all of the seats in that year's class are filled. However, applicants can still send admissions packets until February, which just means that the competition for the remaining spots increases.

Think of it this way. The December 1st or 15th admits are the very top students a college wants to enroll and ensure they get a spot. Even so, some of those admits will get multiple offers so there is no real guarantee that they will go to College X, when College Y and College Z are vying for the same student. The student can only accept one of these schools.

Dental schools can accept applicants after May 1st, though some accept waitlist students in May and June. Thus, if you had to delay taking your DAT, do not wait too long. You should take the test the spring or summer before applying. If you write your application in May through August, you can complete your supplementals from August to October, and get Interviewed from October through February. In this way, you can be granted admission in December. Walk back your timeline of where you want to be so that you are not disappointed. Your goal is to get to an interview and show the side of you that cannot shine through in the application. The interview is crucial.

If you are in the planning stages now, the goal is to apply early. The later you take the DAT and the later you apply, the more competitive the process.

As you are aware, the process of getting accepted to dental school is arduous and stressful. However, it is also competitive and uncertain. Dental school admissions rates are low. There are no easy-admit schools like there were when you applied to undergraduate schools. Everyone who applies to attend dental school did well in college, took tough classes, and scored well on the DATs. Very few get accepted without mostly As in the hardest classes.

Almost all dental schools reject 70 – 90% of their applicants. There is no early decision for schools through the ADEA AADSAS. The earliest decision date is December 1st (or 15th). This goes back to giving yourself that early edge and showing that you are truly committed by planning and applying early. Take the test early, turn your application in early, send back your secondaries as soon as you can, interview, and you have the best shot.

Also remember, that more schools are signing on to require the CASPer test. This is just one more requirement to add to a very busy year. It is also why taking a gap year to strengthen your profile might be better than applying late if it looks like you are going to submit your initial application in the middle of the fall.

Thus, you must avoid putting off the test and application for the greatest chance. Besides, you want to make sure that ADEA AADSAS has all of your documents, that you correct any errors, and you have plenty of time to think about what you want to say in your secondaries.

In the end, your December 1st (or 15th) decision has a much better chance of arriving with you yelling out cheers of victory and holding celebrations during the winter holidays if you plan ahead and apply early. Good Luck!

"

If one dream should fall and break into a thousand pieces, never be afraid to pick one of those pieces up and begin again.

– Flavia Weedn

CHAPTER 52

WAITLIST, REJECTION, APPEAL

Decision Day! Congratulations to those accepted. Patience to those who have not yet heard.

Due to COVID-19, "Decision Day" for Fall 2021 admits was pushed back from December 1, 2020, to December 15, 2020. This may not be true for Fall 2012 or 2022. Check the ADEA website for the specific date. Decisions are typically made by a phone call from an admissions committee member. An official letter from the admissions committee is also mailed to the address on the application. Students can be accepted to multiple schools.

Admissions officers or deans will enthusiastically welcome you to next year's class. This call, letter and acceptance is an important milestone since dental schools have now selected their best candidates from the pool. Congratulations if you are one of those selected.

Some students will be put on a high waitlist (HWL), mid/medium waitlist (MWL), or a low waitlist (LWL). This means you are still in the running, but you did not yet make it over the threshold. You may not hear whether or not you got off the waitlist at your top choice school for four months. Some people do not hear until April.

However, you typically have only thirty days to decide about accepting the offer or offers you are given in December. You will need to decide which school you will choose from the offers you are given. Note: Respond to all schools that offer you a spot as to whether or not you will attend. This response allows schools to extend admission to worthy candidates who were put on the waitlist.

You need to be sure where you want to attend too. First, you will spend four years there. You may want to visit with your family members or others very close to you to get second or third opinions. They may be more candid if you are unsure.

Second, since your time will be consumed with dental school, you may have multiple factors that determine which school you choose. Family and personal reasons might influence your decision based upon proximity, your partner's job, or family reponsibilities. Finances might also play into which school you will attend. You could ask any of the schools to which you were accepted if they have scholarships, fellowships, or other financial aid opportunities.

If you are not accepted on "Decision Day", this is not the end. Decisions roll in over the next few months. Be patient. There are a few online discussion boards where students post their angst about being on a waitlist and when they hear. This community makes people feel as if they are not alone.

You are not alone. There are many others who are trying to be patient throughout the process while their future is on the line. Dental schools update your status when it changes. Do not call the admissions offices. Dental schools are flooded with calls. Applications are often still coming in from late applicants who can still file an application until February.

On the other hand, you do want to update your file with a letter of continued interest and possibly any new information about courses, grades, research, service, clinical experiences, or other activities. Dental school committees would not know your true interest otherwise. If you are no longer interested, please tell them. Lots of anxious students would love to know that there is one more spot available.

If you are rejected, you have lots of options. You could change career paths. You could reapply next year. You could also pursue a master's degree. This is not the end of the road. The next chapter of this book discusses some of your options. While it is possible to appeal a decision, with so many students on the waitlist, appeals are less likely to succeed. On the other hand, if you have a compelling reason, and you are confident that dentistry is the field you want to pursue, then you should appeal the decision.

Good luck in your pursuit!

"

Never be afraid to start over, It's a new chance to rebuild what you want.

— Len Schlesinger

CHAPTER 53

POST-BACC PROGRAMS

'Post-bacc' (or post-baccalaureate programs) is a term used to describe coursework completed after the bachelor's degree. Some post-bacc programs are specifically designed for dental schools. Some also enhance academic credentials, prepare students for the DATs, and support underrepresented students in pursuing dentistry. Particularly, if you need a year before undergraduate and graduate education or are not accepted after applying, these programs are a great option. Some students enroll in post-bacc programs because they did not complete the pre-dental academic requirements or did not get stellar undergraduate grades.

ONE-YEAR NON-DEGREE POST-BACC PROGRAMS

The Creighton University School of Dentistry Post-Baccalaureate Program is a one-year biomedical sciences program where students prepare for the DAT and learn the foundational knowledge to excel in dental school. Students who complete the requirements and display the achievement and qualities necessary will be guaranteed a spot in Creighton's dental school and will receive scholarship support.

The Ohio State University Dent Path Program is a one-year program designed to increase the number of students from underserved or underrepresented backgrounds to strengthen competency in the core sciences and improve both hand skills and perceptual ability. Successful students are automatically accepted to The Ohio State University DDS program. Students acclimate to the Ohio State campus and the surrounding city before beginning dental school. Students must complete the AADSAS application and indicate on the supplemental application that they are interested in the DentPath Program.

Marquette University College of Health Sciences Biomedical Sciences' Pre-Dental Post-Baccalaureate Program is a one-year program associated with the Marquette University School of Dentistry. The program is designed to prepare students who already have a strong science background to be more competitive in the dental school application process.

The UCLA School of Dentistry offers a one-year, non-degree pathway for students to pursue dental school. This program offers underrepresented, disadvantaged college students throughout the dental school preparation and application process. Students are allowed to take dental school classes alongside UCLA dental school students. Three-fourths of the students who have completed this program have been accepted to dental school.

These are just a few post-bacc programs. Also, there are types of post-baccalaureate programs, including master's programs in biomedical sciences, public health, or healthcare administration.

MASTER'S DEGREE CONSIDERATIONS

There are numerous master's programs. This list only contains ten options. The completion times vary from nine months to three years. Your job is to earn almost all As and prove that you can handle graduate-level coursework. While most of the programs offer master's degrees, some also offer guaranteed interviews and access to take dental school classes while in the program. Some require comprehensive exams for completion.

PROGRAMS

Barry University offers an MS in Biomedical Sciences that can take between one and two years, depending upon a student's academic background. To complete the program students are required to pass comprehensive exams in the biomedical sciences.

Boston University offers a one-year (July-July) full-time MS in Oral Health Sciences program on the Boston University Medical Campus in which 90% of its graduates matriculate to dental school. Courses are taken through the Boston University School of Dental Medicine. A thesis or capstone is required. Students can complete their studies in July and begin dental school shortly afterward.

Case Western University offers a rigorous one-year MS in Physiology. Approximately 150-175 students are enrolled each year. Before completion, students must complete comprehensive exams in Physiology and Neurophysiology.

Mercer University School of Medicine offers a one year MS in Preclinical Sciences focused on biomedical practices and research. Students gain the foundation they need for healthcare sciences including dentistry.

Nova Southeastern University (NSU) offers a one-year, 30-credit Master's in Biomedical Sciences program with fall and winter start dates. DAT test preparation is offered along with cutting-edge research labs. Students are guaranteed an interview by completing this program.

Rutgers University offers a one-year MS in Biomedical Sciences in a specialized Dental Scholars Track with an option to concentrate in Oral Biology. Students are guaranteed a dental school interview if they earn a 3.7 GPA. During the program, students are offered the option to take dental school courses. More than half of the graduates are accepted to dental school.

Tufts University Masters in Biomedical Sciences is a rigorous program designed for students planning to apply for medical, dental, or other health science program. The curriculum aligns with Tufts health science programs. Admissions is on a rolling basis until the class fills.

Tulane University offers a MS in Cell and Molecular Biology that can be completed in nine months. Approximately thirty students are accepted to the medical, dental, and research track.

University of South Florida offers a one-year MS in Medical Sciences degree with coursework that is comparable to a first-year dental program.

The University of Washington offers a MS in Oral Biology. With topics spanning molecular biology, microbiology, craniofacial biology, basic and applied behavioral science, dental public health, dental hygiene, clinical research, epidemiology, and biostatistics, students learn more about the field while collaborating with other students and participating in clinical research.

" Failure doesn't mean the game is over; it means try again with experience.

— Len Schlesinger

CHAPTER 54
REAPPLY

D eciding to reapply is the first step toward your goal of becoming a dentist. Reapplying is a big decision and shows a genuine commitment to dentistry. You could have easily quit and gone another direction. Some people do because they are not that committed to this career. Now, you need to determine what you will do differently this time.

WHY WAS I NOT ACCEPTED?

There are numerous reasons why you were not accepted that may not be on your radar. Some of those include institutional priorities. You might have been a highly desirable candidate. Still, they may have needed to accept a student of a particular type to ensure that they were fair in their admissions process and accepted students from diverse backgrounds. They may have had a late applicant who completely wowed the committee.

You can contact the school and ask them to provide you with a post-rejection interview with one of their admissions staff members. Many dental schools offer this option. You should ask and not just assume that you know why. These admissions committee members can tell you the weaknesses you had in your application and what you can do to improve. This call may be the key to success in your reapplication and admissions process.

Maybe you did not show enough experience in dentistry or commitment to the field. In your secondaries, you may not have shown an understanding of the institution, program, and student body. Maybe you picked the wrong schools. Last year, one of my students applied to top schools that did not require the DATs since she did not have a score. Her grades were good, but she had little experience in dentistry. When she called a dental school admissions staff member, the person explained that her background did not show significant commitment to dentistry.

You need to be brutally honest and figure out what you need to do to improve your application. Realistically assess your situation, consider what you plan to pursue passionately, and determine if dentistry is truly your path,

Review your application. Be critical. You are a year older and a year wiser. This review opportunity offers you a sobering maturity about how you consider the activities, interests, academics, letters of recommendation, DAT, essays, and even the schools you chose. You will need to strengthen areas where you are weak and add to those areas where you are stronger.

YOU HAVE A YEAR. THE LOOMING QUESTION IS, WHAT WILL YOU DO WITH THAT TIME?

If your GPA is low, particularly your science GPA, enroll in classes to lay a stronger foundation in biochemistry, immunology, human physiology, microbiology, or genetics. There is always more to learn in any field of your interest. Another option is to pursue a post-baccalaureate program specifically for dental school applicants that possibly has a summer DAT prep option. The challenge is that many of these programs have deadlines from December to March, and you may not hear until May 1. This timing is quite late, so you may have to convince a school to let you apply past the deadline. Whether you take science classes to learn and improve your science GPA or pursue a post-bacc dental program to strengthen your science foundation and prepare anew for the DAT, you should consider alternatives if your grades are low.

Though some people will dissuade you about retaking the DAT, this test is one of the critical components of your application. Carefully evaluate whether this is the right decision and do not rush to take the test. An improvement in your score by a point or two can make a significant difference and put your test results closer to the range of applicants. Retaking the DAT will take some time since you want to be sure you are prepared. After all, you are eight months to two years away from when you took the test. You may need to relearn the material covered on the test if you are not enrolled in school.

If you did not have much in the way of dental experiences, you want to build on that area and learn more about the field you intend to enter. Apply for positions in dental offices. Any chance to learn more about the dental office experience, lifestyle, terminology, acronyms, procedures, referrals, emergencies, and outcomes would be valuable. Clinical exposure is often difficult to manage while in college, though with additional time, more healthcare settings may be available. Dental schools want to ensure that you are committed and you know what to expect. Students do drop out of dental school because they do not like dentistry. Even if you previously volunteered, shadowed, or worked in a clinic or dental office, additional experiences show that you are committed to making dentistry your career.

Write a new personal statement. First, you will be different a year later. Second, you will have new activities to describe. Third, your frame of mind is in a different place. With your commitment and personal growth, you will see the world in a different light. This light will shine through in your personal statement. Finally, demonstrate what you did over this period that reawakened your commitment to dentistry and made you feel that you are more prepared than ever to pursue your chosen field of study.

Finally, write an entirely new personal statement and incorporate elements and experiences learned during that additional year. Do whatever you can to strengthen your application as this will help demonstrate to admissions committees your commitment to becoming a dentist.

YOUR GAP YEAR

This time between the end of school and the beginning of dental school is crucial. Think of this year as a "growth" year. Besides, about half of all dental school applicants take a gap year. So, do not consider this year a detriment to your application. In many ways, it is an enhancement. How can you grow to be a more competitive applicant?

- Clinical Experiences
- Coursework and Science Knowledge
- Retake the DAT
- Research Projects
- Develop Interview Skills
- Improve Your Health
- Lead a Service Project
- Fulbright Scholar
- Peace Corps

- Overseas Dental Support Teams
- Develop Greater Self-Awareness

Consider the possibility of gaining certifications in areas around the healthcare field to learn more about medicine, emergency care, and patient support. These include Basic Life Support (BLS), Lifesaving, Phlebotomy, Cardiopulmonary Resuscitation (CPR), Automated External Defibrillator (AED), Emergency Medical Technician (EMT), Certified Medical Assistant, Certified Nursing Assistant (CNA), Certified Dental Assistant, Certified Paraoptometric or Certified Paraoptometric Technician.

Jobs in the healthcare industry allow prospective applicants the chance to experience dentistry with and without certifications like working as a medical scribe, phlebotomist, clinical research assistant, hospital administration staff member, or clinic assistant. Volunteer or paid work with the community may be of interest to you with local or national organizations like The Red Cross, Muscular Dystrophy Association, United Cerebral Palsy, March of Dimes, Alzheimer's Association, Autism Speaks, and the American Association of People with Disabilities.

Although you will take an additional year, this may be the time you need to be better prepared and truly know this is the direction you want to head. Seek out your pre-health advisor for more information, add letters to your "letter packet" or ensure that you have updated transcripts or revised documents available if this service, like Interflio, is available. If not, organize your files so that you have everything ready for your application when it opens again in May.

PART 9

DENTAL EDUCATION

I was created to create beautiful smiles.

— *Unknown*

CHAPTER 55

THE LANDSCAPE OF DENTAL EDUCATION

On March 11, 2020, the World Health Organization declared the COVID-19 virus outbreak a global pandemic. [1] Dental schools instituted several actions to control the spread of the virus, including a quarantine, social distancing, travel bans, and other regulations. These control measures halted everyday activities in most parts of the world in 2020 and 2021, including educational institutions and in-person visits to healthcare professionals. The pandemic has also created unique challenges that necessitated changes in how these institutions and practices function.

Dental schools adapted to these changes by adopting a wide range of measures, including virtual learning, social distancing, grading systems, and changes to long-held admission processes. U.S. dental schools faced unprecedented challenges outside of clinical training in the admission process for new dental students. Online symposia brought faculty and administrators together to brainstorm and share innovations in virtual experiences and dental practices.

Since the novel coronavirus was present in nasopharyngeal and salivary secretions of those with COVID-19, clinical training exposed students to fluids that risked transmitting the infection and spreading the virus.

---

1   Domenico Cucinotta and Maurizio Vanelli, "WHO Declares COVID-19 A Pandemic," *Acta Biomedica* 91, no. 1 (2020): 157–160, https://doi.org/10.23750/abm.v91i1.9397

CHANGES IN ACADEMIC EXPERIENCES

One of the most notable changes was in laboratory experiences. Challenges abounded for college leaders who needed to quickly determine innovative ways of providing instruction. Social experiences transitioned from in-person to online with the goal of keeping a safe social distance, avoiding close contact, and preventing infection. Most dental schools locked down to minimize the spread.

With the closure of classroom meetings, dental schools transitioned online. As the months passed, the CDC revised its guidelines for dental school education based upon risk levels – online, 6-foot distance activities, hybrid, and fully in-person. These new rules were implemented through video lectures, demonstrations, and case study discussions.

Virtual reality simulations allowed students to visualize teeth, instruments, and procedures on a 3-D screen. Haptic technology was instituted to create the look and feel of the dental experience. Some innovations, previously created, were implemented at schools, while improved technologies were invented. One offered a virtual reality patient with a 360 degree walk-through.

CLINICAL EXPERIENCES

Another significant impact was in the ability to work directly with patients. Changes were needed to protect and shield patients. COVID-19 tests were administered to students before entering the dental science buildings. Only a 'safe' number of patients were allowed into the clinics, limiting patient-student contact. Personal Protective Equipment (PPE) was required for patients, providers, staff, and community members. Safety procedures were instituted at each university.

In March 2020, the Center for Disease Control and Prevention (CDC) provided guidelines for dental practices in general and limited treatments to essential or emergency procedures. Furthermore, the CDC made recommendations regarding faculty supervision and student-patient contact in clinical settings to avoid risk.

Since dental schools locked down and close contact is typically made between patient and dentist, the traditional learning process needed to be adjusted. At the onset, clinical experiences were stopped. During the following academic year, 2020-2021, they continued to be disrupted. For those needing to complete clinical requirements for graduation and take board exams. Extensions were granted, requirements modified, and adaptations were made to the model of educational practice.

The goal was to provide a safe and robust clinical environment to gain the full experience of the practice of dentistry. One "augmented reality advanced dental training simulator" allows students to sit at a manikin and have the actions "optically tracked and analyzed in real-time," providing instant feedback using hand skills, mental imagery, and lab integration.[2]

LICENSURE

The American Dental Education Association (ADEA) created guidelines to support dental schools in managing the challenges. ADEA encouraged dental schools to work with regulatory agencies and ensure flexible options for licensure exams and competency assessments.

MENTAL HEALTH

In a survey of 145 students along the dental education track, 23 to 39 years old, respondents expressed concerns about emotional health, motivation to study, physical health, clinical education, and curricular education.[3] Dental students faced personal, academic, emotional, and financial stress. The survey had mixed results on institutional factors such as masks, gloves, COVID-19 testing, social distancing, online teaching, clinical practice, and technology.

CONCLUSION

The COVID-19 pandemic significantly changed dental education during the later 2019-2020 academic year and the entire 2020-2021 school year. Most students experienced increased levels of stress during the transition. Most students felt that their academic and clinical experiences suffered. Although faculty, staff, and students adapted to the new requirements and abided by policies regarding masks, social distancing, and sanitizing, students had fewer contact hours with faculty and patients.

2   Image Navigation, "DentSim," *Image Navigation*, n.d., https://image-navigation.com/home-page/dentsim/
3   Man Hung et al., "In an Era of Uncertainty: Impact of COVID-19 on Dental Education," *Journal of Dental Education 85*, no. (2): 148-156, https://onlinelibrary.wiley.com/doi/full/10.1002/jdd.12404

I hated every minute of training, but I said, don't quit. Suffer now and live the rest of your life as a champion.

— Muhammad Ali

CHAPTER 56

WHAT TO EXPECT IN DENTAL SCHOOL

THE PEOPLE

Many new dental students, especially those who matriculate directly out of college, may be surprised by the wide spectrum of ages, origins, and skill sets to be found in an entering DMD or DDS class. You will find a significant number of young adults who finished their undergraduate degrees within the prior few years. Also, most classes enjoy the presence of some nontraditional applicants.

More than a few international students enroll in U.S. dental schools. The average age of an entering class approaches the mid-twenties, but new students might be in their thirties or even their forties. They come from military service, from careers in dental hygiene, even from time spent at home raising children. More than a few dental students will arrive in the dental school's city with spouses and kids in tow.

All newly-enrolled DMD/DDS students, of course, have done the requisite work to earn a spot in the class. The point is, 21st-century students appreciate diversity, and dental admissions committees work to build classes not only characterized by differences in socioeconomic status and ethnicities, but also by differences in age, in life experiences, and in places of residence.

Much is demanded from the dental student, and very few, if any, people are wired to do it all well. After all, such a student would be able to carve wax like an artisan, memorize thousands of anatomical details, and complete clinical requirements flawlessly.

You will almost certainly encounter classmates who either believe they can handle all the tasks ahead of them without any help or who want you to think they can. Fortunately, most of these students drop the act by the end of the first semester and the class becomes a collaborative whole.

You may learn in time that some of the students who are most confident and seem to know all the dental lingo, grew up in dental families or already worked in a dental practice. If you feel overwhelmed or intimidated from the outset, take heart; everyone will be equally conversant.

YOUR PROFESSORS

When you get to know your dental school faculty, you are likely to encounter an equal mix of full- and part-time instructors. You will find that a number of these dentists have retired from practice but teach to stay active within the profession.

If you come to dental school from a large university, you may feel that your world paradoxically grows smaller as you step into your future. Life in dental school may actually *feel* more restrictive than your undergraduate experience because you work in close quarters and under supervision.

You will probably run across some instructors who seem to harbor a grudge of mysterious origin against you. Or maybe against your whole class. They will soften as time passes and you prove yourself a competent student dentist.

YOUR COURSE WORK

Dental school is a year-round endeavor, with most schools meeting throughout the summer as well as during the fall and spring semesters.

No matter how demanding the core curriculum is at an undergraduate institution, at least some--and often a great deal--of flexibility is possible in course selection. By contrast, dental coursework is highly prescriptive. Most classes must be taken in a particular order and by a certain point in time. Depending on the size of the entering class, there may be multiple sections of a course, but students will track similarly. Enjoy it. For once, you will have a reprieve from decision fatigue.

Dental school weekdays are busier and more structured than those at an undergraduate institution. While you may miss having any free time, it is wise to embrace the structure as built-in accountability.

Your chances for individualization of your experiences are most likely to come through hands-on externships at off-site locations. Also, the specific faculty members who know you best may approach you about research to be done or clinical experiences for which they think you are well-suited.

WHAT MAKES IT SO DIFFICULT?

In a word, *volume*.

There are a **lot of classes**. Below, see the list of required courses for first-year dental students at the University of Louisville. It looks like one class after another of lecture halls.

There is a **lot of time spent in class.** You will think wistfully about the 2- and 3-hour periods between some of your undergraduate classes because dental school is a full-time gig. You will be in the dental school from 8am to 5pm almost every day. It's pretty hard to get a jump on your anticipated workload when your schedule offers only a handful of unscheduled minutes.

Word to the wise: Whether or not your dental school professors require attendance in their classes, you need to show up or you will fall behind. Go to every session of every class.

When you do get back home, you'll have a **lot of work** in front of you. Plan to study each evening. You will be assessed, formally and informally, on a regular basis, so you will be motivated to know the material.

First year coursework at the University of Louisville School of Dentistry

Survey of Gross and Neuroanatomy	Head & Neck Anatomy
Histology (General and Oral)	Biochemistry
Physiology	Preclinical Operative Dentistry I, lecture and lab
Dental Anatomy & Occlusion lecture and	Intro to Clinical Dentistry I
Correlated Sciences	Growth, Development & Aging
Oral Radiology I	Periodontics I
	Preventive Dentistry
	Cariology

You will have a **lot to organize and manage**. Even if all the classes above were easy, keeping track of the details would tax you a bit.

Eventually, you will have a **lot of clinical requirements**. Sometimes you may find yourself so overwhelmed by expectations and deadlines that you lose a little perspective. Fortunately, your classmates usually come to the rescue. With them, after all, you will have a **lot of fun!**

Rules of thumb about your coursework

Your exact curriculum will, of course, depend on your chosen dental school, but you can count on some generalities:

- Scientific classes are grounded in the understanding of healthy tissue, with pathologies addressed later;
- The ratio of time in class to time with patients will decrease as you progress through your program;
- DMD and DDS candidates will be exposed to both didactic and clinical experiences, not only in general dentistry, but also in most of the specialty fields.

LABS AND CLINICS

When you begin dental school, you will be issued a large inventory of equipment and assigned an individual lab space. The labs are busy places, and your unit lab will begin to feel like a home away from home. You will learn to do some things the old-school way but will also be introduced to state-of-the-art technology.

In the clinics, though, you become a dentist.

Clinical experiences abound from the first day of dental school. And, from that first day, there are four words to live by, because they will serve you well: Follow. All. The. Rules.

Seriously. Even pre-pandemic, your future dental school clinic was already run by a tightly-knit set of complex regulations. Sterile instruments, the orderly inventory of expensive equipment, rules about who can see patients when and where, how records must be kept, who has to check off your work--all are subject to some rules in the name of everyone's safety.

We give you just three more words of advice: Stay on track. During your four years as a DMD/DDS candidate, you will very gradually be granted autonomy and flexibility. It is easy to procrastinate and leave yourself with too much to do as graduation gets closer. Pace yourself, do your best, and you will graduate with the rest of your classmates one day in May, not too long from now.

Social Life

Because of the myriad life experiences mentioned at the beginning of the chapter, some students have less time for social lives than others. A dental student with four children at home, for example, has plenty of family responsibilities to juggle along with her dental school responsibilities. Single students, on the other hand, enjoy less pressure and fewer expenses. They are more likely to organize social gatherings.

As you might imagine, dental school is not characterized by 7-day-a-week partying. Drug and alcohol issues may be present among some students, but the demands of the program, taken together with the pressures of expense, keep most students focused on their studies during the week and most of the weekend.

Recap

There you go--introductory words about your class, your professors, your homework, your stress, your clinical and lab experiences, and even your social life. Are you more excited than ever to be on your way?

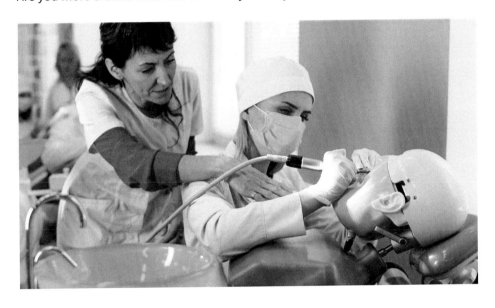

" "

*As to diseases,
make a habit of
two things — to
help, or at least,
to do no harm.*

– Hippocrates

CHAPTER 57

YOUR DENTAL CAREER

How early does a dental student begin planning the next steps beyond earning the DMD/DDS?

Some students enter dental school convinced of their post-graduate intentions. Perhaps they plan to join practices established by a parent or other relative who is eager for them to get back home. Others have an eye on a particular specialty or see themselves remaining in academia.

Needless to say, it is perfectly fine, and maybe preferable, for students to begin their training with open minds about their futures. The objectives for everyone are to achieve excellence in the classroom and establish a reputation as a dependable, compassionate clinician. By meeting those goals, few doors will be closed when the student assesses their options.

Upon graduation, two paths are most common: starting work as a general dentist or continuing into a residency program.

I.   Going to Work--But Where?

The ADEA provides extensive detail about the many kinds of general dentistry chosen by new DMD/DDS graduates. The dentist with decisions to make about where to practice upon graduation would be wise to begin by asking him or herself the following questions:

- How much do I need to make, not just to cover expenses, but also to pay off student debt and begin to save?
- What role(s) appeal to me? Boss? Partner? Employee?
- How important is autonomy to me early in my career?
- How much financial risk will be comfortable for me?

After reflecting on the questions above, the dentist can check out the following options:

Individually- or group-owned practice--This is the most traditional form of dental practice. Individual and group practitioners enjoy lots of autonomy, along with plenty of risks and expenses. Business expertise is critically important to the success of practice owners.

Dental Service Organization/DSO--DSOs are companies that contract with dental offices to provide administrative and business services, leaving the dentist(s) with more time to focus on their patients and skills. More and more young dentists avail themselves of employment opportunities within DSOs.[1] In this growth market, dentists can find mentorship and support as they launch their careers. An employee of a DSO incurs less risk at the sacrifice of maximizing income.

Non-DSO Group--In addition to DSOs, there are non-DSO group practices, often with multiple locations. Dentists are usually hired as employed or contract workers for such groups.

Additional options for dental careers include but are not limited to the military, government, non-profit clinics, and academia. Sometimes it is prudent for a new dentist to begin by practicing in two or more different jobs, but most find that they want to settle into a steady location and regular schedule within a few years.

II. Residencies

The Big Picture

There are just over 750 dental residency programs in the United States, spread across several hundred locations.

How is this possible, with fewer than 100 dental schools in the U.S.? First, remember that there are twelve specialty areas of dentistry (see Ch 10), and more than twelve types of residency programs exist because some programs modify or combine the areas of specialization. Also, many residencies are hosted away from dental schools. Military bases, hospitals, VA hospitals, and governmental agencies are among the types of facilities where residency programs are conducted.

---

1   Brian Colao and Meredith Tavallaee, "The DSO Model Offers Advantages to Dentists," *Dentistry Today*, October 15, 2019, https://www.dentistrytoday.com/news/todays-dental-news/item/5486-the-dso-model-offers-advantages-to-dentists

Breakdown and Duration

The greatest number of residency options, and those which are most likely to be found outside of dental schools, are programs created for general dentists. There are almost a hundred AEGD (Advanced Education in General Dentistry) options and almost two hundred GPR (General Practice Residency) options. With the exception of only a handful, AEGD and GPR residencies are one-year programs, typically beginning in July and wrapping up in June.

In the chart below, you can see the number of residency options for each specialty type. Also included is a typical number of years one might spend completing the program.

Type of residency	Number of programs	Duration (years)
AEGD	92	1
Dental Anesthesiology	8	3
Dental Public Health	14	1
Endodontics	55	2
GPR	177	1
Oral and Maxillofacial Pathology	15	3
Oral and Maxillofacial Radiology	10	2
Oral and Maxillofacial Surgery	100	4-6
Oral Medicine	6	2
Orofacial Pain	12	2
Orthodontics & Dentofacial Orthopedics	68	3
Pediatric Dentistry	80	2
Periodontics	56	3
Prosthodontics	55	3
Source: ADA.org (https://www.ada.org/en/coda/find-a-program)		

The Most Selective?

Most students are curious about which residency spots are the toughest to earn. In all realms of academic selectivity, admit rates can be misleading and should not be conflated with the quality or desirability of the experience sought. That said, here are the latest available statistics relating to selectivity by specialty area.

Type of residency	Applicants	Enrollees	% enrolled
Dental Public Health	195	38	19%
Endodontics	4743	218	5%
GPR and AEGD	16996	1882	11%
Oral and Maxillofacial Pathology	78	18	23%
Oral and Maxillofacial Radiology	213	18	8%
Oral and Maxillofacial Surgery	10564	264	2%
Orthodontics & Dentofacial Orthopedics	9935	393	4%
Pediatric Dentistry	9221	479	5%
Periodontics	3001	192	6%
Prosthodontics	2438	160	7%
Source (CODA Survey of Advanced Dental Education Report, 2019-2020)			

If you begin dental school and become interested in pursuing a specialty area of practice, you will be well served to connect with the faculty members within that department of your dental school. They are the logical mentors to help you understand the path that lies ahead.

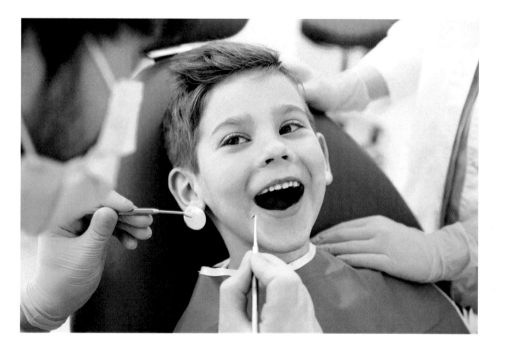

*There are
two ways of
spreading light:
to be the candle
or the mirror that
reflects it.*

— Edith Wharton

CHAPTER 58

TRENDS IN DENTAL EDUCATION: THE HORIZON

While dental education constantly evolves to keep pace with technological advances, its most noticeable trends can be categorized as *pandemic, people,* and *price.*

I. Pandemic

The effects of the COVID-19 pandemic are sure to reverberate throughout dentistry and dental schools for years to come.

As the spring of 2020 progressed, dental schools managed to graduate their seniors, although probably not on schedule or as anticipated. According to the ADEA, 23% of graduating seniors changed post-graduation plans.[1] Having received almost all of their scheduled training prior to the onset of pandemic, the class of 2020 received their degrees relatively unscathed.

But what about the classes of 2021 and beyond? We cannot forecast the extent to which their educations have been altered. Our first meaningful information will come with ADEA's release of the 2021 senior survey results. It will be telling to compare the responses elicited by that survey, particularly concerning the Class of 2021's self-assessments of readiness for

---

1   2020 ADEA Survey of U.S. Dental School Seniors Summary Report

licensed practice. Dental educators then must determine whether or not course corrections or intervention would benefit the Classes of 2022, 2023, and 2024.

Everyone who earns a dental degree between 2021 and 2028 will have encountered substantial disturbances en route to graduation. Assessing the preparedness of dental applicants will pose complexities not seen previously in dental admissions.

II. People

Gender shift

It's hard to believe there was a time when women were a distinct minority within dental classes because females easily outnumber males in U.S. dental schools today. According to data from the American Dental Education Association, women occupied only 40% of dental school seats in the year 2000. Their ascendance into the majority has happened quickly, and the momentum continues. Over 55% of applicants for the dental school class of 2024 were female.

In the world of undergraduate admissions, institutions work hard to keep their female populations below 60%; if the female applicant percentage continues to swell, we can logically assume that males will have a slight competitive advantage during the application process.

Female faculty members are beginning to catch up as well. Necessarily, their process comes more slowly, but women approach the 40% mark in terms of their representation within the dental academe.

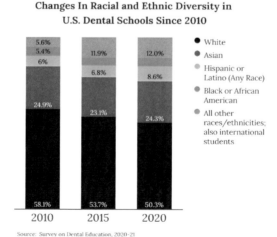

Changes In Racial and Ethnic Diversity in U.S. Dental Schools Since 2010

- White
- Asian
- Hispanic or Latino (Any Race)
- Black or African American
- All other races/ethnicities; also international students

	2010	2015	2020
White	58.1%	53.7%	50.3%
Asian	24.9%	23.1%	24.3%
Hispanic or Latino	6%	6.8%	8.6%
Black or African American	5.4%	11.9%	12.0%
All other	5.6%		

Source: Survey on Dental Education, 2020-21
ADA.org

Ethnic/racial diversity

Racial and ethnic diversity is also seen in DMD/DDS application pools and incoming dental classes. However, these cohorts lack the momentum women have experienced. Thus, continued diversification of incoming classes is a top-of-mind, an institutional priority at all U.S. dental schools, in residency programs, and across various disciplines in the field.

III. Price

According to the ADEA, the "average educational debt for all indebted dental school graduates in the Class of 2019 was $292,169, with the average for public and private schools at $261,305 and $321,184 respectively." [2] Compare that figure to the average amount of debt incurred by students who borrow to pay undergraduate expenses--usually anywhere between $30,000-$40,000.[3]

Dentists will have a marketable, dependable set of high-value skills. They will have job offers and options for further study. What they will not have under a debt load of $300,000+ is much freedom or financial margin.

Given the amount of energy colleges rightly invest in diversity, an obvious societal issue is posed by the matter of exorbitant costs. How much real diversity might a dental school cultivate when the cost for first-year students is as much as $153,555? [4]

Prospective dental students cannot resolve such communal cognitive dissonance. They have a more practical and time-sensitive mandate-- to think critically about the personal and financial investments required to earn a DMD or DDS diploma. Can the student's family bear the cost without the student incurring debt? Even if the parents can pay outright, how will parental retirement accounts be affected, thus eventually impacting the student?

We seek not to discourage but to guide, by asking the hard questions. Dental school will be demanding on its best days, and a student must be able to draw on a deep well of proper motivation and resolution to succeed.

---

2   ADEA, "Educational Debt," *ADEA*, n.d., https://www.adea.org/godental/money_matters/educational_debt.aspx

3   Undergraduate debt is rightly lamented across theU.S. but averages only 10-20% as much as dental school debt.

4   University of Southern California's Herman Ostrow School of Dentistry webpage, sum of direct and indirect costs for the first year of DDS education. USC, "Admission: Paying for Dental School," *USC*, n.d., https://dentistry.usc.edu/admission/paying-for-dental-school/

That which is used - develops. That which is not used wastes away.

— Hippocrates

CHAPTER 59

LIFELONG EDUCATION

I n her 2006 book, *Mindset: The New Psychology of Success*, Dr. Carol Dweck introduced the concept of the growth mindset. In it, she argued that success is less a function of innate ability than of a true commitment to discovery. The opposite of a growth mindset is a fixed mindset, the belief that one's destiny is limited by intelligence, access to formal education, or past failures. Dr. David Burns, another popular therapist, author, and podcaster, uses a helpful metaphor for visualizing growth itself. He says people are rivers, not statues.[1] Rivers never stop moving. They change the environment along their course and are, likewise, changed by the continuous flow. In contrast, the only change accessible to statues is destruction.

It is beyond the scope of this book to prove the negative power of a fixed mindset or the culpability of the achievement culture in cultivating it. New dentists arrive in their chosen career by jumping over one hurdle after another in a complex system of requirements, metrics, and rankings. They have come to rely on grades, test scores, and accomplishments to carry them to the goal. Fortunately, they have done pretty well for themselves, or else they would not have become serious candidates for dental admissions and proceeded through dental school.

However, what happens after receiving one's degree, a DMD, DDS, or advanced residency degree? No matter how high you climb, how much you

---

1   David Burns, Feeling Good: The New Mood Therapy (Harper, 2008).

achieve, to advance professionally, the "fixed", unchangeable perspective must be left behind in favor of lifelong learning.

There is great news at this juncture: finally, you can be a student without the burdens of deadlines, grades, and being evaluated in comparison to others!

Discovering Continuing Education Opportunities

You will have no trouble whatsoever finding continuing education opportunities. Providers offer credit, also called continuing education units (CE or CEUs). The American Dental Association, the American Dental Education Association, and other organizations and websites referenced in this book are packed with offerings.

Be sure to join local affiliate groups of the ADA and groups within your advanced area of focus. That way, you can be informed about national conferences and classes or workshops in your area. Going a bit further afield, you will find in-person events at annual meetings as well as conferences at the local, regional, national, and international levels.

Think Categorically When Choosing CE Opportunities

Category 1: Professional Requirements

Once you have passed your state requirements for certification to practice dentistry, you *must* fulfill a required minimum number of hours of continuing education at the prescribed frequency.

The chart displays every state's CE requirement (in hours) for dentists. The number of required hours varies by state. Also, the length of the renewal period is determined on a state-by-state basis. **The requirement shown is the annual average number of hours required per year of the cycle.** For instance, Kentucky's requirement for dentists is 30 hours every 2 years. The "annual" minimum, therefore, is 15 hours. More restrictions can come into play, such as the percentage of the classes which may be taken remotely. To investigate the details for any state's dental CE requirements, look on the website of each board of dentistry. A helpful site for finding these resources is www.mydentalce.com.

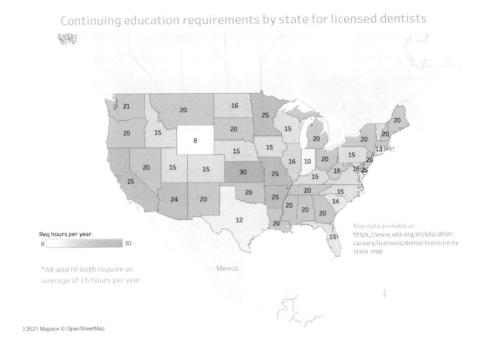

Continuing education requirements by state for licensed dentists

Req hours per year
8 — 30

*AK and HI both require an average of 16 hours per year.

Map data available at: https://www.ada.org/en/education-careers/licensure/dental-licensure-by-state-map

Mexico

© 2021 Mapbox © OpenStreetMap

Category 2: Enhancing Your Dental Education

To remain licensed, you must complete at least the minimum amount of CE. Do not let minimum CE requirements limit you. The more you learn, the more you are in tune with the profession and are able to serve your patients.

New dentists, especially, should remember that dental school is meant to be foundational. You learn enough in dental school to be a confident, safe dentist, but the DDS or DMD diploma does not make you an expert practitioner. Thinking critically about your skills, interests, and goals, you must honestly consider your weaknesses and assiduously strive to turn these into strengths.

When you reflect on your dental school career, were there any classes, either clinical or didactic, which did not come naturally to you? What kinds of situations cause anxiety for you as a practitioner? CE opportunities are available within all areas of dentistry and patient care. Thus, consider and pursue the classes which are most likely to fill gaps in your training.

Category 3: Establishing Yourself in the World of Dentistry

This is where good dentists become great, by targeting interests and going deep into personal and professional skills. In doing so, you can carve a niche for yourself as an expert dentist. Because dentistry is ever-advancing, nothing limits your possible areas of focus.

You can always find an excuse *not* to pursue continuing education beyond that which is mandated. You must take the long view and be intentional about planning--and budgeting for--continuing education.

Three Tiers of Pricing

Most newly-minted dentists appreciate the value of an educational investment. However, many will be paying off debt for years and are understandably hesitant to incur costs that could be avoided. The wise practitioner seeks out opportunities where possible and budgets accordingly.

CE Costs by Category

Tier 1: Free or Almost Free

The financially, strapped dentist can take heart. Many continuing education opportunities are available at no cost, or at no additional cost with a particular organizational membership or professional periodical subscription.

Journal articles are sometimes designated as CE eligible; the dentist pays a nominal fee ($5 or so), reads the article, and then answers some questions to verify that the content has been digested.

(Comment: After surviving gross anatomy, oral pathology, and countless tricky multiple-choice questions in every dental discipline, it's time to relax. CE questions are strictly a matter of validation. In other words, they are easy to answer correctly once you have read the article.)

Dental vendors may also offer free CE credits. With these events or opportunities, the dentist's only cost is the time required to attend. These vendor sales classes include information about products, equipment, software, training, or insurance plans. While dentists may find particular vendor classes very helpful, they should remember that not all CE classes are created equally and some sales pitches may be of limited benefit or interest.

Tier 2: Budget

Some training opportunities cost a bit more money but do not break the bank. Annual meetings hosted by professional organizations fall into this category. Whichever association, academy, or local group you choose, there is a good chance you can pick up CE credits during such events. Registration fees may run you a few hundred dollars, and you will need to cover travel expenses. Most significant, though, will probably be the cost incurred by being away from your office.

Such gatherings can be valuable beyond the CE earned. A benefit that cannot be quantified is the networking associated with these events. The value of a strong professional relationship with a colleague is incalculable.

Tier 3: Deluxe

There are several highly reputable dental institutes that are popular with dentists who go deep in their CE, offering top-tier speakers and appealing venues. When it comes to dental training, some dentists believe that if they are going to take a week off, the overall experience should be worth the time in terms of experiential training, professional reinvention, and maybe even quality relaxation.

The *Pankey Institute*, near Miami, FL, and the *Interdisciplinary Dental Education Academy,* near San Francisco, CA, are two such programs. They offer world-class instruction in small class settings. Networking happens organically. Additionally, institute participants enjoy beautiful surroundings and refreshing ways to spend free time. However, participants pay for the high quality and must budget accordingly. Plan to spend anywhere between $2,000-$10,000 for each visit, depending on the length of the course.

Find Your Inspiration

Dentists committed to excellence will find continuing education a valuable addition to their routines. There is no secret recipe for success. Discover your professional niche and find joy in performing it well.

5
Regions

61
Programs

PART 10
COLLEGE PROFILES AND REQUIREMENTS

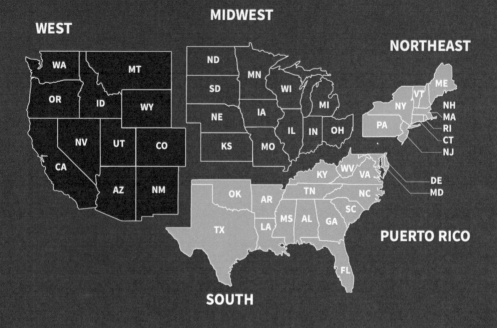

DMD/DDS PROGRAMS BY REGION
U.S. CENSUS BUREAU CLASSIFICATIONS

REGION 1 — NORTHEAST

Connecticut, Maine, Massachusetts, New Hampshire, New Jersey, New York, Pennsylvania, Rhode Island, and Vermont

REGION 2 — MIDWEST

Illinois, Indiana, Iowa, Kansas, Michigan, Minnesota, Missouri, Nebraska, North Dakota, Ohio, South Dakota, and Wisconsin

REGION 3 — SOUTH

Alabama, Arkansas, Delaware, District of Columbia, Florida, Georgia, Kentucky, Louisiana, Maryland, Mississippi, North Carolina, Oklahoma, South Carolina, Tennessee, Texas, Virginia, and West Virginia

REGION 4 — WEST

Alaska, Arizona, California, Colorado, Hawaii, Idaho, Montana, Nevada, New Mexico, Oregon, Utah, Washington, and Wyoming

REGION 5 — U.S. TERRITORIES

Puerto Rico

LIST OF DMD AND DDS PROGRAMS

T he programs listed in the following pages include DMD and DDS programs. Following this list, this book provides lists of MD, DO, dental, PharmD, and vet schools, since many students interested in medical school are also interested in healthcare. There are many facets of the healthcare world. One of these other areas might be a good option for you.

Dental school is not for everyone.

Thus, this book aims to provide you with a more comprehensive set of lists so that you can explore your options. Keep the book handy. You may find that even after you begin college, if you choose a traditional pre-dental path, you may find the list of additional programs in the back a good option for you.

Lists are often tedious to find and take a while to pull together. These lists were gathered to help you with this task.

Descriptions of the college programs, tuition, requirements, and deadlines are accurate as of April 2021. Requirements may have changed somewhat due to the pandemic, but all of this information is a great place to start!

Note: To simplify the text and fit information into the charts and descriptions, abbreviations were used as well as shortened sentences and acronyms.

REGION ONE

NORTHEAST

CONNECTICUT

MAINE

MASSACHUSETTS

NEW HAMPSHIRE

NEW JERSEY

NEW YORK

PENNSYLVANIA

RHODE ISLAND

VERMONT

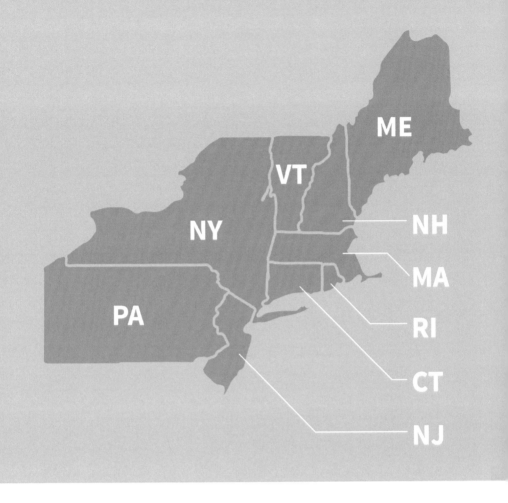

14 Programs | 9 States

1. CT – University of Connecticut School of Dental Medicine
2. ME - University of New England College of Dental Medicine
3. MA - Boston University Henry M. Goldman School of Dental Medicine
4. MA - Harvard School of Dental Medicine
5. MA - Tufts University School of Dental Medicine
6. NJ - Rutgers, The State University of New Jersey, School of Dental Medicine
7. NY - Columbia University College of Dental Medicine
8. NY - NYU College of Dentistry
9. NY - Stony Brook University School of Dental Medicine
10. NY - Touro College of Dental Medicine at New York Medical College
11. NY - University at Buffalo School of Dental Medicine
12. PA - The Maurice H. Kornberg School of Dentistry, Temple University
13. PA - University of Pennsylvania School of Dental Medicine
14. PA - University of Pittsburgh School of Dental Medicine

Dental School	Ave. Gpa & Dat Early Decision (Ed) : Yes/No	Admissions Statistics	Science Req. Other Than Gen Chem, Ochem, Physics, Bio
University of Connecticut 263 Farmington Avenue, Farmington, CT 06030	3.70 (overall) 3.63 (science) DAT: 22 ED: No	**(2019)** Apps Received: 1,456 Admission Offered: 99 Number Enrolled: 48 Acceptance Rate: 6.8% **(2020)** Apps Received: 1,286 Admission Offered: 91 Number Enrolled: 54 Acceptance rate: 7.1%	Biochem.
University of New England 716 Stevens Ave., Portland, ME, 04103	3.41 (overall) 3.33 (science) DAT: 19.1 ED: No	**(2019)** Apps Received: 1,814 Admission Offered: 173 Number Enrolled: 64 Acceptance Rate %: 9.5% **(2020)** Apps Received: 1,085 Admission Offered: 206 Number Enrolled: 64 Acceptance Rate: 19.0%	Zoology (sub. Bio) Anatomy w/Lab Microbio. w/Lab Biochem. Additional Bio., Chem., Calc., or Physics (12 cred.)
Boston University 635 Albany Street, Boston, MA 02118	3.44 (overall) 3.34 (science) DAT: 20 ED: No	**(2019)** Apps Received: 2,626 Admission Offered: 239 Number Enrolled: 117 Acceptance Rate: 9.1% **(2020)** Apps Received: 2,515 Admission Offered: 335 Number Enrolled: 117 Acceptance Rate: 13.3%	Math: At least 1 calculus course. Social Sciences
Harvard School of Dental Medicine 188 Longwood Avenue, Boston, MA 02115	3.89 (overall) 3.87 (science) DAT: 25 ED: No	**(2019)** Apps Received: 1,013 Admission Offered: 49 Number Enrolled: 36 Acceptance Rate: 4.8% **(2020)** Apps Received: 958 Admission Offered: 56 Number Enrolled: 35 Acceptance Rate: 5.8%	Biochem. Calc. 1 & 2 Stats.

Dental School	Ave. Gpa & Dat / Early Decision (Ed) : Yes/No	Admissions Statistics	Science Req. Other Than Gen Chem, Ochem, Physics, Bio
Tufts University 1 Kneeland Street, Boston, MA 02111	3.33 (overall) 3.42 (science) DAT: 20 ED: No	**(2019)** Apps Received: 2,123 Admission Offered: 230 Number Enrolled: 92 Acceptance Rate: 10.8% **(2020)** Apps Received: 2,174 Admission Offered: 235 Number Enrolled: 92 Acceptance Rate: 10.8%	N/A
Columbia University 630 West 168th Street, New York, NY 10032	3.67 (overall) 3.60 (science) DAT: 23.6 ED: No	**(2019)** Apps Received: 1,660 Admission Offered: 168 *Interview Received: 261 Number Enrolled: 84 Acceptance Rate: 10.1% **(2020)** Apps Received: 1,661 Admission Offered: 179 Number Enrolled: 84 Acceptance Rate: 10.8%	Biochem.
NYU College of Dentistry 345 E. 24th Street, New York, NY 10010	3.29 (overall) 3.40 (science) DAT: 21 ED: No	**(2019)** Apps Received: 3,411 Admission Offered: 636 Number Enrolled: 380 Acceptance Rate: 18.6% **(2020)** Apps Received: 3,267 Admission Offered: 664 Number Enrolled: 383 Acceptance Rate: 20.3%	N/A
Stony Brook University 101 Nicolls Road, Stony Brook, NY 11794	3.7 (overall) 3.63 (science) DAT: 22.2 ED: No	**(2019)** Apps Received: 1,065 Admission Offered: 133 Number Enrolled: 46 Acceptance Rate: 12.5% **(2020)** Apps Received: 1,065 Admission Offered: 133 Number Enrolled: 46 Acceptance Rate: 12.5%	Prereqs. Must be completed prior to app submission. Biochem. Calc 1 & 2 or Calc 1 and Stats.

NORTHEAST

DENTAL PROGRAMS

Dental School	Ave. Gpa & Dat / Early Decision (Ed) : Yes/No	Admissions Statistics	Science Req. Other Than Gen Chem, Ochem, Physics, Bio
Touro College of Dental Medicine at New York Medical College 19 Skyline Dr., Hawthorne, NY 10532	3.52 (overall) 3.41 (science) DAT: 21.3 ED: No	**(2019)** Apps Received: 2,573 Admission Offered: N/A Interviews Received: 538 Number Enrolled: 112 Acceptance Rate: 14.4% **(2020)** Apps Received: 2,574 Admission Offered: 379 Number Enrolled: 114 Acceptance Rate: 14.7%	Biochem.
University at Buffalo, South Campus, Buffalo, NY 14215	3.58 (overall) 3.47 (science) DAT: 20.2 ED: No	**(2019)** Apps Received: 1,327 Admission Offered: 149 Number Enrolled: 93 Acceptance Rate: 11.2% **(2020)** Apps Received: 2,005 Admission Offered: 165 Number Enrolled: 93 Acceptance Rate: 8.2%	Biochem.
Temple University 3223 North Broad Street, Philadelphia, PA 19140	3.51 (overall) 3.39 (science) DAT: 21.1 ED: No	**(2019)** Apps Received: 3,173 Admission Offered: 365 Number Enrolled: 140 Acceptance Rate: 11.5% **(2020)** Apps Received: 3,048 Admission Offered: 366 Number Enrolled: 142 Acceptance Rate: 12.0%	N/A, See Chart for details on recommended coursework.
University of Pennsylvania 240 South 40th Street, Philadelphia, PA 19104	3.66 (overall) 3.73 (science) DAT: 22.2 ED: No	**(2019)** Apps Received: 2,183 Admission Offered: 293 Number Enrolled: 134 Acceptance Rate: 13.4% **(2020)** Apps Received: 2,072 Admission Offered: 314 Number Enrolled: 136 Acceptance Rate: 15.2%	Biochem. Math (Calc. preferred)

Dental School	Ave. Gpa & Dat Early Decision (Ed) : Yes/No	Admissions Statistics	Science Req. Other Than Gen Chem, Ochem, Physics, Bio
University of Pittsburgh 3501 Terrace Street, Pittsburgh, PA 15261	University of Pittsburgh 3501 Terrace Street, Pittsburgh, PA 15261	**(2019)** Apps Received: 1,497 Admission Offered: 225 Number Enrolled: 77 Acceptance Rate: 15.0% **(2020)** Apps Received: 1,925 Admission Offered: 345 Number Enrolled: 80 Acceptance Rate: 17.9%	Biochem.

UNIVERSITY OF CONNECTICUT SCHOOL OF DENTAL MEDICINE

Address: 263 Farmington Avenue, Farmington, CT 06030
Website: *https://dentalmedicine.uconn.edu/*
Contact: *https://dentalmedicine.uconn.edu/about-us/contact-us/*
Phone: (860) 679-3170

COST OF ATTENDANCE

In-State Tuition: $37,063
Fees & Indirect Costs: $40,229
Total: $77,292

Out-of-State Tuition: $74,817
Fees & Indirect Costs: $40,229
Total: $115,046

*Note: Reduced tuition for New England residents ($64,861).
Financial Aid: https://health.uconn.edu/student-services/financial-aid/types-of-financial-aid/

CONNECTICUT

MAINE

MASSACHUSETTS

NEW HAMPSHIRE

NEW JERSEY

NEW YORK

PENNSYLVANIA

RHODE ISLAND

VERMONT

ADDITIONAL INFORMATION

Interesting tidbit: As the only public dental school in New England, the School of Dental Medicine participates in the New England Regional Program and gives preference and reduced tuition rate to residents of Connecticut and the rest of New England (i.e., Maine, Vermont, New Hampshire, Massachusetts, Connecticut and Rhode Island).

What international experiences are available? International and domestic service trip opportunities available.

What dual degree options exist? DMD/PhD available. For more information, visit: https://dentalmedicine.uconn.edu/programs-and-admissions/advanced-education/

What service learning opportunities exist? UConn is the "largest provider of dental care to the underserved in the State of Connecticut." A student may apply to participate in the Urban Service Track, whose commitment is to serve Connecticut's urban underserved population. Participants are selected from students enrolled in the UConn School of Pharmacy, Nursing, Medicine and Dental Medicine.

Important Updates due to COVID-19: N/A

Were tests required? All applicants are required to take the Dental Admission Test (DAT).

Are tests expected next year? Yes.

UNIVERSITY OF NEW ENGLAND COLLEGE OF DENTAL MEDICINE

Address: 716 Stevens Ave., Portland, ME, 04103
Website: *https://www.une.edu/dentalmedicine*
Contact: *https://www.une.edu/admissions/grad-inquiry*
Phone: (207) 221-4225

COST OF ATTENDANCE

Tuition: $66,550
Fees & Indirect Costs: $30,025
Total: $96,575
Financial Aid: https://www.une.edu/sfs/graduate/financing-your-education/scholarships-and-grants

ADDITIONAL INFORMATION

Interesting tidbit: The College of Dental Medicine offers a community-based education program, which begins with service learning and public health coursework during the first three years at the College.

What international experiences are available? N/A

What dual degree options exist? No dual degree options listed.

What service learning opportunities exist? N/A

Important Updates due to COVID-19: If a candidate's application is missing one or more required components due to extenuating circumstances caused by COVID-19 (e.g., DAT scores or 30 hours of clinical dental experience) but the application is otherwise complete and verified, the candidate should provide a statement explaining the situation and their plan/timeline for submitting the missing components.

Were tests required? DAT required.

Are tests expected next year? Yes.

CONNECTICUT

MAINE

MASSACHUSETTS

NEW HAMPSHIRE

NEW JERSEY

NEW YORK

PENNSYLVANIA

RHODE ISLAND

VERMONT

NORTHEAST

CONNECTICUT

MAINE

MASSACHUSETTS

NEW HAMPSHIRE

NEW JERSEY

NEW YORK

PENNSYLVANIA

RHODE ISLAND

VERMONT

BOSTON UNIVERSITY HENRY M. GOLDMAN SCHOOL OF DENTAL MEDICINE

Address: 635 Albany Street, Boston, MA 02118
Website: *http://www.bu.edu/dental/*
Contact: *http://www.bu.edu/dental/about/contact/*
Phone: (617) 358-8300

COST OF ATTENDANCE

Tuition: $82,500
Fees & Indirect Costs: $39,107
Total: $121,607

Financial Aid: https://www.bu.edu/dental/admissions/dmd/financial-assistance-2/

ADDITIONAL INFORMATION

Interesting tidbit: Boston University has a long tradition of service learning. GSDM has achieved national recognition for its community outreach programs with its students participating in more than 60 programs and 100 events each year.

What international experiences are available? International elective externships. For more information, visit: http://www.bu.edu/dental/about/offices/global-population-health/

What dual degree options exist? No dual degree options listed.

What service learning opportunities exist? Goldman School of Dental Medicine provides service learning opportunities through a variety of community service programs. For more information, visit: http://www.bu.edu/dental/community/

Important Updates due to COVID-19: BU is flexible in consideration of COVID-19 related limitations, such as extending the application deadline, evaluating pass/fail grading and online prerequisite courses, and considering unofficial DAT scores.

Were tests required? DAT required.

Are tests expected next year? Yes.

HARVARD SCHOOL OF DENTAL MEDICINE

Address: 188 Longwood Avenue, Boston, MA 02115
Website: *https://hsdm.harvard.edu/*
Contact: *https://hsdm.harvard.edu/contact-and-directions*
Phone: (617) 432-1443

COST OF ATTENDANCE

Tuition: $66,284
Fees & Indirect Costs: $35,375
Total: $101,659
Financial Aid: https://hsdm.harvard.edu/dmd-program-financial-aid

ADDITIONAL INFORMATION

Interesting tidbit: The Pathways curriculum at HSDM is an interdisciplinary format, which includes a first-year primary care medical rotation as part of the introduction to clinical dentistry, removing the distinction between oral and systemic health.

What international experiences are available? Global Health Projects: https://hsdm.harvard.edu/global-health

What dual degree options exist? Dual degree programs available. For more information, visit: https://hsdm.harvard.edu/phd-biological-sciences-dental-medicine

What service learning opportunities exist? Community Health Projects and Programs: https://hsdm.harvard.edu/community-health

Important Updates due to COVID-19: HSDM will accept pass/fail credit and unofficial DAT scores. However, the Admissions Committee will require official DAT scores prior to releasing admissions decisions.

Were tests required? DAT required.

Are tests expected next year? Yes.

CONNECTICUT

MAINE

MASSACHUSETTS

NEW HAMPSHIRE

NEW JERSEY

NEW YORK

PENNSYLVANIA

RHODE ISLAND

VERMONT

NORTHEAST

CONNECTICUT

MAINE

MASSACHUSETTS

NEW HAMPSHIRE

NEW JERSEY

NEW YORK

PENNSYLVANIA

RHODE ISLAND

VERMONT

TUFTS UNIVERSITY SCHOOL OF DENTAL MEDICINE

Address: 1 Kneeland Street, Boston, MA 02111
Website: *https://dental.tufts.edu/*
Contact: Via phone or Email: *denadmissions@tufts.edu*
Phone: (617) 636-6828

COST OF ATTENDANCE

Tuition: $82,368
Fees & Indirect Costs: $48,553
Total: $130,921

Financial Aid: https://dental.tufts.edu/academics/financial-aid

ADDITIONAL INFORMATION

Interesting tidbit: Tufts University School of Dental Medicine is dedicated to educating competent clinicians who are also skilled communicators, health advocates and compassionate caregivers. Its curriculum includes behavioral sciences to promote professionalism and communication, and emphasizes culturally competent care to patients with diverse backgrounds.

What international experiences are available? Students are involved in global initiatives in locations such as Africa, South America, and the Caribbean.

What dual degree options exist? Dual degree programs available. For more information on the DMD/MS, visit: https://dental.tufts.edu/academics/graduate-programs/dmdmaster-science-dental-research-program

DMD/MPH: https://dental.tufts.edu/academics/graduate-programs/dmdmaster-public-health

What service learning opportunities exist? Community-based oral health promotion, community service, and other opportunities available. For more information, visit: https://dental.tufts.edu/academics/departments/department-public-health-and-community-service

Other: Tufts offers a Dental International Student Program to help internationally-prepared dentists receive the credentials to practice dentistry in the U.S. For more information, visit: https://dental.tufts.edu/academics/dental-international-student-program

Tufts also offers an 8-year early assurance program for undergraduate sophomores. For more information on this program, visit: https://dental.tufts.edu/academics/graduate-programs/tufts-eight-year-early-assurance

Important Updates due to COVID-19: DAT scores between June 2017 and May 2018 will be considered if the Academic Average, Reading Comprehension and Total Science sections have scores of 20 or above. Applicants may submit unofficial DAT scores directly to the admissions office until the official scores are available through the AADSAS application. Spring and Summer 2020 coursework is acceptable Pass/Fail (including prerequisite courses) if it was school policy for that time period. There will be a section on the AADSAS application where applicants can share obstacles they have faced due to the coronavirus.

Were tests required? DAT required.

Are tests expected next year? Yes.

RUTGERS, THE STATE UNIVERSITY OF NEW JERSEY, SCHOOL OF DENTAL MEDICINE

Address: 110 Bergen Street, Newark, NJ 07101
Website: *http://sdm.rutgers.edu/*
Contact: *http://sdm.rutgers.edu/about/contacts.html*
Phone: (973) 972-5362

COST OF ATTENDANCE

In-State Tuition: $53,164
Fees & Indirect Costs: $47,589
Total: $100,753

Out-of-State Tuition: $86,137
Fees & Indirect Costs: $47,589
Total: $133,726

Financial Aid: https://financialaid.rutgers.edu/types-of-aid/scholarships/rbhs-students/

ADDITIONAL INFORMATION

Interesting tidbit: Rutgers School of Dental Medicine Gateway Programs are unique community outreach programs designed to introduce students from elementary school to college to the wide range of career options in dentistry.

What international experiences are available? Community health activities both locally and globally are available.

What dual degree options exist? DMD/MS or DMD/PhD available in conjunction with Rutgers School of Graduate Studies, DMD/MPH with Rutgers School of Dental Health, and DMD/MBA with Rutgers Business School.

What service learning opportunities exist? Community-Oriented Dental Education (CODE) program.

Other: Pipeline programs: http://sdm.rutgers.edu/pipeline/index.htm

BS/DMD program: http://sdm.rutgers.edu/admissions/predoctoral/bs-dmd.htm

Important Updates due to COVID-19: RSDM is flexible regarding grading for pre-requisites/interrupted coursework if an applicant attended a school that made system-wise grading changes due to COVID-19. In addition, Pass/Fail grades and course interruption for Spring 2020 are considered at the discretion of the admissions committee.

Were tests required? DAT required.

Are tests expected next year? Yes.

CONNECTICUT

MAINE

MASSACHUSETTS

NEW HAMPSHIRE

NEW JERSEY

NEW YORK

PENNSYLVANIA

RHODE ISLAND

VERMONT

NORTHEAST

COLUMBIA UNIVERSITY COLLEGE OF DENTAL MEDICINE

Address: 630 West 168th Street, New York, NY 10032
Website: *https://www.dental.columbia.edu/*
Contact: *https://www.dental.columbia.edu/about-us/contact-us*
Phone: (212) 305-3478

COST OF ATTENDANCE

Tuition: $97,027
Fees & Indirect Costs: $25,740
Total: $122,767

Financial Aid: https://www.ps.columbia.edu/student-financial-aid-and-planning

ADDITIONAL INFORMATION

Interesting tidbit: Columbia University College of Dental Medicine is the major provider of much-needed oral health care services to the underserved populations of Harlem, Inwood, and Washington Heights through its clinics and a variety of free services.

What international experiences are available? Global programs available. For more information, visit: https://www.dental.columbia.edu/education/global-programs

What dual degree options exist? Dual degree programs available. For more information, visit: https://www.dental.columbia.edu/education/dds-program/dual-degree-programs

What service learning opportunities exist? See Global health programs above.

Important Updates due to COVID-19: CDM will accept Pass/Fail grades for Spring and Summer 2020 coursework taken due to the COVID-19 pandemic as well as online prerequisite courses for Spring and Summer 2020 semesters. It will accept applications from applicants who were unable to take the DAT due to COVID-related test cancellations. However, when DAT testing resumes, it will require applicants to have taken the DAT.

Were tests required? No if applicants were unable to take the DAT due to COVID-related cancellations.

Are tests expected next year? Yes.

CONNECTICUT

MAINE

MASSACHUSETTS

NEW HAMPSHIRE

NEW JERSEY

NEW YORK

PENNSYLVANIA

RHODE ISLAND

VERMONT

NYU COLLEGE OF DENTISTRY

Address: 345 E. 24th Street, New York, NY 10010
Website: *https://dental.nyu.edu/*
Contact: *https://dental.nyu.edu/aboutus/contact.html*
Phone: (212) 998-9800

COST OF ATTENDANCE

Tuition: $85,288
Fees & Indirect Costs: $56,088
Total: $141,376

Financial Aid: https://dental.nyu.edu/student-life/financial-services.html

ADDITIONAL INFORMATION

Interesting tidbit: The NYU College of Dentistry is the third oldest and the largest dental school in the United States, educating nearly 10 percent of the nation's dentists.

What international experiences are available? Global outreach programs. For more information, visit: https://dental.nyu.edu/globalreach/global-student-outreach-program.html

What dual degree options exist? Dual degree programs available. For more information, visit: https://dental.nyu.edu/academicprograms/dds-program.html

What service learning opportunities exist? Local outreach including educational presentations, oral screenings, and providing care in the Going Places mobile care van and Smiling Faces.

Important Updates due to COVID-19: The NYU College of Dentistry will accept Pass/Fail grades for prerequisite courses taken during the Spring or Summer 2020 academic terms as well as online courses. Official DAT scores are still required to complete and review your application.

Were tests required? DAT required.

Are tests expected next year? Yes.

CONNECTICUT

MAINE

MASSACHUSETTS

NEW HAMPSHIRE

NEW JERSEY

NEW YORK

PENNSYLVANIA

RHODE ISLAND

VERMONT

NORTHEAST

STONY BROOK UNIVERSITY SCHOOL OF DENTAL MEDICINE

Address: 101 Nicolls Road, Stony Brook, NY 11794
Website: *https://dentistry.stonybrookmedicine.edu/*
Contact: Contact via phone.
Phone: (631) 632-8989

COST OF ATTENDANCE

In-State Tuition: $36,900
Fees & Indirect Costs: $50,494
Total: $87,394

Out-of-State Tuition: $62,950
Fees & Indirect Costs: $50,494
Total: $113,444

Financial Aid: https://dentistry.stonybrookmedicine.edu/student/financialaid

ADDITIONAL INFORMATION

Interesting tidbit: Stony Brook's values are "WE LEAD," Welcoming, Exceptional Care, Leaders of Innovation, Ethics and Accountability, Advocacy and Diversity.

What international experiences are available? Dental outreach missions available.

What dual degree options exist? Dual degree programs available. For more information, visit: https://dentistry.stonybrookmedicine.edu/dentalresearch/students/graduate/dds

What service learning opportunities exist? Fellowship opportunity to train fellows in the provision of dental care for those with developmental disabilities. For more information, visit: https://dentistry.stonybrookmedicine.edu/dentalprograms/disable

Other: The Dental Care Center Volunteer Program is an opportunity for students aged 18+ to observe/shadow pre- and post-doctoral dental students in a dental setting. For more information, visit: https://dentistry.stonybrookmedicine.edu/SDM-Volunteer

Important Updates due to COVID-19: Stony Brook University SDM will consider pass/fail grades and online courses for Spring 2020.

Were tests required? DAT required.

Are tests expected next year? Yes.

TOURO COLLEGE OF DENTAL MEDICINE AT NEW YORK MEDICAL COLLEGE

Address: 19 Skyline Dr., Hawthorne, NY 10532
Website: *https://dental.touro.edu/*
Contact: *https://dental.touro.edu/about/contact-us/*
Phone: (914) 594-2638

COST OF ATTENDANCE

Tuition: $86,255
*Fees & Indirect Costs: $31,670
Total: $117,925

Financial Aid: https://dental.touro.edu/admissions/financial-aid/

*Fees & Indirect Costs are based on off-campus estimates.

ADDITIONAL INFORMATION

Interesting tidbit: Touro College of Dental Medicine (TCDM) is a pioneer in many ways. It is the 66th dental school to open in the United States, the first new one to open in New York State in more than 50 years, and the first one in the U.S. under Jewish auspices.

What international experiences are available? N/A

What dual degree options exist? No dual degree options listed.

What service learning opportunities exist? Give Kids a Smile Program & Annual Smiles for Veterans event

Important Updates due to COVID-19: Pass/Fail coursework as well as online and lab coursework for Winter & Spring 2020, including prerequisite courses are accepted.

Were tests required? DAT required.

Are tests expected next year? Yes.

CONNECTICUT

MAINE

MASSACHUSETTS

NEW HAMPSHIRE

NEW JERSEY

NEW YORK

PENNSYLVANIA

RHODE ISLAND

VERMONT

NORTHEAST

UNIVERSITY AT BUFFALO SCHOOL OF DENTAL MEDICINE

Address: University at Buffalo, South Campus, Buffalo, NY 14215
Website: *http://dental.buffalo.edu/*
Contact: *http://dental.buffalo.edu/about-us/contact-us.html*
Phone: (716) 829-2839

COST OF ATTENDANCE

In-State Tuition: $36,900
Fees & Indirect Costs: $50,607
Total: $87,507

Out-of-State Tuition: $62,950
Fees & Indirect Costs: $50,607
Total: $113,557

Financial Aid: http://dental.buffalo.edu/education/dds-program/
dds-program/doctor-of-dental-surgery--dds-/costs-and-financial-
aid/scholarships.html

ADDITIONAL INFORMATION

Interesting tidbit: The University at Buffalo School of Dental
Medicine plays a critical role in advancing oral health in Buffalo-
Niagara and around the world. It is the largest Medicaid provider in
the region.

What international experiences are available? Global Miles for
Smiles. For more information, visit: http://dental.buffalo.edu/
community-outreach/global-miles-for-smiles.html

What dual degree options exist? Dual degree programs available.
For more information, visit: http://dental.buffalo.edu/education/
dds-program/dds-program/dual-degree-program--dds-mba-.html

What service learning opportunities exist? Various programs and
opportunities. For more information, visit: http://dental.buffalo.
edu/community-outreach/about-community-outreach/serving-the-
community.html

Other: Early Assurance Program available to undergraduate
students at the end of their second year. For more information, visit:
http://dental.buffalo.edu/education/dds-program/dds-program/
early-assurance-program--dds-.html

International Dentist Program available for dentists trained
internationally who seek to practice in the U.S. For more
information, visit: http://dental.buffalo.edu/education/dds-
program/dds-program/international-dentist-program.html

Important Updates due to COVID-19: Pass/Fail coursework as well
as online coursework for prerequisite courses are considered.

Were tests required? DAT required.

Are tests expected next year? Yes.

THE MAURICE H. KORNBERG SCHOOL OF DENTISTRY, TEMPLE UNIVERSITY

Address: 3223 North Broad Street, Philadelphia, PA 19140
Website: *https://dentistry.temple.edu/*
Contact: *https://dentistry.temple.edu/kornberg-school-dentistry-information-request*
Phone: (800) 441-4363

COST OF ATTENDANCE

In-State Tuition: $61,452
Fees & Indirect Costs: $890*
Total: $62,342

Out-of-State Tuition: $69,398
Fees & Indirect Costs: $890*
Total: $70,288

*Only University Fees information is available. Indirect costs and expenses information is unavailable.

Financial Aid: https://dentistry.temple.edu/admissions-academics-0/cost-financial-aid

ADDITIONAL INFORMATION

Interesting tidbit: As the second-oldest dental school in the United States, Temple University's Maurice H. Kornberg School of Dentistry has been educating dentists since 1863. It has a longstanding commitment to treating underserved patients in North Philadelphia.

What international experiences are available? N/A

What dual degree options exist? No dual degree options listed.

What service learning opportunities exist? Community Health Engagement course available.

Important Updates due to COVID-19: N/A

Were tests required? DAT required.

Are tests expected next year? Yes.

CONNECTICUT

MAINE

MASSACHUSETTS

NEW HAMPSHIRE

NEW JERSEY

NEW YORK

PENNSYLVANIA

RHODE ISLAND

VERMONT

NORTHEAST

UNIVERSITY OF PENNSYLVANIA SCHOOL OF DENTAL MEDICINE

Address: 240 South 40th Street, Philadelphia, PA 19104
Website: *https://www.dental.upenn.edu/*
Contact: *https://www.dental.upenn.edu/contacts-visitor-info/*
Phone: (215) 898-8943

COST OF ATTENDANCE

Tuition: $77,612
Fees & Indirect Costs: $48,829
Total: $126,441

Financial Aid: https://www.dental.upenn.edu/admissions-academics/financial-aid/

ADDITIONAL INFORMATION

Interesting tidbit: Penn Dental Medicine is one of 12 schools within the University of Pennsylvania, all of which are located on a singular campus within walking distance of one another.

What international experiences are available? N/A

What dual degree options exist? Dual degree programs available. For more information, visit: https://www.dental.upenn.edu/admissions-academics/dmd-program/dual-degree-options/

What service learning opportunities exist? Community-based activities are required. For more information on opportunities, visit: https://www.dental.upenn.edu/admissions-academics/dmd-program/community-outreach-service-learning/

Other: Bio-Dental Programs for High School Students: https://www.dental.upenn.edu/admissions-academics/bio-dental-consortial-programs-for-high-school-students/

DMD with Honors in areas of research, community health, and more. For more information on this program, visit: https://www.dental.upenn.edu/admissions-academics/dmd-program/honors-degree-program/

Important Updates due to COVID-19: Pass/Fail grades for courses as well as online courses taken during the Spring, Summer, and Fall 2020 and 2021 terms are accepted and considered.

Were tests required? DAT required.

Are tests expected next year? Yes.

UNIVERSITY OF PITTSBURGH SCHOOL OF DENTAL MEDICINE

Address: 3501 Terrace Street, Pittsburgh, PA 15261
Website: *https://www.dental.pitt.edu/*
Contact: *https://pitt.co1.qualtrics.com/jfe/form/SV_8kKBJsunINwYxg1*
Phone: (412) 648-7471

COST OF ATTENDANCE

In-State Tuition: $50,370
Fees & Indirect Costs: $43,130
Total: $93,500

Out-of-State Tuition: $60,396
Fees & Indirect Costs: $42,314
Total: $103,526

Financial Aid: https://www.dental.pitt.edu/students/dmd/financing-your-dental-education

*Note: Scholarships are offered at the time of admission to "those in the top 10% of their Class who do not have current scholarship funding."

ADDITIONAL INFORMATION

Interesting tidbit: The school's general dental clinics and 11 speciality clinics play an integral role in improving the oral health of the patient population of southwestern Pennsylvania and beyond. Some patients travel hundreds of miles to access the high-quality care Pitt Dental Medicine provides every day.

What international experiences are available? Mission trips available.

What dual degree options exist? Dual degree programs available. For more information, visit: https://www.dental.pitt.edu/joint-degreeearly-admission

What service learning opportunities exist? Student Community Outreach Program and Education (SCOPE) available. For more information, visit: https://www.dental.pitt.edu/scope

Other: Several research opportunities. For more information, visit: https://www.dental.pitt.edu/research

Important Updates due to COVID-19: Pass/Fail credits for prerequisite coursework are accepted for courses completed during the spring and summer 2020 semester. DAT scores may not be more than three years old at the application deadline.

Were tests required? DAT required.

Are tests expected next year? Yes.

CONNECTICUT

MAINE

MASSACHUSETTS

NEW HAMPSHIRE

NEW JERSEY

NEW YORK

PENNSYLVANIA

RHODE ISLAND

VERMONT

NORTHEAST

ILLINOIS

INDIANA

IOWA

KANSAS

MICHIGAN

MINNESOTA

MISSOURI

NEBRASKA

NORTH DAKOTA

OHIO

SOUTH DAKOTA

WISCONSIN

REGION TWO
MIDWEST

15 *Programs* | **12** *States*

DENTAL PROGRAMS

Medical School	Ave. Gpa & Dat Early Decision (Ed) : Yes/No	Admissions Statistics	Science Req. Other Than Gen Chem, Ochem, Physics, Bio
Midwestern University - Illinois 555 31st Street, Downers Grove, IL 60515	3.37 (overall) 3.23 (science) DAT: 19.6 ED: No	**(2010)** Apps Received: 2,196 Admission Offered: 319 Number Enrolled: 131 Acceptance Rate: 14.5% **(2020)** Apps Received: 2204 Admission Offered: 319 Number Enrolled: 135 Acceptance Rate: 14.5%	Anatomy Microbio. Physiology Biochem.
Southern Illinois University 2800 College Avenue, Alton, IL 62002	3.60 (overall) 3.49 (science) DAT: 20.1 ED: No	**(2019)** Apps Received: 642 Admission Offered: 99 Number Enrolled: 50 Acceptance Rate: 15.4% **(2020)** Apps Received: 625 Admission Offered: 88 Number Enrolled: 50 Acceptance Rate: 14.1%	Biochem.
University of Illinois at Chicago 801 S. Paulina St., Chicago, IL 60612	3.60 (overall) 3.52 (science) DAT: 21 ED: No	**(2019)** Apps Received: 1,472 Admission Offered: 102 Number Enrolled: 70 Acceptance Rate: 6.9% **(2020)** Apps Received: 1312 Admission Offered: 112 Number Enrolled: 70 Acceptance Rate: 8.5%	Biochem.
Indiana University 1121 W. Michigan Street, Indianapolis, IN 46202	3.55 (overall) 3.45 (science) DAT: 20.1 ED: No	**(2019)** Apps Received: 1,120 Admission Offered: 215 Number Enrolled: 106 Acceptance Rate: 19.2% **(2020)** Apps Received: 1208 Admission Offered: 241 Number Enrolled: 105 Acceptance Rate: 20%	Bio. must include Anatomy, Physio., Microbio, and more. See Chart for details.

DENTAL PROGRAMS

Medical School	Ave. Gpa & Dat Early Decision (Ed) : Yes/No	Admissions Statistics	Science Req. Other Than Gen Chem, Ochem, Physics, Bio
The University of Iowa 801 Newton Rd., Dental Science Building, Iowa City, IA 52242	3.70 (overall) 3.62 (science) DAT: 21 ED: No	**(2019)** Apps Received: 774 Admission Offered: 109 Number Enrolled: 82 Acceptance Rate: 14.1% **(2020)** Apps Received: 836 Admission Offered: 158 Number Enrolled: 81 Acceptance Rate: 18.9%	Biochem. Electives
University of Detroit 2700 Martin Luther King Jr. Blvd., Detroit, MI 48208	3.60 (overall) 3.55 (science) DAT: 20 ED: No	**(2019)** Apps Received: 1,621 Admission Offered: 338 Number Enrolled: 144 Acceptance Rate: 20.9% **(2020)** Apps Received: 1557 Admission Offered: 447 Number Enrolled: 144 Acceptance Rate: 28.7%	Biochem. Microbio.
University of Michigan 1011 North University Ave, Ann Arbor, MI 48109	3.69 (overall) 3.60 (science) DAT: 21.4 ED: No	(2019) Apps Received: 1,893 Admission Offered: 185 Number Enrolled: 109 Acceptance Rate: 9.7% (2020) Apps Received: 1747 Admission Offered: 204 Number Enrolled: 109 Acceptance Rate: 11.7%	Biochem. Microbio. Psych. Sociology
University of Minnesota 515 Delaware St. SE, Minneapolis, MN 55455	3.59 (overall) 3.50 (science) DAT: 20.6 ED: No	**(2019)** Apps Received: 1,198 Admission Offered: 216 Number Enrolled: 110 Acceptance Rate: 18% **(2020)** Apps Received: 576 Admission Offered: 222 Number Enrolled: 109 Acceptance Rate: 38.5%	Biochem. Math Applied Human Psych.

MIDWEST

DENTAL PROGRAMS

Medical School	Ave. Gpa & Dat Early Decision (Ed) : Yes/No	Admissions Statistics	Science Req. Other Than Gen Chem, Ochem, Physics, Bio
Missouri School of Dentistry & Oral Health* 800 W. Jefferson St., Kirksville, MO 63501	3.46 (overall) 3.34 (science) DAT: 18.7 ED: No Int'l App: No	**(2019)** Apps Received: 1,257 Admission Offered: 119 Number Enrolled: 42 Acceptance Rate: 9.5% **(2020)** Apps Received: 1308 Admission Offered: 169 Number Enrolled: 63 Acceptance Rate: 12.9%	Zoology or Microbio. acceptable alternatives to Bio. Biochem. Human Anatomy
University of Missouri-Kansas City* 650 E. 25th St., Kansas City, MO 64108	3.71 (overall) 3.67 (science) DAT: 20 ED: No Int'l App: No	**(2019)** Apps Received: 776 Admission Offered: 145 Number Enrolled: 109 Acceptance Rate: 18.7% **(2020)** Apps Received: 894 Admission Offered: 156 Number Enrolled: 109 Acceptance Rate: 17.4%	Anatomy Physio. Biochem.
Creighton University 2500 California Plaza, Omaha, NE 68178	3.67 (overall) 3.49 (science) DAT: 19.6 ED: No	**(2019)** Apps Received: 1,986 Admission Offered: 215 Number Enrolled: 116 Acceptance Rate: 10.8% **(2020)** Apps Received: 2065 Admission Offered: 227 Number Enrolled: 119 Acceptance Rate: 11%	See Chart for recommendations.
University of Nebraska 4000 East Campus Loop South, Lincoln, NE 68583	3.69 (overall) 3.59 (science) DAT: 20.5 ED: Yes	**(2019)** Apps Received: 603 Admission Offered: 70 Number Enrolled: 51 Acceptance Rate: 11.6% **(2020)** Apps Received: 530 Admission Offered: 80 Number Enrolled: 52 Acceptance Rate: 15.1%	See Chart for recommendations.

Medical School	Ave. Gpa & Dat Early Decision (Ed) : Yes/No	Admissions Statistics	Science Req. Other Than Gen Chem, Ochem, Physics, Bio
Case Western Reserve University 9601 Chester Ave., Cleveland, OH 44106	3.60 (overall) 3.53 (science) DAT: 20.8 ED: No	**(2019)** Apps Received: 2,593 Admission Offered: 297 Number Enrolled: 75 Acceptance Rate: 11.5% **(2020)** Apps Received: 2452 Admission Offered: 314 Number Enrolled: 77 Acceptance Rate: 12.8%	See Chart for recommendations.
The Ohio State University 305 W 12th Ave, Columbus, OH 43210	3.59 (overall) 3.51 (science) DAT: 21 ED: No	**(2019)** Apps Received: 1163 Admission Offered: N/A Number Enrolled: 120 Acceptance Rate: 20.7%** **(2020)** Apps Received: 797 Admission Offered: 162 Number Enrolled: 120 Acceptance Rate: 20.3%	See Chart for recommendations
Marquette University 1801 West Wisconsin Ave., Milwaukee, WI 53233	3.64 (overall) 3.56 (science) DAT: 21 ED: No	**(2019)** Apps Received: 2,353 Admission Offered: 199 Number Enrolled: 100 Acceptance Rate: 8.5% **(2020)** Apps Received: 2316 Admission Offered: 198 Number Enrolled: 100 Acceptance Rate: 8.5%	Biochem.

* Indicates that the school does not accept international applications.
**This figure is based off 2018 data of accepted students (168) divided by applications received (811).

MIDWEST

ILLINOIS

INDIANA

IOWA

KANSAS

MICHIGAN

MINNESOTA

MISSOURI

NEBRASKA

NORTH DAKOTA

OHIO

SOUTH DAKOTA

WISCONSIN

MIDWESTERN UNIVERSITY COLLEGE OF DENTAL MEDICINE - ILLINOIS

Address: 555 31st Street, Downers Grove, IL 60515
Website: *https://www.midwestern.edu/academics/our-colleges/college-of-dental-medicine.xml*
Contact: *https://online.midwestern.edu/public/reqinfo.cgi*
Phone: (630) 515-6171
Other Campus Locations: Glendale, AZ

COST OF ATTENDANCE

Tuition: $82,148
Fees & Indirect Costs: $45,438
*Total: $127,586

*Note: This figure reflects living on-campus. MU's off-campus estimate total is $133,851.

Financial Aid: https://www.midwestern.edu/admissions/tuition-and-financial-aid/scholarships.xml

ADDITIONAL INFORMATION

Interesting tidbit: Midwestern University is organized primarily to provide graduate and postgraduate education in the health sciences. The University has adopted One Health Initiative philosophy that recognizes that the health of humans is connected to the health of animals and the environment and incorporated it into the curriculum where there is a natural fit.

What international experiences are available? N/A

What dual degree options exist? No dual degree options listed.

What service learning opportunities exist? Community outreach opportunities available. For more information, visit: https://www.midwestern.edu/about/who-we-are/community-outreach.xml

NBDE 1 Pass Rate: 100%

NBDE 2 Pass Rate: 99%

Important Updates due to COVID-19: N/A

Were tests required? DAT required.

Are tests expected next year? Yes.

SOUTHERN ILLINOIS UNIVERSITY SCHOOL OF DENTAL MEDICINE

Address: 2800 College Avenue, Alton, IL 62002
Website: *http://www.siue.edu/dental/*
Contact: *https://siue.edu/contact/index.shtml*
Phone: (800) 447-7483

COST OF ATTENDANCE

Tuition: $29,998
*Fees & Indirect Costs: $31,712
Total: $61,710

*Note: This figure is based on the university's estimation of Annual average living and personal expenses for the Alton, IL area.

Financial Aid: http://www.siue.edu/dental/doctor-dental-medicine/financial-aid.shtml

ADDITIONAL INFORMATION

Interesting tidbit: The SIU School of Dental Medicine is the only dental school in Illinois that is outside the Chicago metropolitan area and has the lowest dental school tuition in Illinois.

What international experiences are available? N/A

What dual degree options exist? No dual degree options listed.

What service learning opportunities exist? "Give Kids a Smile Day", National Children's Dental Health Month, and Veterans Dental Care Day. For more information, visit: http://www.siue.edu/dental/campus-community/community-dentistry.shtml

Other: International Advanced Placement Program (IAPP) available for internationally-trained dentists. For more information, visit: http://www.siue.edu/dental/iapp/index.shtml

Important Updates due to COVID-19: N/A

Were tests required? DAT required.

Are tests expected next year? Yes.

ILLINOIS

INDIANA

IOWA

KANSAS

MICHIGAN

MINNESOTA

MISSOURI

NEBRASKA

NORTH DAKOTA

OHIO

SOUTH DAKOTA

WISCONSIN

MIDWEST

UNIVERSITY OF ILLINOIS AT CHICAGO
COLLEGE OF DENTISTRY

Address: 801 S. Paulina St., Chicago, IL 60612
Website: *https://dentistry.uic.edu/*
Contact: Refer to "Contact Us" section at the bottom of the page: *https://dentistry.uic.edu/programs/doctor-dental-medicine-dmd*
Phone: *(312) 355-4815*

COST OF ATTENDANCE

In-State Tuition: $35,636
Fees & Indirect Costs: $12,996
Total: $48,632

Out-of-State Tuition: $64,126
Fees & Indirect Costs: $12,996
Total: $77,122

Financial Aid: Refer to "Financial Planning Issues for Dental Students guide" under "Tuition", https://dentistry.uic.edu/programs/doctor-dental-medicine-dmd

ADDITIONAL INFORMATION

Interesting tidbit: UI Chicago College of Dentistry is the largest oral heal college and patient care provider in the state of Illinois offering outstanding education, research and patient care.

What international experiences are available? International rotation opportunities available.

What dual degree options exist? Dual degree programs available. For more information, visit: https://dentistry.uic.edu/dmd-mph

What service learning opportunities exist? Community outreach opportunities available. For more information, visit: https://dentistry.uic.edu/community-health

Important Updates due to COVID-19: N/A

Were tests required? DAT required.

Are tests expected next year? Yes.

INDIANA UNIVERSITY SCHOOL OF DENTISTRY

Address: 1121 W. Michigan Street, Indianapolis, IN 46202
Website: *https://dentistry.iu.edu/*
Contact: *https://dentistry.iu.edu/about/contact.html*
Phone: (317) 274-7957

COST OF ATTENDANCE

In-State Tuition: $38,973
Fees & Indirect Costs: $19,489.64
Total: $58,462.64

Out-of-State Tuition: $86,798
Fees & Indirect Costs: $19,489.64
Total: $106,287.64

Financial Aid: Donor-funded scholarships available to a few dental students. For more information, visit: https://dentistry.iu.edu/admissions/cost-financial-aid/dds-cost.html

ADDITIONAL INFORMATION

Interesting tidbit: Indiana University School of Dentistry is the only dental school in Indiana, and it trains 80 percent of the state's dentists.

What international experiences are available? Global service learning opportunities.

What dual degree options exist? For information on the DDS/MPH program, visit: https://dentistry.iu.edu/admissions/how-to-apply/dds-mph-dual-degree.html

For information on the DDS/PhD program, visit: https://dentistry.iu.edu/admissions/how-to-apply/dds-phd-dual-degree.html

What service learning opportunities exist? Community outreach locally, nationally, and internationally. For more information, visit: https://dentistry.iu.edu/academics/student-experience/service-learning-opportunities.html

Other: International Dentist Program available for international dental graduates seeking to practice in the U.S. For more information, visit: https://dentistry.iu.edu/admissions/how-to-apply/international-dentist-program.html

Important Updates due to COVID-19: N/A

Were tests required? DAT required.

Are tests expected next year? Yes.

ILLINOIS

INDIANA

IOWA

KANSAS

MICHIGAN

MINNESOTA

MISSOURI

NEBRASKA

NORTH DAKOTA

OHIO

SOUTH DAKOTA

WISCONSIN

MIDWEST

ILLINOIS

INDIANA

IOWA

KANSAS

MICHIGAN

MINNESOTA

MISSOURI

NEBRASKA

NORTH DAKOTA

OHIO

SOUTH DAKOTA

WISCONSIN

THE UNIVERSITY OF IOWA COLLEGE OF DENTISTRY & DENTAL CLINICS

Address: 801 Newton Rd., Dental Science Building, Iowa City, IA 52242
Website: *https://www.dentistry.uiowa.edu/*
Contact: *https://www.dentistry.uiowa.edu/contact-us*
Phone: (319) 335-7157

COST OF ATTENDANCE

In-State Tuition: $50,791.50
*Fees & Indirect Costs: $18,474.64
Total: $69,266.14

Out-of-State Tuition: $75,930
*Fees & Indirect Costs: $18,474.64
Total: $94,404.14

*Note: This figure does not include room and board.

Financial Aid: https://www.dentistry.uiowa.edu/admissions-costs-and-financial-aid

ADDITIONAL INFORMATION

Interesting tidbit: The College of Dentistry and Dental Clinics is one of only two dental schools in the nation to offer advanced education in nine ADA-recognized dental specialties.

What international experiences are available? International opportunities available, no listed specifics.

What dual degree options exist? No dual degree options listed.

What service learning opportunities exist? Extramural programs available. For more information, visit: https://www.dentistry.uiowa.edu/academics-extramurals

Important Updates due to COVID-19: If you attend an institution that has mandated that all coursework change to Pass/Fail during the spring or summer 2020 sessions due to COVID-19, the University of Iowa College of Dentistry expects that your institution annotates this mandate on your transcripts.

Were tests required? DAT required.

Are tests expected next year? Yes.

UNIVERSITY OF DETROIT MERCY SCHOOL OF DENTISTRY

Address: 2700 Martin Luther King Jr. Blvd., Detroit, MI 48208
Website: *https://dental.udmercy.edu/*
Contact: Contact via phone
Phone: (313) 494-6611

COST OF ATTENDANCE

Tuition: $74,260
Fees & Indirect Costs: $39,074
*Total: $115,334

Financial Aid: https://dental.udmercy.edu/admission/financial/index.php

ADDITIONAL INFORMATION

Interesting tidbit: Community service is an integral component of the Detroit Mercy Dental's mission to develop socially and ethically sensitive dental professionals. Since 2006 it has been cultivating a Community Based Dental Education (CBDE) course to provide students with unique experiences, making a difference in underserved communities throughout Michigan.

What international experiences are available? Mission trips.

What dual degree options exist? No dual degree options listed.

What service learning opportunities exist? Community-based dental education, outreach initiatives, and mobile programs available. For more information, visit: https://dental.udmercy.edu/community/index.php

Other: Accelerated track available to select students. This program allows students to obtain their BS in Biology or BA in Chemistry and DDS in 7 years. For more information, visit: https://eng-sci.udmercy.edu/academics/science/pre-health/seven-year-dental.php

Accelerated Dental Program available for foreign-trained dentists seeking the credentials to practice in the U.S. For more information, visit: https://dental.udmercy.edu/programs/dental/accelerated/index.php

Important Updates due to COVID-19: Pass/Fail grading for the Spring or Summer 2020 academic semester(s), are accepted. Unofficial DAT scores are accepted for review.

Were tests required? DAT required.

Are tests expected next year? Yes.

ILLINOIS

INDIANA

IOWA

KANSAS

MICHIGAN

MINNESOTA

MISSOURI

NEBRASKA

NORTH DAKOTA

OHIO

SOUTH DAKOTA

WISCONSIN

MIDWEST

UNIVERSITY OF MICHIGAN SCHOOL OF DENTISTRY

Address: 1011 North University Ave, Ann Arbor, MI 48109
Website: *https://www.dent.umich.edu/*
Contact: *https://dent.umich.edu/people*
Phone: (734) 763-6933

COST OF ATTENDANCE

In-State Tuition: $16,423
*Fees & Indirect Costs: $24,482.19
Total: $40,905.19

Out-of-State Tuition: $22,509
*Fees & Indirect Costs: $24.482.19
Total: $46,991.19

*Note: Mandatory fees of $214.19 is information provided by School of Dentistry while the remaining costs ($24,268) estimates are information from the College of Literature, Science and the Arts.

*Note: A student may be charged a laboratory or other supplemental fee per class.

Financial Aid: https://finaid.umich.edu/dental-dds-students/

ADDITIONAL INFORMATION

Interesting tidbit: The Sindecuse Museum of Dentistry, housed within the School of Dentistry, is one of a handful of museums throughout the world devoted to preserving and exhibiting the history of dentistry.

What international experiences are available? Global Initiatives Program available. For more information, visit: https://www.dent.umich.edu/about#global-initiatives

What dual degree options exist? Dual degree programs available. For more information, visit: https://www.dent.umich.edu/education/dual-degree-programs

What service learning opportunities exist? Global Initiatives Program.

Other: Internationally Trained Dentist Program available for foreign-trained dentists seeking to practice in the U.S. For more information, visit: https://www.dent.umich.edu/education/internationally-trained-dentist-program-itdp

Important Updates due to COVID-19: Coursework taken online through accredited colleges and universities for the Fall 2020 and Winter 2021 terms accepted. Any/all courses graded this term on a Pass/Fail basis are accepted with caveats.

Were tests required? DAT required.

Are tests expected next year? Yes.

UNIVERSITY OF MINNESOTA SCHOOL OF DENTISTRY

Address: 515 Delaware St. SE, Minneapolis, MN 55455
Website: *https://www.dentistry.umn.edu/*
Contact: *https://www.dentistry.umn.edu/about/contact-us*
Phone: (612) 625-7477

COST OF ATTENDANCE

In-State Tuition: $39,538
Fees & Indirect Costs: $26,315.51
Total: $65,853.51

Out-of-State Tuition: $73,246
Fees & Indirect Costs: $26,315.51
Total: $99,561.51

Financial Aid: https://www.dentistry.umn.edu/sites/dentistry.umn.edu/files/dds_class_of_2020_projected_cost_of_attendance.pdf

ADDITIONAL INFORMATION

Interesting tidbit: The University of Minnesota School of Dentistry is the state's only dental school and the only dental school in the northern tier of states between Wisconsin and the Pacific Northwest, making it a regional resource to five states for dental education, consulting services, patient treatment, and ongoing dental education.

What international experiences are available? Student exchange programs in Denmark, Norway, Germany, and the Netherlands.

What dual degree options exist? For information on the DDS/PhD program, visit: https://www.dentistry.umn.edu/degrees-programs/advanced-education-programs/oral-biology/ddsphd-program

For information on the DDS/MPH program, visit: https://www.sph.umn.edu/academics/degrees-programs/dual-degrees/dentistry/

What service learning opportunities exist? Students are required to engage in community outreach as a condition of graduation. For more information on service learning opportunities, visit: https://www.dentistry.umn.edu/degrees-programs/community-outreach-experience

Important Updates due to COVID-19: Pass/Fail grading for prerequisites and online labs for spring and summer 2020 are accepted. The 50-hr Dental shadowing is waived for the 2021-2022 admission cycle.

Were tests required? DAT required.

Are tests expected next year? Yes.

ILLINOIS

INDIANA

IOWA

KANSAS

MICHIGAN

MINNESOTA

MISSOURI

NEBRASKA

NORTH DAKOTA

OHIO

SOUTH DAKOTA

WISCONSIN

MIDWEST

ILLINOIS

INDIANA

IOWA

KANSAS

MICHIGAN

MINNESOTA

MISSOURI

NEBRASKA

NORTH DAKOTA

OHIO

SOUTH DAKOTA

WISCONSIN

MISSOURI SCHOOL OF DENTISTRY & ORAL HEALTH

Address: 800 W. Jefferson St., Kirksville, MO 63501
Website: *https://www.atsu.edu/missouri-school-of-dentistry-and-oral-health*
Contact: *https://www.atsu.edu/connect/contact-atsu*
Phone: (660) 626-2121

COST OF ATTENDANCE

***Tuition:** $87,382
Fees & Indirect Costs: $26,175
Total: $113,557

***Note:** Tuition includes tuition and mandatory fees.

Financial Aid: https://www.atsu.edu/department-of-student-affairs/enrollment-services/types-of-aid/federal-direct-student-loans#cost-attendance

ADDITIONAL INFORMATION

Interesting tidbit: ATSU-MOSDOH rests on an expansive campus, which includes ATSU medical school, ATSU's Gutensohn Clinic, Museum of Osteopathic Medicine, A.T. Still Memorial Library, Missouri Area Health Education Center program office, and A.T. Still Research Institute. It is a hub of comprehensive medical and dental education, research, and healthcare.

What international experiences are available? N/A

What dual degree options exist? No dual degree options listed.

What service learning opportunities exist? Service learning is interweaved throughout the curriculum. For more information, visit: https://www.atsu.edu/missouri-school-of-dentistry-and-oral-health/about-mosdoh/serving-the-underserved

Important Updates due to COVID-19: Due to COVID-19, ATSU-MOSDOH will reivew and interview applicants without a DAT for the 2020-2021 application cycle. However, a successful DAT score is a condition of matriculation. Also, unofficial transcripts are reviewed but official transcripts or a letter of explanation from the school is required for matriculation.

Were tests required? DAT required.

Are tests expected next year? Yes.

UNIVERSITY OF MISSOURI-KANSAS CITY SCHOOL OF DENTISTRY

Address: 650 E. 25th St., Kansas City, MO 64108
Website: *https://dentistry.umkc.edu/*
Contact: https://dentistry.umkc.edu/contact-us/
Phone: (816) 235-2100

COST OF ATTENDANCE

In-State Tuition: $35,860.80
*Fees & Indirect Costs: $676.53
Total: $36,537.33

Out-of-State Tuition: $71,470.20
*Fees & Indirect Costs: $676.53
Total: $72,146.73

*Note: only ancillary fees information available.

Financial Aid: https://dentistry.umkc.edu/academics/doctor-of-dental-surgery/affordability/dds-scholarships/

ADDITIONAL INFORMATION

Interesting tidbit: UMKC School of Dentistry is the only public dental school in Missouri. It is the only institution in Missouri offering advanced educational programs and clinical training in General Dentistry, Oral and Maxillofacial Surgery, Periodontics, Orthodontics and Dentofacial Orthopedics and Endodontics.

What international experiences are available? International and domestic trips available to admitted students.

What dual degree options exist? No dual degree options available.

What service learning opportunities exist? N/A

Other: STAHR Scholars Dentistry Program is a 10-week summer program for culturally diverse candidates. For more information, visit: https://dentistry.umkc.edu/academics/doctor-of-dental-surgery/stahrscholarsdentistry/

Important Updates due to COVID-19: For 2020-2021 application cycle, Pass/Fail grading and online coursework are accepted. Unofficial DAT score report is accepted.

Were tests required? DAT required.

Are tests expected next year? Yes.

ILLINOIS

INDIANA

IOWA

KANSAS

MICHIGAN

MINNESOTA

MISSOURI

NEBRASKA

NORTH DAKOTA

OHIO

SOUTH DAKOTA

WISCONSIN

MIDWEST

ILLINOIS

INDIANA

IOWA

KANSAS

MICHIGAN

MINNESOTA

MISSOURI

NEBRASKA

NORTH DAKOTA

OHIO

SOUTH DAKOTA

WISCONSIN

CREIGHTON UNIVERSITY SCHOOL OF DENTISTRY

Address: 2500 California Plaza, Omaha, NE 68178
Website: *https://dentistry.creighton.edu/*
Contact: *https://www.creighton.edu/ask*
Phone: (402) 280-2700

COST OF ATTENDANCE

Tuition: $69,836
Fees & Indirect Costs: $35,134
Total: $104,979

Financial Aid: https://dentistry.creighton.edu/future-students/tuition-and-aid

ADDITIONAL INFORMATION

Interesting tidbit: The education at Creighton University School of Dentistry is conducted in a culture and learning environment that reflects Ignatian humanism and a Catholic, Jesuit heritage. At Creighton, Jesuit principles are infused into both the curriculum and the student experience.

What international experiences are available? Institute for Latin American Concern (ILAC) dental program. For more information, visit: https://dentistry.creighton.edu/about/community-outreach/institute-latin-american-concern-dental-program

What dual degree options exist? No dual degree options listed.

What service learning opportunities exist? "Give Kids a Smile" program. For more information, visit: https://dentistry.creighton.edu/about/community-outreach/give-kids-smile

Important Updates due to COVID-19: Online coursework for Spring and Fall of 2020 are accepted.

Were tests required? DAT required.

Are tests expected next year? Yes.

UNIVERSITY OF NEBRASKA MEDICAL CENTER COLLEGE OF DENTISTRY

Address: 4000 East Campus Loop South, Lincoln, NE 68583
Website: *https://www.unmc.edu/dentistry/*
Contact: *https://www.unmc.edu/dentistry/about/contact.html*
Phone: (402) 472-1363

COST OF ATTENDANCE

In-State Tuition: $32,360
Fees & Indirect Costs: $69,870
Total: $102,230

Out-of-State Tuition: $67,460
Fees & Indirect Costs: $69,870
Total: $138,830

Financial Aid: https://www.unmc.edu/dentistry/programs/dental/financial.html

ADDITIONAL INFORMATION

Interesting tidbit: The UNMC College of Dentistry established a dental museum in 1977, under Dean Richard E. Bradley. The museum collection represents the history of dentistry in Nebraska, which began in the 1850s.

What international experiences are available? East Meets West Dental Program and annual medical service trips abroad. For more information on these international experiences, visit: https://www.unmc.edu/dentistry/outreach/mission-trips.html

What dual degree options exist? No dual degree options listed.

What service learning opportunities exist? Children's Dental Day, Sealant Program, and more. For more information, visit: https://www.unmc.edu/dentistry/outreach/index.html

Other: UNMC developed the first-ever Health Professions Degree Program for Chinese students. For more information, visit: https://www.unmc.edu/aprdp/csc/professional-degree/index.html

Rural Health Opportunities Program (RHOP) encourages rural NE residents to pursue health-care career. Selected students receive scholarships and guaranteed admission upon completion of requirements. For more information on this program, visit: https://www.unmc.edu/dentistry/programs/ruralhealthprograms.html

Important Updates due to COVID-19: N/A

Were tests required? DAT required.

Are tests expected next year? Yes.

ILLINOIS

INDIANA

IOWA

KANSAS

MICHIGAN

MINNESOTA

MISSOURI

NEBRASKA

NORTH DAKOTA

OHIO

SOUTH DAKOTA

WISCONSIN

MIDWEST

ILLINOIS

INDIANA

IOWA

KANSAS

MICHIGAN

MINNESOTA

MISSOURI

NEBRASKA

NORTH DAKOTA

OHIO

SOUTH DAKOTA

WISCONSIN

CASE WESTERN RESERVE UNIVERSITY SCHOOL OF DENTAL MEDICINE

Address: 9601 Chester Ave., Cleveland, OH 44106
Website: *https://case.edu/dental/*
Contact: *https://case.edu/dental/prospective-students/doctor-dental-medicine-dmd/visitcontact-us*
Phone: (216) 368-3200

COST OF ATTENDANCE

Tuition: $75,136
Fees & Indirect Costs: $42,667.95
Total: $17,803.95

Financial Aid: https://case.edu/dental/prospective-students/doctor-dental-medicine-dmd/financial-aid

ADDITIONAL INFORMATION

Interesting tidbit: CWRU SoDM boasts an award-winning curriculum, The REAL curriculum, which stands for Relevant Experiential Active Learning. It is integrated into all components of the learning culture from classroom, clinic, research, and to community.

What international experiences are available? N/A

What dual degree options exist? Dual degree programs available. For more information, visit:

What service learning opportunities exist? Head Start Outreach Program, Healthy Smiles Sealant Program, Family First Program, and more. For more information, visit: https://case.edu/dental/departments-programs/community-dentistry

Important Updates due to COVID-19: N/A

Were tests required? DAT required.

Are tests expected next year? Yes.

THE OHIO STATE UNIVERSITY COLLEGE OF DENTISTRY

Address: 305 W 12th Ave, Columbus, OH 43210
Website: *https://dentistry.osu.edu/*
Contact: *https://dentistry.osu.edu/about-us/contact-us*
Phone: (614) 292-3361

COST OF ATTENDANCE

In-State Tuition: $38,520
Fees & Indirect Costs: $30,401
Total: $68,921

Out-of-State Tuition: $81,940
Fees & Indirect Costs: $30,401
Total: $112,341

Financial Aid: https://dentistry.osu.edu/prospective-students/doctor-dental-surgery-dds/financial-aid

ADDITIONAL INFORMATION

Interesting tidbit: The Ohio State University College of Dentistry is the fourth largest public dental school in the United States and consists of ten academic divisions representing all major dental specialties. The divisions allow dentists to train as specialists.

What international experiences are available? N/A

What dual degree options exist? Dual degree programs available. For information on the DDS/PhD, visit: https://dentistry.osu.edu/prospective-students/dual-degree-ddsphd

For information on the DDS/MPH, visit: https://dentistry.osu.edu/prospective-students/doctor-dental-surgerymaster-public-health-combined-degree-program

What service learning opportunities exist? OHIO Project and Dental H.O.M.E. (Health Outreach Mobile Experience) Coach are two projects that are within the curriculum. Other outreach activities available as well. For more information, visit: https://dentistry.osu.edu/about-us/community-outreach-education

Other: Commitment to Access Resources and Education (CARE) Program available to students. This program aims to work to address the healthcare need in underserved areas in Ohio. For more information, visit: https://dentistry.osu.edu/prospective-students/CARE-program

Important Updates due to COVID-19: N/A

Were tests required? DAT required.

Are tests expected next year? Yes.

ILLINOIS

INDIANA

IOWA

KANSAS

MICHIGAN

MINNESOTA

MISSOURI

NEBRASKA

NORTH DAKOTA

OHIO

SOUTH DAKOTA

WISCONSIN

MIDWEST

ILLINOIS

INDIANA

IOWA

KANSAS

MICHIGAN

MINNESOTA

MISSOURI

NEBRASKA

NORTH DAKOTA

OHIO

SOUTH DAKOTA

WISCONSIN

MARQUETTE UNIVERSITY SCHOOL OF DENTISTRY

Address: 1801 West Wisconsin Ave., Milwaukee, WI 53233
Website: *https://www.marquette.edu/dentistry/*
Contact: *https://www.marquette.edu/dentistry/resources/contact-us.php*
Phone: (414) 288-3532

COST OF ATTENDANCE

In-State Tuition: $57,450
Fees & Indirect Costs: $38,442
Total: $95,892

Out-of-State Tuition: $66,110
Fees & Indirect Costs: $38,442
Total: $104,552

Financial Aid: https://www.marquette.edu/dentistry/admissions/financial-aid.php

ADDITIONAL INFORMATION

Interesting tidbit: Marquette University School of Dentistry's curriculum is centered in the Catholic, Jesuit belief that the classroom is not the real world. One-fourth of each student's academic career is dedicated to treating patients at urban and rural clinical sites affiliated with Marquette University.

What international experiences are available? N/A

What dual degree options exist? No dual degree options.

What service learning opportunities exist? N/A

Other: Pre-Dental Scholars Program open to high school applicants. This program is a 7-year BS/DDS track. For more information, visit: https://www.marquette.edu/explore/scholarships-pre-dental.php

Important Updates due to COVID-19: Unofficial DAT scores are accepted for review.

Were tests required? DAT required.

Are tests expected next year? Yes.

REGION THREE
SOUTH

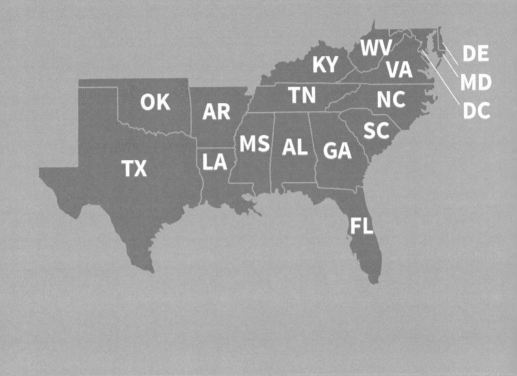

23 Programs | 16 States

DENTAL PROGRAMS

Dental School	Ave. GPA & DAT EARLY DECISION (ED) : YES/NO	Admissions Statistics	Science Req. Other Than Gen Chem, Ochem, Physics, Bio
University of Alabama at Birmingham 1919 7th Ave. S., Birmingham, AL 35233	3.69 (overall) 3.61 (science) DAT: 21.1 ED: No	**(2019)** Apps Received: 1,003 Admission Offered: 91 Number Enrolled: 63 Acceptance Rate: 9.1% **(2020)** Apps Received: 976 Admission Offered: 102 Number Enrolled: 63 Acceptance Rate: 10.5%	Math See Chart for recommendations.
Howard University 600 W Street, NW, Washington, DC 20059	3.26 (overall) 3.12 (science) DAT: 18.4 ED: No	**(2019)** Apps Received: 2,062 Admission Offered: 110 Number Enrolled: 73 Acceptance Rate: 5.3% **(2020)** Apps Received: 1071 Admission Offered: N/A Number Enrolled: 75 Acceptance Rate: 7%**	Biochem. Human Anatomy
Lake Erie College of Osteopathic Medicine* 4800 Lakewood Ranch Boulevard, Bradenton, FL 34211	3.49 (overall) 3.41 (science) DAT: 20 ED: No Int'l App: No	**(2019)** Apps Received: 3,333 Admission Offered: 290 Number Enrolled: 105 Acceptance Rate: 8.7% **(2020)** Apps Received: 3470 Admission Offered: 371 Number Enrolled: 105 Acceptance Rate: 10.7%	Biochem.
Nova Southeastern University 3301 College Avenue, Fort Lauderdale, Florida 33314	3.70 (overall) 3.60 (science) DAT: 21 ED: No	**(2019)** Apps Received: 2,749 Admission Offered: 295 Number Enrolled: 122 Acceptance Rate: 10.7% **(2020)** Apps Received: 2499 Admission Offered: 302 Number Enrolled: 125 Acceptance Rate: 12.1%	Biochem. Microbio.

DENTAL PROGRAMS

Dental School	Ave. GPA & DAT / EARLY DECISION (ED) : YES/NO	Admissions Statistics	Science Req. Other Than Gen Chem, Ochem, Physics, Bio
University of Florida* 1395 Center Drive, Gainesville, FL 32610	3.73 (overall) 3.68 (science) DAT: 22 ED: No Int'l App: No	**(2019)** Apps Received: 1,606 Admission Offered: 156 Number Enrolled: 93 Acceptance Rate: 9.7% **(2020)** Apps Received: 1567 Admission Offered: 158 Number Enrolled: 93 Acceptance Rate: 10.1%	Biochem. Microbio.
Augusta University* 1430 John Wesley Gilbert Drive, Augusta, GA 30912	3.57 (overall) 3.49 (science) DAT: 20 ED: No Int'l App: No	**(2019)** Apps Received: 772 *Interviews Received: 202 Admission Offered: N/A Number Enrolled: 96 Acceptance Rate: 16.7%*** **(2020)** Apps Received: 772 Admission Offered: 124 Number Enrolled: 96 Acceptance Rate: 16.1%	Biochem.
University of Kentucky 800 Rose St., Lexington, KY 40536	3.63 (overall) 3.52 (science) DAT: 19.9 ED: No	**(2019)** Apps Received: 1,838 Admission Offered: 135 Number Enrolled: 65 Acceptance Rate: 7.3% **(2020)** Apps Received: 1273 Admission Offered: 143 Number Enrolled: 65 Acceptance Rate: 11.2%	Biochem. Microbio.
University of Louisville 501 S. Preston St., Louisville, KY 40202	3.61 (overall) 3.49 (science) DAT: 20 ED: No	(2019) Apps Received: 2,400 Admission Offered: 310 Number Enrolled: 120 Acceptance Rate: 12.9% (2020) Apps Received: 2258 Admission Offered: 318 Number Enrolled: 120 Acceptance Rate: 14.1%	Biochem.

SOUTH

DENTAL PROGRAMS

Dental School	Ave. GPA & DAT EARLY DECISION (ED) : YES/NO	Admissions Statistics	Science Req. Other Than Gen Chem, Ochem, Physics, Bio
Louisiana State University Health New Orleans* 1100 Florida Avenue, New Orleans, LA 70119	3.64 (overall) 3.57 (science) DAT: 20.8 ED: No Int'l App: No	**(2019)** Apps Received: 446 Admission Offered: 101 Number Enrolled: 75 Acceptance Rate: 22.6% **(2020)** Apps Received: 448 Admission Offered: 73 Number Enrolled: 76 Acceptance Rate: 16.3%	Biochem. Microbio.
University of Maryland 650 W Baltimore St, Baltimore, MD 21201	3.45 (overall) 3.53 (science) DAT: 20.9 ED: No	**(2019)** Apps Received: 2,188 Admission Offered: 260 Number Enrolled: 130 Acceptance Rate: 11.9% **(2020)** Apps Received: 1649 Admission Offered: 317 Number Enrolled: 129 Acceptance Rate: 16.3%	Biochem.
University of Mississippi Dental Center* 2500 N. State St., Jackson, MS 39216	3.61 (overall) 3.41 (science) DAT: 19 ED: No Int'l App: No	**(2019)** Apps Received: 102 Admission Offered: 55 Number Enrolled: 40 Acceptance Rate: 53.9% **(2020)** Apps Received: 88 Admission Offered: 39 Number Enrolled: 40 Acceptance Rate: 44.3%	Bio or Zoology Microbio. Math. Stats. or Biostats. Biochem.
East Carolina University* 1851 MacGregor Downs Road, Greenville, NC 27834	3.35 (overall) 3.27 (science) DAT: 19.1 ED: No Int'l App: No	**(2019)** Apps Received: 461 Admission Offered: 76 Number Enrolled: 52 Acceptance Rate: 16.5% **(2020)** Apps Received: 397 Admission Offered: 84 Number Enrolled: 52 Acceptance Rate: 21.2%	Math

DENTAL PROGRAMS

Dental School	Ave. GPA & DAT EARLY DECISION (ED) : YES/NO	Admissions Statistics	Science Req. Other Than Gen Chem, Ochem, Physics, Bio
University of North Carolina at Chapel Hill 385 S Columbia St, Chapel Hill, NC 27599	3.62 (overall) 3.50 (science) DAT: 23 ED: No	**(2019)** Apps Received: 1,065 Admission Offered: 101 Number Enrolled: 84 Acceptance Rate: 9.5% **(2020)** Apps Received: 1218 Admission Offered: 104 Number Enrolled: 83 Acceptance Rate: 8.5%	Biochem.
University of Oklahoma 1201 N. Stonewall Ave., Oklahoma City, OK 73117	3.62 (overall) 3.54 (science) DAT: 20 ED: No	**(2019)** Apps Received: 761 Admission Offered: 54 Number Enrolled: 54 Acceptance Rate: 7.1% **(2020)** Apps Received: 803 Admission Offered: 54 Number Enrolled: 53 Acceptance Rate: 6.7%	Biochem. Psych.
Dental University of South Carolina 173 Ashley Avenue, Charleston, SC 29425	3.55 (overall) 3.48 (science) DAT: 20 ED: No	**(2019)** Apps Received: 1,273 Admission Offered: 111 Number Enrolled: 75 Acceptance Rate: 8.7% **(2020)** Apps Received: 1246 Admission Offered: 118 Number Enrolled: 76 Acceptance Rate: 9.5%	Bio. or Zoology Math Science Electives (e.g., Microbio. Biochem, Anatomy, Physio., Genetics)
Meharry Dental College 1005 Dr DB Todd Jr Blvd, Nashville, TN 37208	3.19 (overall) 3.10 (science) DAT: 17.7 ED: No	**(2019)** Apps Received: 2,593 Admission Offered: 61 Number Enrolled: 61 Acceptance Rate: 2.4% **(2020)** Apps Received: 3449 Admission Offered: 115 Number Enrolled: 62 Acceptance Rate: 3.3%	Chem. w/Quantitative Analysis Biochem. Calc. or Stats.

SOUTH

DENTAL PROGRAMS

Dental School	Ave. GPA & DAT / EARLY DECISION (ED) : YES/NO	Admissions Statistics	Science Req. Other Than Gen Chem, Ochem, Physics, Bio
University of Tennessee Health Science Center* 875 Union Avenue, Memphis, TN 38163	3.60 (overall) 3.50 (science) DAT: 20 ED: No Int'l App: No	**(2019)** Apps Received: 1,803 Admission Offered: 244 Number Enrolled: 99 Acceptance Rate: 13.5% **(2020)** Apps Received: 1394 Admission Offered: 132 Number Enrolled: 97 Acceptance Rate: 9.5%	Biochem. Histology, Microbio., or Comparative Anatomy
Texas A&M College of Dentistry 3302 Gaston Ave., Dallas, TX 75246	3.71 (overall) 3.61 (science) DAT: 21.3 ED: No	**(2019)** Apps Received: 1,616 Admission Offered: 146 Number Enrolled: 105 Acceptance Rate: 9% **(2020)** Apps Received: 1605 Admission Offered: 138 Number Enrolled: 106 Acceptance Rate: 8.6%	Stats. Biochem. Anatomy w/Lab Physio. Microbio.
Texas Tech University Health Sciences Center***+ 5001 El Paso Dr., El Paso, TX 79905	N/A DAT: N/A ED: No Int'l App: No	N/A (40 seats available)	Microbio. Biochem. Stats.
The University of Texas at Houston* 7500 Cambridge St., Houston, TX 77054	3.81 (overall) 3.78 (science) DAT: 22 ED: No Int'l App: No	**(2019)** Apps Received: 1,233 Admission Offered: 162 Number Enrolled: 105 Acceptance Rate: 13.1% **(2020)** Apps Received: 1489 Admission Offered: 185 Number Enrolled: 105 Acceptance Rate: 12.4%	Biochem. Stats.

DENTAL PROGRAMS

Dental School	Ave. GPA & DAT EARLY DECISION (ED) : YES/NO	Admissions Statistics	Science Req. Other Than Gen Chem, Ochem, Physics, Bio
UT Health San Antonio* 7703 Floyd Curl Drive, San Antonio, TX 78229	3.71 (overall) 3.63 (science) DAT: 20.8 ED: No Int'l App: No	**(2019)** Apps Received: 1,400 Admission Offered: 218 Number Enrolled: 104 Acceptance Rate: 15.6% **(2020)** Apps Received: 1433 Admission Offered: 218 Number Enrolled: 106 Acceptance Rate: 15.2%	Biochem. Stats.
Virginia Commonwealth University 520 North 12th Street, Richmond, VA 23298	3.63 (overall) 3.51 (science) DAT: 21 ED: No	**(2019)** Apps Received: 1,670 Admission Offered: 214 Number Enrolled: 96 Acceptance Rate: 12.8% **(2020)** Apps Received: 2408 Admission Offered: 250 Number Enrolled: 101 Acceptance Rate: 10.4%	Biochem. Math/Stats.
West Virginia University 1 Medical Center Dr, Morgantown, WV 26505	3.65 (overall) 3.70 (science) DAT: 19 ED: No	**(2019)** Apps Received: 1,018 Admission Offered: 75 Number Enrolled: 48 Acceptance Rate: 7.4% **(2020)** Apps Received: 972 Admission Offered: 80 Number Enrolled: 47 Acceptance Rate: 8.2%	Bio. or Zoology Anatomy Biochem.

* Indicates that the school does not accept international applications.
**This figure is based off 2019 data of enrolled students (75) divided by # of applications (1071).
***This figure is based off 2018 data of accepted students (116) divided by # of applications (695).
+Texas Tech will have their inaugural class in 2021. Therefore, no admissions data yet.

SOUTH

ALABAMA

ARKANSAS

DELAWARE

DISTRICT OF
COLUMBIA

FLORIDA

GEORGIA

KENTUCKY

LOUISIANA

MARYLAND

MISSISSIPPI

NORTH CAROLINA

OKLAHOMA

SOUTH CAROLINA

TENNESSEE

TEXAS

VIRGINIA

WEST VIRGINIA

UNIVERSITY OF ALABAMA AT BIRMINGHAM SCHOOL OF DENTISTRY

Address: 1919 7th Ave. S., Birmingham, AL 35233
Website: *https://www.uab.edu/dentistry/home/*
Contact: *https://www.uab.edu/dentistry/home/about/contact-us*
Phone: (205) 934-3000

COST OF ATTENDANCE

In-State Tuition: $28,000
Fees & Indirect Costs: $17,112
Total: $45,112

Out-of-State Tuition: $65,000
Fees & Indirect Costs: $17,112
Total: $82,112

Financial Aid: Students encouraged to apply for federal financial aid.

ADDITIONAL INFORMATION

Interesting tidbit: In the 1960s, UAB School of Dentistry gave birth to the concept of "four-handed dentistry" by introducing a second person into the practice environment. As a recipient of a seven-year, $22.4 million grant from the National Institute of Dental and Craniofacial Research, part of the National Institutes of Health, UAB leads and oversees six smaller regional research centers located in Birmingham; Rochester, New York; Gainesville, Florida; Minneapolis; San Antonio; and Portland, Oregon.

What international experiences are available? Global outreach available. For more information, see link under "service learning opportunities".

What dual degree options exist? For information on the DMD/PhD program, visit: https://www.uab.edu/dentistry/home/academics/dmd-phd

For information on the DMD/MBA program, visit: https://www.uab.edu/dentistry/home/academics/dmd-mba

For information on the DMD/MD program, visit: https://www.uab.edu/dentistry/home/academics/dmd-md

What service learning opportunities exist? Local and Global Outreach as well as volunteer opportunities available. For more information, visit: https://www.uab.edu/dentistry/home/community/local-global-impact

For more information on volunteer opportunities, visit: https://www.uab.edu/dentistry/home/community/volunteer-outreach

Other: International Dentist Program available for foreign-trained dentists seeking to practice in the U.S. For more information, visit: https://www.uab.edu/dentistry/home/academics/idp

Important Updates due to COVID-19: N/A

Were tests required? DAT required.

Are tests expected next year? Yes.

HOWARD UNIVERSITY COLLEGE OF DENTISTRY

Address: 600 W Street, NW, Washington, DC 20059
Website: *http://healthsciences.howard.edu/education/colleges/dentistry*
Contact: *http://healthsciences.howard.edu/huhealthcare/contact-us*
Phone: (202) 806-0400

COST OF ATTENDANCE

Tuition: $42,632
Fees & Indirect Costs: $46,890
Total: $89,522

Financial Aid: http://healthsciences.howard.edu/education/colleges/dentistry/financial-aid/scholarships-and-loan-programs

ADDITIONAL INFORMATION

Interesting tidbit: The College of Dentistry at Howard University is the fifth oldest dental school in the United States.

What international experiences are available? N/A

What dual degree options exist? Dual degree programs available. For more information, visit: http://healthsciences.howard.edu/education/colleges/dentistry/programs/predoctoral-programs/DDS-MBA-program

What service learning opportunities exist? N/A

Other: BS/DDS program available for undergraduates of Howard University. This is a 6-year program. For more information, visit: http://healthsciences.howard.edu/education/colleges/dentistry/programs/predoctoral-programs/BS-DDS-combined-education-program

International Dentist Program available for foreign-trained dentists seeking to practice in the U.S. For more information on this program, visit: http://healthsciences.howard.edu/education/colleges/dentistry/programs/predoctoral-programs/international-dentist-program

Important Updates due to COVID-19: N/A

Were tests required? DAT required.

Are tests expected next year? Yes.

ALABAMA

ARKANSAS

DELAWARE

DISTRICT OF COLUMBIA

FLORIDA

GEORGIA

KENTUCKY

LOUISIANA

MARYLAND

MISSISSIPPI

NORTH CAROLINA

OKLAHOMA

SOUTH CAROLINA

TENNESSEE

TEXAS

VIRGINIA

WEST VIRGINIA

SOUTH

LAKE ERIE COLLEGE OF OSTEOPATHIC MEDICINE SCHOOL OF DENTAL MEDICINE

Address: 4800 Lakewood Ranch Boulevard, Bradenton, FL 34211
Website: *https://lecom.edu/academics/school-of-dental-medicine/*
Contact: *https://lecom.edu/contact-us/*
Phone: (941) 405-1500

COST OF ATTENDANCE

Tuition: $55,130
Fees & Indirect Costs: $45,893
Total: $101,023

Financial Aid: https://lecom.edu/admissions/tuition-and-financial-aid/school-of-dental-medicine-tuition-financial-aid/financial-aid-outside-scholarshipsawards/

ADDITIONAL INFORMATION

Interesting tidbit: The Lake Erie College of Osteopathic Medicine (LECOM) is the nation's largest Dental college and is the only Academic Health Center in the osteopathic profession. The Doctor of Dental Medicine curriculum is modeled on Problem-Based Learning whose courses emphasize self-directed study with a team approach through mentored case studies.

What international experiences are available? N/A

What dual degree options exist? No dual degree options listed.

What service learning opportunities exist? N/A

Important Updates due to COVID-19: N/A

Were tests required? DAT required.

Are tests expected next year? Yes.

NOVA SOUTHEASTERN UNIVERSITY COLLEGE OF DENTAL MEDICINE

Address: 3301 College Avenue, Fort Lauderdale, Florida 33314
Website: *https://dental.nova.edu/index.html*
Contact: *https://apply.nova.edu/Ellucian.Erecruiting.Web.External/ Pages/prospectinquiry*
Phone: (800) 541-6682

COST OF ATTENDANCE

In-State Tuition: N/A
Fees & Indirect Costs: $37,700
Total: $37,700*

Out-of-State Tuition: N/A
Fees & Indirect Costs: $37,700
Total: $37,700

*Tuition information is not provided.

Financial Aid: https://dental.nova.edu/doctoral/finaid.html

ADDITIONAL INFORMATION

Interesting tidbit: NSU College of Dental Medicine is Florida's first private college of dentistry. It is also the first U.S dental college established in partnership with a College of Osteopathic Medicine.

What international experiences are available? Dental missions available.

What dual degree options exist? Dual degree programs available. For more information, visit: https://dental.nova.edu/doctoral/ dodmd.html

What service learning opportunities exist? Oral cancer walk and other opportunities.

Other: International program available for foreign-trained dentists seeking to practice in the U.S. For more information, visit: https:// dental.nova.edu/international/index.html

Important Updates due to COVID-19: N/A

Were tests required? DAT required.

Are tests expected next year? Yes.

ALABAMA
ARKANSAS
DELAWARE
DISTRICT OF COLUMBIA
FLORIDA
GEORGIA
KENTUCKY
LOUISIANA
MARYLAND
MISSISSIPPI
NORTH CAROLINA
OKLAHOMA
SOUTH CAROLINA
TENNESSEE
TEXAS
VIRGINIA
WEST VIRGINIA

SOUTH

ALABAMA

ARKANSAS

DELAWARE

DISTRICT OF
COLUMBIA

FLORIDA

GEORGIA

KENTUCKY

LOUISIANA

MARYLAND

MISSISSIPPI

NORTH CAROLINA

OKLAHOMA

SOUTH CAROLINA

TENNESSEE

TEXAS

VIRGINIA

WEST VIRGINIA

UNIVERSITY OF FLORIDA COLLEGE OF DENTISTRY

Address: 1395 Center Drive, Gainesville, FL 32610
Website: *https://dental.ufl.edu/*
Contact: *https://dental.ufl.edu/about/contact-information/*
Phone: (352) 273-6700

COST OF ATTENDANCE

In-State Tuition: $37,566
Fees & Indirect Costs: $39,910
Total: $77,476

Out-of-State Tuition: $64,046
Fees & Indirect Costs: $39,910
Total: $103,956

Financial Aid: https://admissions.dental.ufl.edu/financial-aid/d-m-d/scholarships-d-m-d/

ADDITIONAL INFORMATION

Interesting tidbit: UF College of Dentistry is the only publicly-funded dental school in Florida. For the sixth consecutive year the college received the Higher Education Excellence in Diversity Award (HEED Award), making it one of 45 HEED Award winners.

What international experiences are available? Service trips abroad. For more information, visit: https://dental.ufl.edu/education/dmd-program/service-opportunities-international-experience/

What dual degree options exist? Dual degree programs available. For more information, visit: https://research.dental.ufl.edu/student-resource/dmd-phd-program/

What service learning opportunities exist? See international experiences.

Other: BS/DMD accelerated 7-year program available for college freshmen. For more information, visit: https://admissions.dental.ufl.edu/d-m-d/combined-programs/b-s-d-m-d/

Important Updates due to COVID-19: N/A

Were tests required? DAT required.

Are tests expected next year? Yes.

DENTAL COLLEGE OF GEORGIA AT AUGUSTA UNIVERSITY

Address: 1430 John Wesley Gilbert Drive, Augusta, GA 30912
Website: *https://www.augusta.edu/dentalmedicine/*
Contact: *https://www.augusta.edu/about/contact.php*
Phone: (706) 721-3587

COST OF ATTENDANCE

In-State Tuition: $25,544
Fees & Indirect Costs: $17,343
Total: $43,341

Out-of-State Tuition: $62,816
Fees & Indirect Costs: $17,343
Total: $80,613

Financial Aid: https://www.augusta.edu/finaid/dental medicine

ADDITIONAL INFORMATION

Interesting tidbit: The Dental College of Georgia is the state's sole dental college. The DCG boasts one of the most impressive clinical buildings in the country that has won engineering and construction management awards for best project and is silver-LEED certified.

What international experiences are available? International exchange program available.

What dual degree options exist? Oral Biology MS/PhD available. For more information, visit: https://www.augusta.edu/dentalmedicine/academics/departments/oralbio/programs.php

DMD/MBA program available. For more information, visit: http://catalog.augusta.edu/preview_program.php?catoid=30&poid=4725&returnto=3565

What service learning opportunities exist? Dental students have a 25-hour community service requirement each year.

Important Updates due to COVID-19: N/A

Were tests required? DAT required.

Are tests expected next year? Yes.

ALABAMA
ARKANSAS
DELAWARE
DISTRICT OF COLUMBIA
FLORIDA
GEORGIA
KENTUCKY
LOUISIANA
MARYLAND
MISSISSIPPI
NORTH CAROLINA
OKLAHOMA
SOUTH CAROLINA
TENNESSEE
TEXAS
VIRGINIA
WEST VIRGINIA

SOUTH

ALABAMA

ARKANSAS

DELAWARE

DISTRICT OF
COLUMBIA

FLORIDA

GEORGIA

KENTUCKY

LOUISIANA

MARYLAND

MISSISSIPPI

NORTH CAROLINA

OKLAHOMA

SOUTH CAROLINA

TENNESSEE

TEXAS

VIRGINIA

WEST VIRGINIA

UNIVERSITY OF KENTUCKY COLLEGE OF DENTISTRY

Address: 800 Rose St., Lexington, KY 40536
Website: *https://dentistry.uky.edu/*
Contact: *https://dentistry.uky.edu/prospective-student-inquiry*
Phone: (859) 323-3368

COST OF ATTENDANCE

In-State Tuition: $34,822
Fees & Indirect Costs: $14,426
Total: $49,248

Out-of-State Tuition: $75,922
Fees & Indirect Costs: $14,426
Total: $90,348

Financial Aid: https://dentistry.uky.edu/scholarships

ADDITIONAL INFORMATION

Interesting tidbit: Incoming DMD students interested in taking part in an intensive research experience in conjunction with their dental curriculum have the option of applying for theU.K. College of Dentistry Research Track program of study.

What international experiences are available? Humanitarian trips available.

What dual degree options exist? No dual degree options listed.

What service learning opportunities exist? Saturday Morning Clinics, volunteer work at local clinics, and school-based trips to Eastern Kentucky available.

Important Updates due to COVID-19: N/A

Were tests required? DAT required.

Are tests expected next year? Yes.

UNIVERSITY OF LOUISVILLE SCHOOL OF DENTISTRY

Address: 501 S. Preston St., Louisville, KY 40202
Website: *https://louisville.edu/dentistry*
Contact: *https://louisville.edu/dentistry/degrees/dmd/contact*
Phone: (502) 852-5081

COST OF ATTENDANCE

In-State Tuition: $35,532
Fees & Indirect Costs: $7,801*
Total: $42,299

Out-of-State Tuition: $74,128
Fees & Indirect Costs: $7,801*
Total: $79,771

*Note: This figure is only for mandatory fees and does not include other indirect costs.

Financial Aid: https://louisville.edu/dentistry/financialaid

ADDITIONAL INFORMATION

Interesting tidbit: University of Louisville School of Dentistry is a proponent of competency-based dental education - what students learn is based upon clearly articulated competencies. Its curriculum assumes that all behaviors/abilities are supported by foundation knowledge and psychomotor skills in bioDental, behavioral, ethical, clinical dental science and information management that are essential for independent and unsupervised performance.

What international experiences are available? Interdisciplinary healthcare missions abroad available. For more information, visit: https://louisville.edu/dentistry/outreach/international-service-learning

What dual degree options exist? DMD/PhD program available. For more information, visit: https://louisville.edu/dentistry/degrees/oralbiology/dmd-phd

For information on the DMD/MS, visit: https://louisville.edu/dentistry/degrees/oralbiology/dmd-msob

For information on the DMD/MBA, visit: https://business.louisville.edu/academics-programs/graduate-programs/dualmba/

What service learning opportunities exist? Various opportunities available. For more information, visit: https://louisville.edu/dentistry/outreach/community-dental-health-service-learning

Other: Early admission opportunity (ULEAD) for high school seniors. For more information, visit: https://louisville.edu/dentistry/degrees/dmd/ulead

Important Updates due to COVID-19: ULSD amended its admissions policy to accept both letter grades and pass/fail (satisfactory/unsatisfactory) marks for the Spring/Winter 2020 semester. Also, it recommended applicants consider submitting their applications without DAT scores and take the test at the earliest possible future date.

Were tests required? DAT required.

Are tests expected next year? Yes.

ALABAMA
ARKANSAS
DELAWARE
DISTRICT OF COLUMBIA
FLORIDA
GEORGIA
KENTUCKY
LOUISIANA
MARYLAND
MISSISSIPPI
NORTH CAROLINA
OKLAHOMA
SOUTH CAROLINA
TENNESSEE
TEXAS
VIRGINIA
WEST VIRGINIA

SOUTH

ALABAMA

ARKANSAS

DELAWARE

DISTRICT OF
COLUMBIA

FLORIDA

GEORGIA

KENTUCKY

LOUISIANA

MARYLAND

MISSISSIPPI

NORTH CAROLINA

OKLAHOMA

SOUTH CAROLINA

TENNESSEE

TEXAS

VIRGINIA

WEST VIRGINIA

LOUISIANA STATE UNIVERSITY HEALTH NEW ORLEANS SCHOOL OF DENTISTRY

Address: 1100 Florida Avenue, New Orleans, LA 70119
Website: *https://www.lsusd.lsuhsc.edu/*
Contact: *https://www.lsusd.lsuhsc.edu/contact.html*
Phone: (504) 941-8124

COST OF ATTENDANCE

In-State Tuition: $28,418
Fees & Indirect Costs: $26,772
Total: $55,190

Out-of-State Tuition: $57,146
Fees & Indirect Costs: $26,772
Total: $83,981

Financial Aid: https://www.lsuhsc.edu/financialaid/

ADDITIONAL INFORMATION

Interesting tidbit: Three out of every four dentists and dental hygienists practicing in Louisiana today are graduates of the LSU School of Dentistry. LSUSD is committed to educating dentists throughout their careers and enjoys a national reputation for its continuing education program, which attracts dentists from throughout the United States.

What international experiences are available? N/A

What dual degree options exist? No dual degree options listed.

What service learning opportunities exist? Outreach programs to educate the community about oral health.

Important Updates due to COVID-19: The deadline for application submission was extended from September 1st to November 30th. The general dentistry shadowing hours requirement was reduced from 50 to 25 (minimum). It recommended applicants choose to receive a letter grade rather than a P/F grade when given the option, particularly for courses that are considered pre-requisites. It accepted unofficial DAT scores while waiting for verification in AADSAS.

Were tests required? DAT required.

Are tests expected next year? Yes.

UNIVERSITY OF MARYLAND SCHOOL OF DENTISTRY

Address: 650 W Baltimore St, Baltimore, MD 21201
Website: *https://www.dental.umaryland.edu/*
Contact: *https://www.dental.umaryland.edu/about/contact-us/*
Phone: (410) 706-7472

COST OF ATTENDANCE

In-State Tuition: $42,080.50
*Fees & Indirect Costs: $21,501
Total: $63,581.50

Out-of-State Tuition: $78,237.60
*Fees & Indirect Costs: $21,501
Total: $99,738.60

*Note: These figures do not include living or other indirect costs.

Financial Aid: https://www.umaryland.edu/fin/school-specific-information/dentistry/

ADDITIONAL INFORMATION

Interesting tidbit: As the world's first dental college, the University of Maryland School of Dentistry played a seminal role in the development of science-based dental education. The present dental school evolved through a series of consolidations involving the Baltimore College of Dental Surgery (BCDS), a school that engendered the practice of dentistry 177 years ago by establishing and promoting formal dental education and in the development of dentistry as a profession.

What international experiences are available? Global Dental Organization available. For more information, visit: https://www.dental.umaryland.edu/studentaffairs/student-organizations/global-dental-organization/

What dual degree options exist? Dual degree programs available. For more information, visit: https://www.dental.umaryland.edu/admissions/programs/dds-dual-degree-program/

What service learning opportunities exist? For information on community service opportunities, visit: https://www.dental.umaryland.edu/studentaffairs/community-service-/

Important Updates due to COVID-19: The school accepted P/F grading for SPRING 2020 and FALL 2021. It also placed application files on hold as applicants awaited their official DAT scores and modified its admissions cycle to accommodate the late receipt of some DAT scores.

Were tests required? DAT required.

Are tests expected next year? Yes.

ALABAMA
ARKANSAS
DELAWARE
DISTRICT OF COLUMBIA
FLORIDA
GEORGIA
KENTUCKY
LOUISIANA
MARYLAND
MISSISSIPPI
NORTH CAROLINA
OKLAHOMA
SOUTH CAROLINA
TENNESSEE
TEXAS
VIRGINIA
WEST VIRGINIA

SOUTH

ALABAMA

ARKANSAS

DELAWARE

DISTRICT OF
COLUMBIA

FLORIDA

GEORGIA

KENTUCKY

LOUISIANA

MARYLAND

MISSISSIPPI

NORTH CAROLINA

OKLAHOMA

SOUTH CAROLINA

TENNESSEE

TEXAS

VIRGINIA

WEST VIRGINIA

UNIVERSITY OF MISSISSIPPI DENTAL CENTER SCHOOL OF DENTISTRY

Address: 2500 N. State St., Jackson, MS 39216
Website: *https://www.umc.edu/sod/SOD_Home.html*
Contact: *https://www.umc.edu/sod/About%20Us/Contact%20Us.html*
Phone: (601) 984-6155

COST OF ATTENDANCE

Tuition: $31,166
Fees & Indirect Costs: $36,450
Total: $67,616

Financial Aid: https://www.umc.edu/Office%20of%20Academic%20Affairs/For-Students/Student%20Financial%20Aid/Student-Financial-Aid.html

ADDITIONAL INFORMATION

Interesting tidbit: The University of Mississippi School of Dentistry is the state's only dental school. The School of Dentistry is one of seven schools at The University of Mississippi Dental Center (UMC), which functions as a separately funded, semi-autonomous unit from eight state institutions of higher learning in Mississippi.

What international experiences are available? Global Health Student Association available.

What dual degree options exist? No dual degree options listed.

What service learning opportunities exist? For information on community oral health, visit: https://www.umc.edu/sod/Departments/Pediatric-Dentistry-and-Community-Oral-Health/Outreach.html

Important Updates due to COVID-19: N/A

Were tests required? DAT required.

Are tests expected next year? Yes.

EAST CAROLINA UNIVERSITY SCHOOL OF DENTAL MEDICINE

Address: 1851 MacGregor Downs Road, Greenville, NC 27834
Website: *https://www.ecu.edu/cs-dhs/dental/*
Contact: *https://www.ecu.edu/cs-dhs/dental/contactus.cfm*
Phone: (252) 737-7000

COST OF ATTENDANCE

Tuition: $36,689
Fees & Indirect Costs: $37,978
Total: $74,667

Financial Aid: https://www.ecu.edu/cs-acad/financial/availableaid.cfm

ADDITIONAL INFORMATION

Interesting tidbit: The East Carolina University School of Dental Medicine is a state-supported professional school. Enrollment is limited to residents of North Carolina only.

What international experiences are available? Global outreach opportunities available. For more information, visit: https://www.ecu.edu/cs-dhs/dental/abroad.cfm

What dual degree options exist? No dual degree options listed.

What service learning opportunities exist? For information on community service learning opportunities, visit: https://www.ecu.edu/cs-dhs/dental/cslc.cfm

Important Updates due to COVID-19: N/A

Were tests required? DAT required.

Are tests expected next year? Yes.

ALABAMA
ARKANSAS
DELAWARE
DISTRICT OF COLUMBIA
FLORIDA
GEORGIA
KENTUCKY
LOUISIANA
MARYLAND
MISSISSIPPI
NORTH CAROLINA
OKLAHOMA
SOUTH CAROLINA
TENNESSEE
TEXAS
VIRGINIA
WEST VIRGINIA

SOUTH

ALABAMA

ARKANSAS

DELAWARE

DISTRICT OF COLUMBIA

FLORIDA

GEORGIA

KENTUCKY

LOUISIANA

MARYLAND

MISSISSIPPI

NORTH CAROLINA

OKLAHOMA

SOUTH CAROLINA

TENNESSEE

TEXAS

VIRGINIA

WEST VIRGINIA

UNIVERSITY OF NORTH CAROLINA AT CHAPEL HILL ADAMS SCHOOL OF DENTISTRY

Address: 385 S Columbia St, Chapel Hill, NC 27599
Website: *https://www.dentistry.unc.edu/*
Contact: *https://www.dentistry.unc.edu/contact/*
Phone: (919) 962-2211

COST OF ATTENDANCE

In-State Tuition: $35,607
*Fees & Indirect Costs: $5,038.14
Total: $40,645.14

Out-of-State Tuition: $62,124
*Fees & Indirect Costs: $5,038.14
Total: $67,162.14

*Note: These figures only include required fees and do not include other indirect costs.

Financial Aid: https://www.dentistry.unc.edu/academicprograms/ dds/tuition-and-financial-aid/

ADDITIONAL INFORMATION

Interesting tidbit: The University of North Carolina at Chapel Hill Adams School of Dentistry is North Carolina's first dental school. Its curriculum is based on the Advocate-Clinician-Thinker framework: advocating for your patients, providing clinical care at the top of the profession, and staying mentally agile so you can critically think while determining a course of care.

What international experiences are available? International service and outreach available. For more information, visit: https:// www.dentistry.unc.edu/service/international/

What dual degree options exist? Dual degree programs available. For more information, visit:

What service learning opportunities exist? Student-led Service and Outreach, Dentistry in Service to Communities (DISC) Program, and other opportunities. For more information, visit: https://www. dentistry.unc.edu/service/

Other: Advanced Standing Program for International Dentists available. For more information, visit: https://www.dentistry.unc. edu/academicprograms/dds/advanced-standing-for-international-dentists/

Important Updates due to COVID-19: The school accepted Pass/ Fail grades for prerequisite courses. It also temporarily suspended our DAT testing requirement for the 2020-2021 application cycle.

Were tests required? DAT not required for the 2020-2021 application cycle.

Are tests expected next year? Yes.

UNIVERSITY OF OKLAHOMA COLLEGE OF DENTISTRY

Address: 1201 N. Stonewall Ave., Oklahoma City, OK 73117
Website: *https://dentistry.ouhsc.edu/*
Contact: *Contact via phone.*
Phone: (405) 271-7744

COST OF ATTENDANCE

In-State Tuition: $48,072
*Fees & Indirect Costs: $28,322
Total: $76,394

Out-of-State Tuition: $81,208
*Fees & Indirect Costs: $28,322
Total: $109,530

*Note: These figures include mandatory fees only and do not include other indirect costs.

Financial Aid: http://www.ou.edu/admissions/affordability/financial-aid

ADDITIONAL INFORMATION

Interesting tidbit: A high priority is placed on the integration of research with the educational mission of the OU College of Dentistry. A Student Research Program provides stipends and other support for students to participate in meaningful research activities under faculty mentorship.

What international experiences are available? N/A

What dual degree options exist? No dual degree options listed.

What service learning opportunities exist? N/A

Other: Advanced Standing Program for foreign-trained dentists available. For more information, visit: https://dentistry.ouhsc.edu/Prospective-Students/Programs-Offered/ASPID

Important Updates due to COVID-19: N/A

Were tests required? DAT required.

Are tests expected next year? Yes.

ALABAMA

ARKANSAS

DELAWARE

DISTRICT OF COLUMBIA

FLORIDA

GEORGIA

KENTUCKY

LOUISIANA

MARYLAND

MISSISSIPPI

NORTH CAROLINA

OKLAHOMA

SOUTH CAROLINA

TENNESSEE

TEXAS

VIRGINIA

WEST VIRGINIA

SOUTH

ALABAMA

ARKANSAS

DELAWARE

DISTRICT OF
COLUMBIA

FLORIDA

GEORGIA

KENTUCKY

LOUISIANA

MARYLAND

MISSISSIPPI

NORTH CAROLINA

OKLAHOMA

SOUTH CAROLINA

TENNESSEE

TEXAS

VIRGINIA

WEST VIRGINIA

DENTAL UNIVERSITY OF SOUTH CAROLINA JAMES B. EDWARDS COLLEGE OF DENTAL MEDICINE

Address: 173 Ashley Avenue, Charleston, SC 29425
Website: *https://dentistry.musc.edu/*
Contact: *https://dentistry.musc.edu/about/contact*
Phone: (843) 792-4892

COST OF ATTENDANCE

In-State Tuition: $69,010
Fees & Indirect Costs: $35,170
Total: $104,180

Out-of-State Tuition: $104,885
Fees & Indirect Costs: $35,170
Total: $140,055

Financial Aid: https://dentistry.musc.edu/programs/admissions/scholarships

ADDITIONAL INFORMATION

Interesting tidbit: As South Carolina's only dental school, the MUSC College of Dental Medicine is an important source of dentists in a state that is currently under-served in terms of dental care.

What international experiences are available? Mission trips available.

What dual degree options exist? No dual degree options listed.

What service learning opportunities exist? Oral cancer screenings, community outreach, etc. For more information, visit: https://education.musc.edu/students/spsd/musc-gives-back

Important Updates due to COVID-19: N/A

Were tests required? DAT required.

Are tests expected next year? Yes.

MEHARRY DENTAL COLLEGE SCHOOL OF DENTISTRY

Address: 1005 Dr DB Todd Jr Blvd, Nashville, TN 37208
Website: *https://home.mmc.edu/school-of-dentistry/*
Contact: *Contact via phone*
Phone: (615) 327-6207

COST OF ATTENDANCE

Tuition: $55,598
Fees & Indirect Costs: $45,218
Total: $100,816

Financial Aid: https://home.mmc.edu/financial-aid/

ADDITIONAL INFORMATION

Interesting tidbit: Meharry Dental College is the nation's largest private, historically black academic health sciences center. Meharry is a United Methodist Church-affiliated institution whose motto is "Worship of God Through Service to Mankind."

What international experiences are available? N/A

What dual degree options exist? DDS/PhD program available.

What service learning opportunities exist? Adopt-a-Grandparent program to provide dental care to low income seniors. For more information on community initiatives, visit: https://home.mmc.edu/community-initiatives/

Important Updates due to COVID-19: N/A

Were tests required? DAT required.

Are tests expected next year? Yes.

ALABAMA
ARKANSAS
DELAWARE
DISTRICT OF COLUMBIA
FLORIDA
GEORGIA
KENTUCKY
LOUISIANA
MARYLAND
MISSISSIPPI
NORTH CAROLINA
OKLAHOMA
SOUTH CAROLINA
TENNESSEE
TEXAS
VIRGINIA
WEST VIRGINIA

SOUTH

ALABAMA

ARKANSAS

DELAWARE

DISTRICT OF
COLUMBIA

FLORIDA

GEORGIA

KENTUCKY

LOUISIANA

MARYLAND

MISSISSIPPI

NORTH CAROLINA

OKLAHOMA

SOUTH CAROLINA

TENNESSEE

TEXAS

VIRGINIA

WEST VIRGINIA

UNIVERSITY OF TENNESSEE HEALTH SCIENCE CENTER COLLEGE OF DENTISTRY

Address: 875 Union Avenue, Memphis, TN 38163
Website: *https://www.uthsc.edu/dentistry/*
Contact: *https://www.uthsc.edu/contacts/*
Phone: (901) 448-6200

COST OF ATTENDANCE

In-State Tuition: $30,388
Fees & Indirect Costs: $43,768
Total: $74,156

Out-of-State Tuition: $69,148
Fees & Indirect Costs: $43,768
Total: $112,916

Financial Aid: https://uthsc.edu/financial-aid/

ADDITIONAL INFORMATION

Interesting tidbit: The UTHSC College of Dentistry is the oldest dental college in the South, and the third oldest public college of dentistry in the United States. It interacts with simulated patients in the Kaplan Clinical Skills Center to practice scenarios with patients that they may encounter in actual practice.

What international experiences are available? N/A

What dual degree options exist? No dual degree options listed.

What service learning opportunities exist? Tennessee Smiles Oral Health Outreach Initiative and other opportunities available.

Important Updates due to COVID-19: If submitting P/F grading or online coursework, applicants must provide documentation from their school's Registrar or Academic Counselor that earning a letter grade was not possible or the course/lab was not offered in a face-to-face format.

Were tests required? DAT required.

Are tests expected next year? Yes.

TEXAS A&M COLLEGE OF DENTISTRY

Address: 3302 Gaston Ave., Dallas, TX 75246
Website: *https://dentistry.tamu.edu/*
Contact: *https://dentistry.tamu.edu/about/contacts.html*
Phone: (214) 828-8100

COST OF ATTENDANCE

In-State Tuition: $37,754
Fees & Indirect Costs: $29,811
Total: $67,565

Out-of-State Tuition: $48,554
Fees & Indirect Costs: $29,811
Total: $78,771

Financial Aid: https://financialaid.tamu.edu/Graduate/Types-of-Aid

ADDITIONAL INFORMATION

Interesting tidbit: Texas A&M College of Dentistry participates in the Texas Dental and Dental Schools Application Service (TMDSAS), a central processing service that allows the applicant to apply to any or all of the dental schools in the State of Texas. Texas Residents must apply through the TMDSAS. Out-of-state applicants have three application options: they may apply through the TMDSAS, through AADSAS or with the College of Dentistry's online application. However, out-of-state applicants who apply through AADSAS must also submit the Texas A&M College of Dentistry application.

What international experiences are available? N/A

What dual degree options exist? No dual degree options listed.

What service learning opportunities exist? Outreach opportunities available. For more information, visit: https://dentistry.tamu.edu/outreach/index.html

Important Updates due to COVID-19: N/A

Were tests required? DAT required.

Are tests expected next year? Yes.

ALABAMA
ARKANSAS
DELAWARE
DISTRICT OF COLUMBIA
FLORIDA
GEORGIA
KENTUCKY
LOUISIANA
MARYLAND
MISSISSIPPI
NORTH CAROLINA
OKLAHOMA
SOUTH CAROLINA
TENNESSEE
TEXAS
VIRGINIA
WEST VIRGINIA

SOUTH

ALABAMA

ARKANSAS

DELAWARE

DISTRICT OF
COLUMBIA

FLORIDA

GEORGIA

KENTUCKY

LOUISIANA

MARYLAND

MISSISSIPPI

NORTH CAROLINA

OKLAHOMA

SOUTH CAROLINA

TENNESSEE

TEXAS

VIRGINIA

WEST VIRGINIA

TEXAS TECH UNIVERSITY HEALTH SCIENCES CENTER EL PASO WOODY L. HUNT SCHOOL OF DENTAL MEDICINE

Address: 5001 El Paso Dr., El Paso, TX 79905
Website: *https://elpaso.ttuhsc.edu/sdm/*
Contact: *Contact on sidebar of page: https://elpaso.ttuhsc.edu/sdm/ admissions/default.aspx*
Phone: (915) 215-8000

COST OF ATTENDANCE

In-State Tuition: $39,171
Fees & Indirect Costs: $35,860
Total: $75,031

Out-of-State Tuition: $59,171
Fees & Indirect Costs: $35,860
Total: $95,031

Financial Aid: https://elpaso.ttuhsc.edu/sdm/admissions/financial-aid.aspx

ADDITIONAL INFORMATION

Interesting tidbit: The Woody L. Hunt School of Dental Medicine curriculum adopts an integrative model that will implement a symptoms-based approach for learning throughout its behavioral, bioDental, and clinical courses. In addition to earning a DMD, students will graduate with a community health certificate, having completed the first 15 hours toward a Master of Public Health degree.

What international experiences are available? N/A

What dual degree options exist? No dual degree options.

What service learning opportunities exist? Oral Health Clinic. For more information, visit: https://elpaso.ttuhsc.edu/sdm/oral-health-clinic.aspx

Note: Texas Tech will admit their inaugural class in 2021. Therefore, limited data is available. The inaugural class will seat 40 students. Each year after that, 60 students will be seated.

Important Updates due to COVID-19: WLHSDM accepted all courses graded as pass/fail or credit/no-credit as equivalent to graded courses during the COVID-19 pandemic, specifically the spring 2020 academic term (including winter 2020 quarter term). It accepted online/hybrid prerequisite coursework for Fall 2020 and Spring 2021. It extended the application and interview timelines to accommodate DAT testing disruption.

Were tests required? DAT required.

Are tests expected next year? Yes.

THE UNIVERSITY OF TEXAS SCHOOL OF DENTISTRY AT HOUSTON

Address: 7500 Cambridge St., Houston, TX 77054
Website: *https://dentistry.uth.edu/*
Contact: *https://dentistry.uth.edu/about/contact-us.htm*
Phone: (713) 486-4000

COST OF ATTENDANCE

In-State Tuition: $30,869
Fees & Indirect Costs: $45,234
Total: $76,103

Out-of-State Tuition: $47,510
Fees & Indirect Costs: $45,234
Total: $92,744

Financial Aid: https://www.uth.edu/sfs/financial-aid/types-of-financial-aid/scholarships.htm

ADDITIONAL INFORMATION

Interesting tidbit: The University of Texas School of Dentistry at Houston was the first dental school in Texas and was a founding institution of the world-renowned Texas Dental Center. The School of Dentistry comprises three research centers: the Center for Craniofacial Research, the Center for Oral Health Quality and Research Informatics and the Houston Center for Biomimetic and Biomaterials.

What international experiences are available? N/A

What dual degree options exist? No dual degree options listed.

What service learning opportunities exist? Service learning opportunities through coursework (e.g., Geriatric Oral Health Care Needs in the Community).

Important Updates due to COVID-19: N/A

Were tests required? DAT required.

Are tests expected next year? Yes.

ALABAMA

ARKANSAS

DELAWARE

DISTRICT OF COLUMBIA

FLORIDA

GEORGIA

KENTUCKY

LOUISIANA

MARYLAND

MISSISSIPPI

NORTH CAROLINA

OKLAHOMA

SOUTH CAROLINA

TENNESSEE

TEXAS

VIRGINIA

WEST VIRGINIA

SOUTH

ALABAMA

ARKANSAS

DELAWARE

DISTRICT OF
COLUMBIA

FLORIDA

GEORGIA

KENTUCKY

LOUISIANA

MARYLAND

MISSISSIPPI

NORTH CAROLINA

OKLAHOMA

SOUTH CAROLINA

TENNESSEE

TEXAS

VIRGINIA

WEST VIRGINIA

UT HEALTH SAN ANTONIO SCHOOL OF DENTISTRY

Address: 7703 Floyd Curl Drive, San Antonio, TX 78229
Website: *https://www.uthscsa.edu/academics/dental*
Contact: *https://www.uthscsa.edu/academics/dental/school-dentistry-administration*
Phone: (210) 567-7000

COST OF ATTENDANCE

In-State Tuition: $24,150
Fees & Indirect Costs: $44,490
Total: $68,640

Out-of-State Tuition: $34,950
Fees & Indirect Costs: $44,490
Total: $79,440

Financial Aid: https://www.uthscsa.edu/academics/dental/tuition-and-financial-aid

ADDITIONAL INFORMATION

Interesting tidbit: One goal of the School of Dentistry is to provide community-based services with a focus on South Texas. Patients in underserved areas of South Texas find that dental care from UT Dentistry can come to them on wheels.

What international experiences are available? N/A

What dual degree options exist? Dual degree programs available. For more information, visit: https://www.uthscsa.edu/academics/dental/programs/phd-in-dentistry

What service learning opportunities exist? Community-based dental training programs. For more information, visit: https://www.uthscsa.edu/academics/dental/deon/dental-education-outreach-network-deon

Other: Dental Early Acceptance (3+4) Program available to high school applicants. For more information, visit: https://www.uthscsa.edu/academics/dental/programs/deap-program

Important Updates due to COVID-19: UT Health San Antonio School of Dentistry was flexible in the graded requirements for prerequisite coursework if an applicant attends a school which made system-wide online format changes for the spring 2020 (including winter 2020 quarter term) and summer 2020 academic terms. It also accepted pass/fail grades for Spring 2020 coursework.

Were tests required? DAT required.

Are tests expected next year? Yes.

VIRGINIA COMMONWEALTH UNIVERSITY SCHOOL OF DENTISTRY

Address: 520 North 12th Street, Richmond, VA 23298
Website: *https://dentistry.vcu.edu/*
Contact: *https://dentistry.vcu.edu/contacts/*
Phone: (804) 828-9196

COST OF ATTENDANCE

In-State Tuition: $41,615
Fees & Indirect Costs: $53,953
Total: $95,568

Out-of-State Tuition: $73,325
Fees & Indirect Costs: $53,953
Total: $127,938

Financial Aid: https://intranet.dentistry.vcu.edu/incoming/dds/financial-aid-information/

ADDITIONAL INFORMATION

Interesting tidbit: The curriculum in the dental school is organized into a competency-based four-year program and emphasizes study in three broad areas: bioDental sciences, clinical sciences and behavioral sciences.

What international experiences are available? Study abroad programs available. For more information, visit: https://dentalpublichealth.vcu.edu/abroad/

What dual degree options exist? No dual degree options listed.

What service learning opportunities exist? Various community outreach opportunities. For more information, visit: https://dentistry.vcu.edu/community/

Other: Guaranteed Admissions Program available for five high school students.

For information on the Advanced Standing Program, visit: https://dentistry.vcu.edu/programs/dds/advanced/

For information on the International Dentist Program, visit: https://dentistry.vcu.edu/programs/internationaldentists/

Important Updates due to COVID-19: N/A

Were tests required? DAT required.

Are tests expected next year? Yes.

ALABAMA
ARKANSAS
DELAWARE
DISTRICT OF COLUMBIA
FLORIDA
GEORGIA
KENTUCKY
LOUISIANA
MARYLAND
MISSISSIPPI
NORTH CAROLINA
OKLAHOMA
SOUTH CAROLINA
TENNESSEE
TEXAS
VIRGINIA
WEST VIRGINIA

SOUTH

ALABAMA

ARKANSAS

DELAWARE

DISTRICT OF
COLUMBIA

FLORIDA

GEORGIA

KENTUCKY

LOUISIANA

MARYLAND

MISSISSIPPI

NORTH CAROLINA

OKLAHOMA

SOUTH CAROLINA

TENNESSEE

TEXAS

VIRGINIA

WEST VIRGINIA

WEST VIRGINIA UNIVERSITY SCHOOL OF DENTISTRY

Address: 1 Medical Center Dr, Morgantown, WV 26505
Website: *https://dentistry.wvu.edu/*
Contact: *https://dentistry.wvu.edu/about/contact-us/*
Phone: (304) 293-6646

COST OF ATTENDANCE

Tuition: $25,506
Fees & Indirect Costs: $26,930
Total: $52,436

Financial Aid: https://graduateadmissions.wvu.edu/cost-and-aid

ADDITIONAL INFORMATION

Interesting tidbit: It is one of only 115 higher education institutions in the U.S. to receive the Carnegie R1 designation for the level of scientific activity and graduate education on campus. It boasts that 100% of its graduates receive immediate job offers.

What international experiences are available? Mission trip to Guatemala.

What dual degree options exist? No dual degree options listed.

What service learning opportunities exist? Several community service projects available. For more information, visit: https://dentistry.wvu.edu/outreach/

Dental students must complete rural rotations to serve in underserved communities. For more information, visit: https://dentistry.wvu.edu/outreach/rural-rotation/

Other: Early Admission Programs available. For more information, visit: https://dentistry.wvu.edu/students/doctor-of-dental-surgery-dds/early-admission-programs/

Important Updates due to COVID-19: N/A

Were tests required? DAT required.

Are tests expected next year? Yes.

REGION FOUR
WEST

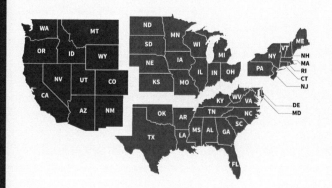

ALASKA

ARIZONA

CALIFORNIA

COLORADO

HAWAII

IDAHO

MONTANA

NEVADA

NEW MEXICO

OREGON

UTAH

WASHINGTON

WYOMING

15 *Programs* | **13** *States*

1. AZ – Arizona School of Dentistry & Oral Health
2. AZ - Midwestern University College of Dental Medicine-Arizona
3. CA - California Northstate College of Dental Medicine
4. CA - Herman Ostrow School of Dentistry of USC
5. CA - Loma Linda University School of Dentistry
6. CA - University of California, Los Angeles, School of Dentistry
7. CA - University of California, San Francisco, School of Dentistry
8. CA - University of the Pacific Arthur A. Dugoni School of Dentistry
9. CA - Western University of Health Sciences College of Dental Medicine
10. CO - University of Colorado School of Dental Medicine
11. NV - University of Nevada, Las Vegas, School of Dental Medicine
12. OR - Oregon Health & Science University School of Dentistry
13. UT - Roseman University of Health Sciences College of Dental Medicine – South Jordan, Utah
14. UT - University of Utah School of Dentistry
15. WA - University of Washington School of Dentistry

Dental School	Ave. GPA & DAT EARLY DECISION (ED) : YES/NO	Admissions Statistics	Science Req. Other Than Gen Chem, Ochem, Physics, Bio
Arizona School of Dentistry & Oral Health 5850 E. Still Circle, Mesa, AZ 85206	3.7 (overall) 3.23 (science) DAT: 19.6 ED: N	**(2019)** Apps Received: 2,236 Admission Offered: 150 Number Enrolled: 76 Acceptance Rate: 6.7% **(2020)** Apps Received: 2,323 Admission Offered: 171 Number Enrolled: 77 Acceptance Rate: 7.4%	Human Physio. Biochem. Human Anatomy
Midwestern University College of Dental Medicine-Arizona 19555 N 59th Ave., Glendale, AZ 85308	3.49 (overall) 3.41 (science) DAT: 20 ED: N	**(2019)** Apps Received: 2,267 Admission Offered: 335 Number Enrolled: 143 Acceptance Rate: 14.8% **(2020)** Apps Received: 2,204 Admission Offered: 319 Number Enrolled: 135 Acceptance Rate: 14.5%	Anatomy w/Lab Physio. Biochem.
California Northstate College of Dental Medicine* 9700 W Taron Dr., Elk Grove, CA 95757	N/A	N/A	Math (Stats./Calc. preferred) Biochem.
Herman Ostrow School of Dentistry of USC 925 W. 34th St., Los Angeles, CA 90089	3.59 (overall) 3.51 (science) DAT: 19.9 ED: N	**(2019)** Apps Received: 2,990 Admission Offered: 242 Number Enrolled: 144 Acceptance Rate: 8% **(2020)** Apps Received: 2,387 Admission Offered: 300 Number Enrolled: 144 Acceptance Rate: 12.6%	See Chart for recommendations.

Dental School	Ave. GPA & DAT EARLY DECISION (ED) : YES/NO	Admissions Statistics	Science Req. Other Than Gen Chem, Ochem, Physics, Bio
Loma Linda University 11092 Anderson St., Loma Linda, CA 92350	3.51 (overall) 3.36 (science) DAT: 20 ED: N	**(2019)** Apps Received: 1,617 Admission Offered: 156 Number Enrolled: 100 Acceptance Rate: 9.6% **(2020)** Apps Received: 1,179 Admission Offered: 137 Number Enrolled: 102 Acceptance Rate: 11.6%	Biochem.
University of California, Los Angeles 714 Tiverton Ave, Los Angeles, CA 90024	3.77 (overall) 3.73 (science) DAT: 23 ED: N	**(2019)** Apps Received: 1,447 Admission Offered: 165 Number Enrolled: 88 Acceptance Rate: 11.4% **(2020)** Apps Received: 1,309 Admission Offered: 133 Number Enrolled: 88 Acceptance Rate: 10.2%	Biochem.
University of California, San Francisco 513 Parnassus Ave, San Francisco, CA 94143	3.62 (overall) 3.56 (science) DAT: 22 ED: N	**(2019)** Apps Received: 1,540 Admission Offered: 145 Number Enrolled: 89 Acceptance Rate: 9.4% **(2020)** Apps Received: 1,412 Admission Offered: 162 Number Enrolled: 88 Acceptance Rate: 11.5%	Biochem. Psych. Additional electives (See Chart)
University of the Pacific 155 Fifth St., San Francisco, CA 94103	3.51 (overall) 3.43 (science) DAT: 22 ED: N	**(2019)** Apps Received: 2,337 Admission Offered: 234 Number Enrolled: 145 Acceptance Rate: 9.9% **(2020)** Apps Received: 2,173 Admission Offered: 250 Number Enrolled: 145 Acceptance Rate: 11.5%	See Chart for recommendations.

WEST

Dental School	Ave. GPA & DAT EARLY DECISION (ED) : YES/NO	Admissions Statistics	Science Req. Other Than Gen Chem, Ochem, Physics, Bio
Western University of Health Sciences 309 E. Second St., Pomona, CA 91766	3.33 (overall) 3.18 (science) DAT: 19.8 ED: N	**(2019)** Apps Received: 2,045 *Interview Received: 371 Admission Offered: N/A Number Enrolled: 70 Acceptance Rate: 5.6% **(2020)** Apps Received: 2,945 Admission Offered: 207 Number Enrolled: 70 Acceptance Rate: 7.0%	See Chart for recommendations.
University of Colorado 13065 E. 17th Ave., Aurora, CO 80045	3.56 (overall) 3.46 (science) DAT: 21 ED: N	**(2019)** Apps Received: 2,007 Admission Offered: 80 Number Enrolled: 80 Acceptance Rate: 3.9% **(2020)** Apps Received: 2,172 Admission Offered: 155 Number Enrolled: 80 Acceptance Rate: 7.1%	Microbio. Biochem.
University of Nevada, Las Vegas, 1001 Shadow Ln., Las Vegas, NV 89106	3.48 (overall) 3.37 (science) DAT: 21 ED: N	**(2019)** Apps Received: 1,816 Admission Offered: 147 Number Enrolled: 82 Acceptance Rate: 8.1% **(2020)** Apps Received: 1,718 Admission Offered: 167 Number Enrolled: 82 Acceptance Rate: 9.7%	Human Anatomy Biochem.
Oregon Health & Science University School of Dentistry 3181 S.W. Sam Jackson Park Rd., Portland, OR 97239	3.69 (overall) 3.61 (science) DAT: 20.4 ED: N	**(2019)** Apps Received: 1,108 Admission Offered: 140 Number Enrolled: 76 Acceptance Rate: 12.6% **(2020)** Apps Received: 1,000 Admission Offered: 166 Number Enrolled: 78 Acceptance Rate: 16.6%	Human Anatomy and Physio. w/Labs Biochem. w/Lab

Dental School	Ave. GPA & DAT / EARLY DECISION (ED) : YES/NO	Admissions Statistics	Science Req. Other Than Gen Chem, Ochem, Physics, Bio
Roseman University of Health Sciences 10894 S River Front Pkwy, South Jordan, UT 84095	3.28 (overall) 3.14 (science) DAT: 19.5 ED: N	**(2019)** Apps Received: 2,015 Admission Offered: 181 Number Enrolled: 100 Acceptance Rate: 8.9% **(2020)** Apps Received: 1,785 Admission Offered: 214 Number Enrolled: 100 Acceptance Rate: 12.0%	Biochem.
University of Utah School of Dentistry 530 South Wakara Way, Salt Lake City, UT 84108	3.68 (overall) 3.62 (science) DAT: 21 ED: N	**(2019)** Apps Received: 443 Admission Offered: 118 Number Enrolled: 49 Acceptance Rate: 26.6% **(2020)** Apps Received: 510 Admission Offered: 140 Number Enrolled: 50 Acceptance Rate: 27.5%	Anatomy (Human or Comparative) Biochem. Microbio. w/Lab
University of Washington School of Dentistry 1959 NE Pacific St B-307, Seattle, WA 98195	3.60 (overall) 3.50 (science) DAT: 20.8 ED: N	**(2019)** Apps Received: 486 Admission Offered: 105 Number Enrolled: 63 Acceptance Rate: 21.6% **(2020)** Apps Received: 448 Admission Offered: 101 Number Enrolled: 61 Acceptance Rate: 22.5%	Biochem. Microbio. Bio. or Zoology

*Due to COVID-19, the inaugural class is postponed to 2021, pending accreditation. Therefore, no statistics available.
**This figure is based off 2018 data of accepted students (180) divided by applications received (3230).

WEST

ARIZONA SCHOOL OF DENTISTRY & ORAL HEALTH

Address: 5850 E. Still Circle, Mesa, AZ 85206
Website: *https://www.atsu.edu/arizona-school-of-dentistry-and-oral-health*
Contact: *https://www.atsu.edu/connect/contact-atsu*
Phone: (480) 219-6000

COST OF ATTENDANCE

Tuition: $84,494
Fees & Indirect Costs: $43,906
Total: $128,400

Financial Aid: https://www.atsu.edu/department-of-student-affairs/enrollment-services

ADDITIONAL INFORMATION

Interesting tidbit: A.T. Still University's Arizona School of Dentistry & Oral Health (ATSU-ASDOH) is the first dental school in Arizona. In addition to earning a DDM degree, all ASDOH students earn a certificate in public health core concepts.

What international experiences are available? N/A

What dual degree options exist? dual degree program available. For more information, visit: https://www.atsu.edu/arizona-school-of-dentistry-and-oral-health/academics/dmd-mph-dual-degree

What service learning opportunities exist? For information on serving the underserved, visit: https://www.atsu.edu/arizona-school-of-dentistry-and-oral-health/about-asdoh/serving-the-underserved

Important Updates due to COVID-19: N/A

Were tests required? DAT required.

Are tests expected next year? Yes.

MIDWESTERN UNIVERSITY COLLEGE OF DENTAL MEDICINE-ARIZONA

Address: 19555 N 59th Ave., Glendale, AZ 85308
Website: *https://www.midwestern.edu/academics/our-colleges/college-of-dental-medicine*
Contact: *https://online.midwestern.edu/public/reqinfo.cgi*
Phone: (623) 572-3215

COST OF ATTENDANCE

Tuition: $85,931
Fees & Indirect Costs: $45,142
Total: $131,073

Financial Aid: https://www.midwestern.edu/admissions/tuition-and-financial-aid/scholarships.xml

ADDITIONAL INFORMATION

Interesting tidbit: The core curriculum at Midwestern University CDMA is supplemented with course sequences in ethics and professionalism, practice management, advanced clinical dentistry, and community service.

What international experiences are available? N/A

What dual degree options exist? No dual degree options listed.

What service learning opportunities exist? Community outreach opportunities available. For more information, visit: https://www.midwestern.edu/about/who-we-are/community-outreach.xml

Important Updates due to COVID-19: N/A

Were tests required? DAT required.

Are tests expected next year? Yes.

ALASKA

ARIZONA

CALIFORNIA

COLORADO

HAWAII

IDAHO

MONTANA

NEVADA

NEW MEXICO

OREGON

UTAH

WASHINGTON

WYOMING

WEST

ALASKA

ARIZONA

CALIFORNIA

COLORADO

HAWAII

IDAHO

MONTANA

NEVADA

NEW MEXICO

OREGON

UTAH

WASHINGTON

WYOMING

CALIFORNIA NORTHSTATE COLLEGE OF DENTAL MEDICINE

Address: 9700 W Taron Dr., Elk Grove, CA 95757
Website: *http://dentalmedicine.cnsu.edu/*
Contact: *Email list sign-up at bottom of main page.*
Phone: (916) 686-7300

COST OF ATTENDANCE

Tuition: N/A
Fees & Indirect Costs: N/A
Total: N/A

Financial Aid: http://cnsu.edu/student-financial-aid-offices

ADDITIONAL INFORMATION

Interesting tidbit: California Northstate University College of Dental Medicine is America's youngest dental school. Its inaugural class will start in the fall of 2021.

What international experiences are available? N/A

What dual degree options exist? No dual degree options listed.

What service learning opportunities exist? N/A

Other: 3+4 BS/DMD Pathway available.

Note: CNSU will welcome its inaugural class in 2021. Therefore, there is limited information.

Important Updates due to COVID-19: N/A

Were tests required? DAT required.

Are tests expected next year? Yes.

HERMAN OSTROW SCHOOL OF DENTISTRY OF USC

Address: 925 W. 34th St., Los Angeles, CA 90089
Website: *https://dentistry.usc.edu/*
Contact: *https://dentistry.usc.edu/about/contact-us/*
Phone: (213) 740-2800

COST OF ATTENDANCE

Tuition: $103,167
Fees & Indirect Costs: $50,388
Total: $153,555

Financial Aid: https://dentistry.usc.edu/admission/paying-for-dental-school/

ADDITIONAL INFORMATION

Interesting tidbit: First-year DDS students at Ostrow School of Dentistry benefit from significant preclinical experience, education and training in restorative dentistry using simulators, for a seamless transition to direct patient care by the end of year one.

What international experiences are available? N/A

What dual degree options exist? No dual degree options listed.

What service learning opportunities exist? Mobile Dental Clinics, Oral Health Clinics, and other community initiatives. For more information, visit: https://dentistry.usc.edu/community/

Important Updates due to COVID-19: N/A

Were tests required? DAT required.

Are tests expected next year? Yes.

ALASKA

ARIZONA

CALIFORNIA

COLORADO

HAWAII

IDAHO

MONTANA

NEVADA

NEW MEXICO

OREGON

UTAH

WASHINGTON

WYOMING

WEST

ALASKA

ARIZONA

CALIFORNIA

COLORADO

HAWAII

IDAHO

MONTANA

NEVADA

NEW MEXICO

OREGON

UTAH

WASHINGTON

WYOMING

LOMA LINDA UNIVERSITY SCHOOL OF DENTISTRY

Address: 11092 Anderson St., Loma Linda, CA 92350
Website: *https://dentistry.llu.edu/*
Contact: *https://admissions.llu.edu/register/inquire*
Phone: (909) 558-4222

COST OF ATTENDANCE

Tuition: $74,950
Fees & Indirect Costs: $37,504
Total: $112,454

Financial Aid: https://home.llu.edu/campus-and-spiritual-life/
student-services/financial-life/financial-aid/types-of-financial-
aid?rsource=www.llu.edu/students/financial-aid/types-of-aid.php

ADDITIONAL INFORMATION

Interesting tidbit: Loma Linda University School of Dentistry a part
of the Seventh-day Adventist Church's system of higher education.
It provides an environment for learning that emphasizes individual
commitment to Christ, personal integrity, intellectual development,
and community service.

What international experiences are available? International
mission trips available.

What dual degree options exist? No dual degree options listed.

What service learning opportunities exist? The university's motto
is "Service is our Calling". DDS students are required to complete
120+ hours of community service prior to graduation. For more
information, visit: https://dentistry.llu.edu/current-students/
service-learning-program

Other: International Dentist Program available for foreign-trained
dentists seeking to practice in the U.S. For more information, visit:
https://dentistry.llu.edu/admissions/international-dentist-program-
dds

Important Updates due to COVID-19: N/A

Were tests required? DAT required.

Are tests expected next year? Yes.

UNIVERSITY OF CALIFORNIA, LOS ANGELES, SCHOOL OF DENTISTRY

Address: 714 Tiverton Ave, Los Angeles, CA 90024
Website: *https://www.dentistry.ucla.edu/*
Contact: *https://www.dentistry.ucla.edu/contact*
Phone: (310) 825-9789

COST OF ATTENDANCE

In-State Tuition: $47,624
Fees & Indirect Costs: $47,386
Total: $95,010

Out-of-State Tuition: $58,267
Fees & Indirect Costs: $47,386
Total: $105,653

Financial Aid: https://www.dentistry.ucla.edu/learning/financial-aid

ADDITIONAL INFORMATION

Interesting tidbit: UCLA School of Dentistry established a new unit, Innovative Digital Dentistry Systems (iDDS) to create synergy among its existing digital assets and a strategy to acquire new technology. The core mission of this unit is to lead a digital transformation in dental education and oral health care through creativity, innovation, and research.

What international experiences are available? International experiences available through student associations. For more information, visit: https://www.dentistry.ucla.edu/resources/dental-student-associations

What dual degree options exist? dual degree program available. For more information, visit: https://www.dentistry.ucla.edu/learning/ddsphd-degree

What service learning opportunities exist? Care Harbor and Give Kids a Smile outreach opportunities available. For more information, visit: https://www.dentistry.ucla.edu/service/outreach-events

Important Updates due to COVID-19: N/A

Were tests required? DAT required.

Are tests expected next year? Yes.

ALASKA

ARIZONA

CALIFORNIA

COLORADO

HAWAII

IDAHO

MONTANA

NEVADA

NEW MEXICO

OREGON

UTAH

WASHINGTON

WYOMING

WEST

ALASKA

ARIZONA

CALIFORNIA

COLORADO

HAWAII

IDAHO

MONTANA

NEVADA

NEW MEXICO

OREGON

UTAH

WASHINGTON

WYOMING

UNIVERSITY OF CALIFORNIA, SAN FRANCISCO, SCHOOL OF DENTISTRY

Address: 513 Parnassus Ave, San Francisco, CA 94143
Website: *https://dentistry.ucsf.edu/*
Contact: *https://dentistry.ucsf.edu/about/contact*
Phone: (415) 502-5800

COST OF ATTENDANCE

In-State Tuition: $44,370
Fees & Indirect Costs: $48,418
Total: $92,788

Out-of-State Tuition: $56,615
Fees & Indirect Costs: $48,418
Total: $105,033

Financial Aid: https://dentistry.ucsf.edu/programs/dds/financing-your-dental-education

ADDITIONAL INFORMATION

Interesting tidbit: The Dental College organized and established by the University of California Regents September 7, 1881 with an initial capital budget of $510. The modern day UCSF has ranked as the top U.S. dental school in research funding from the National Institutes of Health for 25 years.

What international experiences are available? N/A

What dual degree options exist? For information on the DDS/MBA program, visit: https://dentistry.ucsf.edu/programs/dds-mba/admissions

For information on the DDS/PhD program, visit: https://dentistry.ucsf.edu/programs/dds-phd/admissions

What service learning opportunities exist? N/A

Other: International Dentist Program available for foreign-trained dentists seeking to practice in the U.S. For more information, visit: https://dentistry.ucsf.edu/programs/international-dentist-pathway/admissions

Important Updates due to COVID-19: UCSF accepted pass/fail grades for courses taken during the COVID-19 pandemic and also accepted online courses for classes that began during or after the start of the pandemic.

Were tests required? DAT required.

Are tests expected next year? Yes.

UNIVERSITY OF THE PACIFIC ARTHUR A. DUGONI SCHOOL OF DENTISTRY

Address: 155 Fifth St., San Francisco, CA 94103
Website: *https://www.dental.pacific.edu/*
Contact: *https://www.dental.pacific.edu/about/locations-and-visitor-information/contact-us*
Phone: (415) 929-6400

COST OF ATTENDANCE

Tuition: $119,360
*Fees & Indirect Costs: $21,741
Total: $141,101

*Note: This figure does not reflect estimated housing/living expenses or other indirect costs.

Financial Aid: https://www.dental.pacific.edu/academic-programs/financial-aid

ADDITIONAL INFORMATION

Interesting tidbit: The Arthur A. Dugoni School of Dentistry is highly regarded for its accelerated year-round predoctoral program where students are able to complete four academic years of instruction in three calendar years.

What international experiences are available? Mission trips and China Student Exchange Program available. For more information, visit: https://www.dental.pacific.edu/about/community-and-regional-impact/outreach-abroad

What dual degree options exist? No dual degree options listed.

What service learning opportunities exist? Student Community Outreach for Public Education (SCOPE) program available. For more information, visit: https://www.dental.pacific.edu/about/community-and-regional-impact/student-community-outreach-for-public-education-(scope)

Other: International Dentist Studies available for foreign-trained dentists seeking to practice in the U.S. For more information, visit: https://www.dental.pacific.edu/academic-programs/international-dental-studies

Project Homeless Connect (PHC) also available. For more information on PHC, visit: https://www.dental.pacific.edu/about/community-and-regional-impact/project-homeless-connect

Important Updates due to COVID-19: For courses taken in Spring and Summer 2020, it accepted pass/no credit grades and online courses, including labs.

Were tests required? DAT required.

Are tests expected next year? Yes.

ALASKA

ARIZONA

CALIFORNIA

COLORADO

HAWAII

IDAHO

MONTANA

NEVADA

NEW MEXICO

OREGON

UTAH

WASHINGTON

WYOMING

WEST

ALASKA

ARIZONA

CALIFORNIA

COLORADO

HAWAII

IDAHO

MONTANA

NEVADA

NEW MEXICO

OREGON

UTAH

WASHINGTON

WYOMING

WESTERN UNIVERSITY OF HEALTH SCIENCES COLLEGE OF DENTAL MEDICINE

Address: 309 E. Second St., Pomona, CA 91766
Website: *https://www.westernu.edu/dentistry/*
Contact: *https://prospective.westernu.edu/dentistry/dmd/contact/*
Phone: (909) 623-6116

COST OF ATTENDANCE

In-State Tuition: $76,325
Fees & Indirect Costs: $41,286
Total: $117,611

Out-of-State Tuition: $85,657
Fees & Indirect Costs: $41,286
Total: $126,946

Financial Aid: https://prospective.westernu.edu/dentistry/dmd/tuition-scholarships/

ADDITIONAL INFORMATION

Interesting tidbit: Western University developed a wide-reaching Interprofessional Education (IPE) curriculum in response to the Institute of Medicine (IOM)'s industry-wide findings of an unacceptable rate of Dental errors prevalent in the United States. WesternU was the first institution to develop a comprehensive program helping students from nine distinct health professions to learn how to work as a cohesive health care team.

What international experiences are available? Global health opportunities available. For more information, visit: https://www.westernu.edu/gch/global-health/

What dual degree options exist? No dual degree options listed.

What service learning opportunities exist? Service learning coursework and opportunities in community-based locations.

Other: International Dentist Program available for foreign-trained dentists seeking to practice in the U.S. For more information, visit: https://prospective.westernu.edu/dentistry/dmd-idp/

Important Updates due to COVID-19: For courses completed in the spring 2020, summer 2020, fall 2020 and spring 2021 semesters, online lab and pass/no pass credit for prerequisite courses were accepted.

Were tests required? DAT required.

Are tests expected next year? Yes.

UNIVERSITY OF COLORADO SCHOOL OF DENTAL MEDICINE

Address: 13065 E. 17th Ave., Aurora, CO 80045
Website: *http://www.ucdenver.edu/academics/colleges/ dentalmedicine/Pages/DentalMedicine.aspx*
Contact: *http://www.ucdenver.edu/academics/colleges/ dentalmedicine/AboutUs/Pages/ContactUs.aspx*
Phone: (303) 724-6900

COST OF ATTENDANCE

In-State Tuition: $40,140
Fees & Indirect Costs: $10,238.40
Total: $50,378.40

Out-of-State Tuition: $65,443
Fees & Indirect Costs: $10,238.40
Total: $78,681.40

Financial Aid: http://www.ucdenver.edu/academics/colleges/ dentalmedicine/ProgramsAdmissions/DoctorDentalSurgery/

ADDITIONAL INFORMATION

Interesting tidbit: The University of Colorado School of Dental Medicine (CU SDM) is a research-intensive, comprehensive dental education institution. It is in the top 10 U.S. dental schools that receive funding from the National Institute of Dental and Craniofacial Research.

What international experiences are available? Opportunities through the Center for Global Outreach. For more information and contact information, visit: http://www.ucdenver.edu/academics/ colleges/PublicHealth/research/centers/globalhealth/about/Pages/ mission.aspx

What dual degree options exist? No dual degree options listed.

What service learning opportunities exist? Community outreach opportunities available. For more information, visit: http://www.ucdenver.edu/academics/colleges/dentalmedicine/ CommunityService/Pages/CommunityService.aspx

Other: Advanced Standing International Student Program available for foreign-trained dentists seeking to practice in the U.S. For more information, visit: http://www.ucdenver.edu/ academics/colleges/dentalmedicine/ProgramsAdmissions/ InternationalStudentProgram/

Important Updates due to COVID-19: N/A

Were tests required? DAT required.

Are tests expected next year? Yes.

409

ALASKA

ARIZONA

CALIFORNIA

COLORADO

HAWAII

IDAHO

MONTANA

NEVADA

NEW MEXICO

OREGON

UTAH

WASHINGTON

WYOMING

WEST

ALASKA

ARIZONA

CALIFORNIA

COLORADO

HAWAII

IDAHO

MONTANA

NEVADA

NEW MEXICO

OREGON

UTAH

WASHINGTON

WYOMING

UNIVERSITY OF NEVADA, LAS VEGAS, SCHOOL OF DENTAL MEDICINE

Address: 1001 Shadow Ln., Las Vegas, NV 89106
Website: *https://www.unlv.edu/dental*
Contact: *https://www.unlv.edu/dental/contact*
Phone: (702) 774-2520

COST OF ATTENDANCE

In-State Tuition: $37,389
Fees & Indirect Costs: $22,577
Total: $59,966

Out-of-State Tuition: $77,124
Fees & Indirect Costs: $22,577
Total: $99,701

Financial Aid: https://www.unlv.edu/dental/financialaid

ADDITIONAL INFORMATION

Interesting tidbit: UNLV School of Dental Medicine is the only accredited dental school in Nevada. It delivered over $3.5 million in free care between 2011 and 2019 to children, homeless persons, veterans, women and children who are victims of domestic violence, those reentering the workforce, and those with special needs through philanthropic support at on-site clinics.

What international experiences are available? Humanitarian trips.

What dual degree options exist? Dual degree program available. For more information, visit: https://www.unlv.edu/dental/admissions

What service learning opportunities exist? UNLV Saturday Morning Community Clinics, Seal Nevada South, Women's Clinic and more opportunities. For more information, visit: https://www.unlv.edu/dental/community-clinics

Other: Two-year Advanced Standing DDS program available for foreign-trained dentists seeking to practice in the U.S.

Important Updates due to COVID-19: For the Spring and Summer 2021 semesters, online courses and Pass/Fail prerequisite coursework were accepted.

Were tests required? DAT required.

Are tests expected next year? Yes.

OREGON HEALTH & SCIENCE UNIVERSITY SCHOOL OF DENTISTRY

Address: 3181 S.W. Sam Jackson Park Rd., Portland, OR 97239
Website: *https://www.ohsu.edu/school-of-dentistry*
Contact: *https://www.ohsu.edu/about/contact-us*
Phone: (503) 494-8311

COST OF ATTENDANCE

In-State Tuition: $46,120
Fees & Indirect Costs: $41,821.83
Total: $87,941.83

Out-of-State Tuition: $74,436
Fees & Indirect Costs: $41,821.83
Total: $116,257.83

Financial Aid: https://www.ohsu.edu/school-of-dentistry/dmd-program-financial-aid

ADDITIONAL INFORMATION

Interesting tidbit: The Oregon Health & Science University School of Dentistry is a publicly supported institution located in Portland.

What international experiences are available? N/A

What dual degree options exist? No dual degree options listed.

What service learning opportunities exist? Community-based rotations and more. For more information, visit: https://www.ohsu.edu/school-of-dentistry/community-dentistry-education

Important Updates due to COVID-19: N/A

Were tests required? DAT required.

Are tests expected next year? Yes.

ALASKA

ARIZONA

CALIFORNIA

COLORADO

HAWAII

IDAHO

MONTANA

NEVADA

NEW MEXICO

OREGON

UTAH

WASHINGTON

WYOMING

WEST

ALASKA

ARIZONA

CALIFORNIA

COLORADO

HAWAII

IDAHO

MONTANA

NEVADA

NEW MEXICO

OREGON

UTAH

WASHINGTON

WYOMING

ROSEMAN UNIVERSITY OF HEALTH SCIENCES COLLEGE OF DENTAL MEDICINE

Address: 10894 S River Front Pkwy, South Jordan, UT 84095
Website: *https://dental.roseman.edu/*
Contact: *https://www.roseman.edu/contact-dental-medicine-program-utah/*
Phone: (801) 878-1200

COST OF ATTENDANCE

Tuition: $79,460
*Fees & Indirect Costs: $48,855
Total: $92,181
*Note: Fees include program fees ($15,555) and general University fees ($5,700). Indirect costs ($2,760/month *10) are based on graduate students not living with parents.

Financial Aid: https://dental.roseman.edu/doctor-dental-medicine-dmd/admissions/financial-aid/

ADDITIONAL INFORMATION

Interesting tidbit: The Roseman University of Health Sciences College of Dental Medicine DMD program's mission is to improve the oral health of the public with special attention to the underserved people in the Intermountain West region.

What international experiences are available? No international programs affiliated with the university, however international service trips organized through the American Student Dental Association. For more information, visit: https://www.utahasda.org/copy-of-global-outreach

What dual degree options exist? No dual degree options listed.

What service learning opportunities exist? Community engagement opportunities such as Give Kids a Smile and Back to School Brush Up available. For more information, visit: https://dental.roseman.edu/doctor-dental-medicine-dmd/student-life/community-engagement/

Important Updates due to COVID-19: N/A

Were tests required? DAT required.

Are tests expected next year? Yes.

UNIVERSITY OF UTAH SCHOOL OF DENTISTRY

Address: 530 South Wakara Way, Salt Lake City, UT 84108
Website: *https://dentistry.utah.edu/*
Contact: *https://dentistry.utah.edu/contact.php*
Phone: (801) 587-6453

COST OF ATTENDANCE

In-State Tuition: $40,538
*Fees & Indirect Costs: $9,595
Total: $50,133

Out-of-State Tuition: $76,745
*Fees & Indirect Costs: $9,595
Total: $86,340

*Note: These figures do not include estimated housing/living expenses or other indirect costs.

Financial Aid: https://dentistry.utah.edu/education/dds-degree/scholarships.php

ADDITIONAL INFORMATION

Interesting tidbit: As part of U of U Health, the School of Dentistry is a member of the Mountain West's only academic Dental center, It serves people in six states - Utah, Idaho, Montana, Wyoming and portions of Nevada and Colorado - nearly 10 percent of the continental United States.

What international experiences are available? N/A

What dual degree options exist? No dual degree options listed.

What service learning opportunities exist? Pediatric Oral Health Outreach Program.

Important Updates due to COVID-19: The University of Utah School of Dentistry was flexible regarding the graded requirements for prerequisite coursework (P/F or C/N). It reviewed applications without DAT scores but applicants were required to submit it at a later date.

Were tests required? DAT required.

Are tests expected next year? Yes.

ALASKA

ARIZONA

CALIFORNIA

COLORADO

HAWAII

IDAHO

MONTANA

NEVADA

NEW MEXICO

OREGON

UTAH

WASHINGTON

WYOMING

WEST

ALASKA

ARIZONA

CALIFORNIA

COLORADO

HAWAII

IDAHO

MONTANA

NEVADA

NEW MEXICO

OREGON

UTAH

WASHINGTON

WYOMING

UNIVERSITY OF WASHINGTON SCHOOL OF DENTISTRY

Address: 1959 NE Pacific St B-307, Seattle, WA 98195
Website: *https://dental.washington.edu/*
Contact: *https://dental.washington.edu/about-us/contact-us/*
Phone: (206) 543-5840

COST OF ATTENDANCE

In-State Tuition: $55,422
Fees & Indirect Costs: $36,871
Total: $92,293

Out-of-State Tuition: $84,926
Fees & Indirect Costs: $36,871
Total: $121,797

Financial Aid: https://dental.washington.edu/students/dds-programs/admissions/financial-aid/

ADDITIONAL INFORMATION

Interesting tidbit: The University of Washington School of Dentistry (UWSOD) has a specific educational track that trains dentists to meet the needs of rural and underserved populations in the state and region. The Regional Initiatives in Dental Education (RIDE) program is operated in conjunction with Eastern Washington University and the UW School of Medicine WWAMI.

What international experiences are available? N/A

What dual degree options exist? DDS/PhD Program available. For more information, visit: https://dental.washington.edu/oral-health-sciences/graduate-program-in-oral-biology/ddsphd/

What service learning opportunities exist? Rural Initiatives in Dental Education (RIDE) Program. For more information, visit: https://dental.washington.edu/ride/

Project H.O.P.E., Latina Health Fair, and more opportunities available. For more information, visit: https://dental.washington.edu/oepd/our-programs/

Other: International DDS Program available for foreign-trained dentists seeking to practice in the U.S. For more information, visit: https://dental.washington.edu/students/dds-programs/international-dds-program/

Important Updates due to COVID-19: N/A

Were tests required? DAT required.

Are tests expected next year? Yes.

REGION FIVE
U.S TERRITORIES

Dental School	Ave. GPA & DAT EARLY DECISION (ED) : YES/NO	Admissions Statistics	Science Req. Other Than Gen Chem, Ochem, Physics, Bio
University of Puerto Rico School of Dental Medicine Paseo Dr. Jose Celso Barbosa, San Juan, 00921, Puerto Rico	3.64 (overall) 3.57 (science) DAT: 18 ED: N	**(2019)** Apps Received: 427 Admission Offered: 42 Number Enrolled: 41 Acceptance Rate: 9.8% **(2020)** Apps Received: 109 Admission Offered: 40 Number Enrolled: 41 Acceptance Rate: 36.7%	Bio. or Zoology Social/Behav. Sciences Spanish

UNIVERSITY OF PUERTO RICO SCHOOL OF DENTAL MEDICINE

Address: Paseo Dr. Jose Celso Barbosa, San Juan, 00921, Puerto Rico
Website: *https://dental.rcm.upr.edu/*
Contact: *https://dental.rcm.upr.edu/contact-us/*
Phone: (787) 758-2525

COST OF ATTENDANCE

Tuition: $17,568
Fees & Indirect Costs: $32,318
Total: $49,886

Financial Aid: N/A

ADDITIONAL INFORMATION

Interesting tidbit: Established in 1957, the School of Dental Medicine of the UPR is the only school of its kind in Puerto Rico. It requires that all students must be proficient in reading, writing and speaking English and Spanish.

What international experiences are available? N/A

What dual degree options exist? No dual degree options listed.

What service learning opportunities exist? N/A

Important Updates due to COVID-19: Deadline was extended to January 4 from December 1.

Were tests required? DAT required.

Are tests expected next year? Yes.

PART 11

DENTAL SCHOOL LISTS

DENTAL SCHOOL ADMISSIONS REQUIREMENTS

ALABAMA

School	Required	Recommended	Notes
University of Alabama at Birmingham School of Dentistry	Bio. or Zoology w/Lab, Chem. w/Lab, OChem. w/Lab, Physics w/Lab, Math, and 30 sem. hrs of non-science coursework (see Recommended)	Biochem. is strongly recommended. Other courses: Cell Bio., Physio., Comparative Anatomy, Embryology, Histology, Human Anatomy, Microbio, Analytic Geometry, Differential and Integral Calc., Engl., Courses in Social Sciences and Humanities, and coursework that enhances manual dexterity (e.g., Sculpting, Painting, etc.)	AP credits accepted as long as they are listed on undergraduate transcript.

ARIZONA

School	Required	Recommended	Notes
Arizona School of Dentistry & Oral Health	Bio. w/Lab, Chem. w/Lab, OChem. w/Lab, Human Physio., Biochem., Physics w/Lab, Engl. Comp./Technical Writing, and Human Anatomy.	N/A	AP credits not accepted.
Midwestern University College of Dental Medicine-Arizona	Bio. w/Lab, Chem. w/Lab, OChem. w/Lab, Anatomy w/Lab, Microbio., w/Lab, Physics, Physio., Biochem., and Engl. Comp./Technical Writing	N/A	No listed information on AP credits. Contact admissions.

CALIFORNIA

School	Required	Recommended	Notes
California North State College of Dental Medicine	Engl. (see Notes), Bio. w/Lab, Chem. w/Lab, OChem. w/Lab, Physics, Math (Stats. and/or Calc. preferred), and Biochem.	Social Sciences, Anatomy, Microbio., Behavior Sciences, Physio., Immunology, Cellular Bio., Molecular Bio., Histology, and Foreign Lang.	AP credits may be accepted for Engl. only.
Herman Ostrow School of Dentistry of Usc	Bio. w/Lab, Physics w/Lab, Chem. w/Lab, OChem. w/Lab, Engl. Comp., and Philosophy, History, or Fine Arts.	Biochem., Anatomy, Histology, and Physiology.	AP credits not accepted.
Loma Linda University School of Dentistry	Bio. w/Lab, Chem. w/Lab, OChem. w/Lab, Biochem., Physics w/Lab, and Engl. Comp.	Science courses (by priority): Histology, Human Gross Anatomy, Systems Physio., Microbio., Cellular & Molecular Bio., Immunology, Neuroscience, Genetics, and Biochem. 2 or 3. Other recommended coursework: Small Business Management, Human Resource Management, Ceramics, Business & the Law, Accounting, Human Development, Marketing, Sculpture, and Interpersonal Communication.	AP credits not accepted for science prerequisites. Contact admissions for more information.

School	Required	Recommended	Notes
University of California, Los Angeles, School of Dentistry	Chem. w/Lab, OChem. w/Lab, Physics w/Lab, Bio. w/Lab, Engl. Comp., Psych., and Biochem.	Histology, Physio., Human or Comparative Anatomy, Social Sciences, Microbio., Communication, Business, Composition, Technical Writing, Fine Arts, Philosophy, Engineering, and Classics.	Max 3 semester/4 quarter units given for each AP subject. Remaining credit hours must be completed at collegel level.
University of California, San Francisco, School of Dentistry	Engl. Comp., Chem. w/Lab, OChem. w/ Lab, Biochem., Physics w/Lab, Bio or Zoology w/Lab (see Recommended), Psych., Social Sciences, Humanities, or Foreign Lang., and additional electives.	Bio.: Vetebrate Zoology is strongly recommended. Additional electives: Embryology, Comparative Vertebrate Anatomy, Genetics, and Stats.	AP credits may only partially fulfill certain prerequisites. For detailed information, visit: *https://dentistry. ucsf.edu/programs/ dds/admissions/ prerequisites*
University of the Pacific Arthur A. Dugoni School of Dentistry	Bio. w/Lab, Physics w/Lab, Chem. w/Lab, OChem., and Engl., Communication, or Speech	Anatomy, Physio., Microbio., Biochem., Histology, and Cell Biology.	No listed information on AP credits. Contact admissions.
Western University of Health Sciences College of Dental Medicine	Bio. w/Lab, Chem. w/Lab, OChem. w/ Lab, Physics w/Lab, and College Engl./ Engl. Comp.,	Biochem., Genetics, Cell Bio., Human Anatomy & Physio., Microbio., Calc. 1, Biometrics, Psych., and Conversational Spanish.	AP credits only accepted for Engl.

COLORADO

School	Required	Recommended	Notes
University of Colorado School of Dental Medicine	Bio. or Zoology w/ Lab, Chem. w/Lab, OChem. w/Lab, Physics w/Lab (Alg. or Calc. based), Microbio., Biochem., and Engl. Comp.	Anatomy, Cell Bio., Histology, Immunology, Physio., Business Management/ Finance, Psych., and Communications.	AP credits accepted on a case-by-case basis.

CONNECTICUT

School	Required	Recommended	Notes
University of Connecticut School of Dental Medicine	Bio. w/Lab, Chem. w/Lab, OChem. w/ Lab, Physics w/Lab, and Biochem.	Cell Bio. and Molecular Genetics	AP credits accepted as long as they are listed on undergraduate transcript.

D.C.

School	Required	Recommended	Notes
Howard University College of Dentistry	Engl. Comp. and Lit., Chem. w/Lab, OChem. w/Lab, Biochem., Human Anatomy, Physics, and Electives	Physiology and Microbiology.	AP credits not accepted.

FLORIDA

School	Required	Recommended	Notes
Lake Erie College of Osteopathic Medicine School of Dental Medicine	Bio. w/Lab, Chem. w/Lab, OChem. w/ Lab, Biochem., and Engl.	Anatomy, Physio., Microbio., and Physics strongly encouraged. Other recommended courses include Cell Bio., Histology, Immunology, and Molecular/Genetic Bio.	AP credits accepted upon review by admissions committee.

School	Required	Recommended	Notes
Nova Southeastern University College of Dental Medicine	Bio. w/Lab, Chem. w/Lab, OChem. w/Lab, Physics w/Lab, Biochem., Microbio., and Engl.	Anatomy, Physio., Cell Bio., Molecular Bio., Histology, Genetics, and Immunology.	No listed information on AP credits. Contact admissions.
University of Florida College of Dentistry	Engl., Bio., Chem., OChem., Physics, Microbio., and Biochem.	N/A	AP credits accepted as long as they are listed on undergraduate transcript.

GEORGIA

School	Required	Recommended	Notes
Dental College of Georgia At Augusta University	Bio. w/Lab, Chem. w/Lab, OChem. w/Lab, Biochem., Physics w/Lab, and Engl.	Human Anatomy, Microbio., Genetics, and Histology	No listed information on AP credits. Contact admissions.

ILLINOIS

School	Required	Recommended	Notes
Midwestern University College of Dental Medicine-Illinois	Bio. w/Lab, Chem. w/Lab, OChem. w/Lab, Physics, Anatomy, Microbio., Physio., Biochem., and Engl. Comp/Technical Writing	N/A	All science courses must be designed for science majors. Anatomy and Physiology requirements may be fulfilled by taking the combined Anatomy and Physiology 1 and Anatomy and Physiology 2 offerings if available. No listed information on AP credits. Contact admissions.

School	Required	Recommended	Notes
Southern Illinois University School of Dental Medicine	Bio. w/Lab, Chem. w/Lab, OChem. w/Lab, Physics w/Lab, Biochem., and Engl.	Anatomy, Physio., Microbio., Cell and Molecular Bio., Histology, Immunology, Genetics, Neural Science/Neural Physio., and Stats.	No listed information on AP credits. Contact admissions.
University Of Illinois At Chicago College 0f Dentistry	Chem., w/Lab, OChem. w/Lab, Physics w/Lab, Bio. w/Lab, Biochem., and Engl.	Human Anatomy, Human Physio., Histology, Microbio., Cell Bio., Molecular Bio., Immunology, and Genetics.	AP credit not accepted as course requirements. If basic Chem., Bio., or Physics is met with AP credit, student must take the required number of credit hours from upper-level courses at a 4-year institution.

INDIANA

School	Required	Recommended	Notes
Indiana University School 0f Dentistry	Bio. w/Lab (see Notes), Chem. w/Lab, OChem. w/Lab, Physics, either Communications or Psych., and Humanities (choose 1: Engl. Comp., Lit., Philosophy, History, or Foreign Lang.)	N/A	Bio. 20 credit hours must include: Human, Mammalian, or Comparative Anatomy or Histology (Lecture and Lab), Human, Mammalian, or Cell Physio., Microbio. or Immunology, and Cell Bio., Biochem., or Molecular Bio. Up to 4 credit hours of non-science AP credit accepted. Only science courses intended for science majors accepted.

IOWA

School	Required	Recommended	Notes
The University of Iowa College of Dentistry & Dental Clinics	Physics w/Lab, Chem. w/Lab, OChem. w/Lab, Biochem., Bio. w/ Lab, Engl., and Electives (see Recommended).	Electives: Social Sciences, Philosophy, History, Foreign Languages, Business and Accounting, and Math.	AP credits accepted.

KENTUCKY

School	Required	Recommended	Notes
University of Kentucky College of Dentistry	Bio. w/Lab, Chem. w/Lab, OChem. w/ Lab, Physics w/ Lab, Microbio., and Biochem.	N/A	No listed information on AP credits. Contact admissions.
University of Louisville School of Dentistry	Bio., Chem. w/ Lab, OChem. w/ Lab, Physics, and Biochem.	Microbio. (*strongly recommended*), Upper-level Human Anatomy, Upper-level Physio., Histology, Immunology, and other upper-level human bio. courses.	AP credits accepted as long as they are listed on undergraduate transcript.

LOUISIANA

School	Required	Recommended	Notes
Louisiana State University Health New Orleans School of Dentistry	Bio. w/Lab, Chem. w/Lab, OChem. w/ Lab, Physics w/Lab, Engl., Biochem., and Microbio.	Comparative Anatomy, Cell and Molecular Bio., Embryology, Histology, Microanatomy, Physio., and Genetics	AP credits accepted as long as they are listed on undergraduate transcript.

MAINE

School	Required	Recommended	Notes
University of New England College of Dental Medicine	Bio. w/Lab or Zoology, Anatomy w/Lab (see Notes), Microbio. w/Lab, Chem. w/Lab, OChem. w/Lab, Biochem., Additional Bio., Chem., Calc., or Physics (12 semester credits), and English Comp./Technical Writing.	Human Physiology and Immunology strongly recommended. Other recommended coursework: Pharmacology, Histology, Genetics, Physics, Business, Computers, 3D Art (e.g., Sculpture), Communications, Ethics, and Public Health.	AP credits not accepted.

MARYLAND

School	Required	Recommended	Notes
University of Maryland School of Dentistry	Bio. w/Lab, Chem. w/Lab, OChem. w/Lab, Physics w/Lab, Biochem., and Engl. Comp	N/A	No listed information on AP credits. Contact admissions.

MASSACHUSETTS

School	Required	Recommended	Notes
Boston University Henry M. Goldman School of Dental Medicine	Bio. w/Lab, Chem., w/Lab, OChem. w/Lab, Physics w/Lab, Math (see Notes), and Engl. or Comp.	Anatomy, Biochem., Cell Bio., Embryology, Genetics, Histology, Immunology, Microbio., Molecular Bio., Physio., Zoology, Humanities, Social Sciences, Arts, Business, and Engineering.	AP credits towards English or Math prerequisites are accepted as long as they are listed on undergraduate transcript. AP credit is not accepted towards science requirements. Math must include at least 1 Calculus course. Biochemistry may count towards Biology or Chemistry prerequisite. Contact admissions for more information.
Harvard School of Dental Medicine	Biochem., Bio. w/Lab, Chem. w/Lab, OChem. w/Lab, Physics w/Lab, Engl., Calc 1 and 2, and Stats.	Although AP credits are accepted, students are strongly encouraged to take science prerequisites at a 4-year college. Recommended courses: Cell Bio. and Microbio.	AP credits accepted as long as they are listed on undergraduate transcript.
Tufts University School of Dental Medicine	Bio. w/Lab, Upper-level Bio., Chem. w/Lab, Physics w/Lab, OChem. w/Lab, Biochem., Writing-intensive Humanities or Social Science.	N/A	AP credits not accepted.

MICHIGAN

School	Required	Recommended	Notes
University Of Detroit Mercy School of Dentistry	Chem. w/Lab, OChem. w/Lab, Bio. or Zoology w/ Lab, Physics w/Lab, Engl., Biochem., and Microbio.	Anatomy, Physio. and Stats.	AP credits accepted as long as they are listed on undergraduate transcript.
University of Michigan School of Dentistry	Biochem., Microbio., Psych., Sociology, Engl. Comp., Bio. w/ Lab, Chem. w/Lab, OChem. w/Lab, and Physics w/Lab.	Anatomy, Physio., Histology, Public Speaking, and Art.	AP credits accepted as long as they are listed on undergraduate transcript.

MINNESOTA

School	Required	Recommended	Notes
University of Minnesota School of Dentistry	Engl. (see Recommended), Bio. or Zoology w/ Lab, Physics w/ Lab, Chem. w/Lab, OChem. w/Lab, Biochem., Math, and Applied Human Psych.	Engl: Two comp. courses preferred; or 1 Comp. course and one additional course in Lit., Humanities, or Public Speaking (writing intensive). Strong science electives strongly encouraged. Preferred electives: Art (3D drawing or sculpture), Cell Bio., Histology, Human Anatomy, Microbio., Physio., Genetics, Immunology, and Stats.	AP credits accepted.

MISSISSIPPI

School	Required	Recommended	Notes
University of Mississippi Medical Center School of Dentistry	Engl., Chem. w/ Lab, OChem. w/Lab, Physics w/Lab, Bio. or Zoology w/Lab, Microbio. w/Lab, Math (College Alg. and Trig. or higher), Stats or Biostats., and Biochem.	Foreign Lang., Sociology, Psych., Speech, Humanities, Philosophy, Embryology, Histology, Immunology, Cell Bio., Physio., Gross Anatomy, and Neuroanatomy.	AP credits not accepted.

MISSOURI

School	Required	Recommended	Notes
Missouri School of Dentistry & Oral Health	Bio. w/Lab, Chem. w/Lab, OChem. w/ Lab, Human Physio., Biochem., Physics w/Lab, Human Anatomy, and Engl. Comp./Technical Writing	N/A	No listed information on AP credits. Contact admissions.
University of Missouri-Kansas City School of Dentistry	Bio. w/Lab, Anatomy, Physio., Cell Bio., Biochem., Chem. w/Lab, OChem. w/Lab, Physics w/Lab, and Engl. Comp	Histology, Immunology, Genetics, Ethics, Stats., Public Health, Social Sciences, Psych., Nutrition, Business, Communications, Art, Ceramics, 3D Design, and Spanish.	AP credits accepted as long as they are listed on undergraduate transcript.

NEBRASKA

School	Required	Recommended	Notes
Creighton University School of Dentistry	Bio., OChem., Physics, Chem., and Engl.	Strongly encouraged: Comparative Anatomy, Econ., History, Math., Modern Languages, Philosophy, Psych., Social Science, and/ or Speech.	AP credits not accepted.

School	Required	Recommended	Notes
University of Nebraska Medical Center College of Dentistry	Engl. Comp., Chem. w/Lab, OChem. w/Lab, Bio. w/Lab, and Physics w/Lab.	Anatomy, Biochem., Cell Bio., Comparative Anatomy, Embryology, Genetics, Histology, Immunology, Microbio., Physio., Psych., Scientific Greek or Latin, and Stats.	No listed information on AP credits. Contact admissions.

NEVADA

School	Required	Recommended	Notes
University of Nevada, Las Vegas, School of Dental Medicine	Bio. w/Lab, Chem. w/Lab, OChem. w/Lab, Physics w/Lab, Human Anatomy, Biochem., and Engl.	N/A	AP credits may be accepted on a case-by-case basis.

NEW JERSEY

School	Required	Recommended	Notes
Rutgers, The State University of New Jersey, School of Dental Medicine	Bio. w/Lab, Engl., Chem. w/Lab, OChem. w/Lab, and Physics w/Lab	N/A	AP credits not accepted.

NEW YORK

School	Required	Recommended	Notes
Columbia University College of Dental Medicine	Engl. Comp or Literature (Writing-intensive), Physics w/Lab, Bio. w/Lab, Chem. w/Lab, OChem. w/Lab, and Biochem. (no lab req.)	Math, Sociology, History, Fine or Industrial Arts, 1+ Foreign Languages	No listed information on AP credits. Contact admissions.

School	Required	Recommended	Notes
Nyu College of Dentistry	Bio. w/Lab, Chem. w/Lab, OChem. w/ Lab, Physics w/Lab, and Engl./Writing-Intensive	Comparative Anatomy, Biochem., Cell Bio., Microbio. Genetics, Histology, Embryology, Physio., Sociology, Philosophy, Psych., and Math	AP credits accepted for half of the prerequisites in any subject with the requirement of one additional course in that subject at a four-year college.
Stony Brook University School of Dental Medicine	Bio. w/Lab, Chem. w/Lab, OChem. w/ Lab, Physics w/Lab, Engl., Biochem., Calc 1 and Calc 2 or Calc 1 and Stats.	N/A	AP credit accepted as long as student scores at least a 4 in the subject. Students are expected to take an additional course of equal level or better to demonstrate scholastic ability.
Touro College of Dental Medicine At New York Medical College	Bio. w/Lab, Chem. w/Lab, OChem. w/ Lab, Biochem. (lab optional), Physics w/ Lab, and Engl.	N/A	AP credits accepted as long as they are listed on undergraduate transcript.
University At Buffalo School of Dental Medicine	Engl. (including Comp.), Chem. w/ Lab, OChem. w/Lab, Bio. w/Lab, Physics w/Lab (algebra or calc.-based), and Biochem.	Histology, Psychology, Sociology, Public Speaking, Composition, and Humanities. Students who do not hold a science-based major should pursue additional coursework in Biology and Chemistry beyond the prerequisites.	AP credit accepted for prerequisites except for Biology.

NORTH CAROLINA

School	Required	Recommended	Notes
East Carolina University School of Dental Medicine	Bio. or Zoology w/Lab, Chem. w/Lab, OChem. w/Lab, Physics w/Lab, Engl. Comp., and Math (College Alg. or higher)	Biochem., Microbio., Comparative Anatomy, Physio., Embryology/Histology, Vertebrate Physio., Anatomy, Genetics and Cell Bio., Stats., Humanities, and Psych.	AP credits accepted as long as they are listed on undergraduate transcript.
University of North Carolina At Chapel Hill Adams School of Dentistry	Bio. and Zoology w/Lab (see Notes), Chem. w/Lab, OChem., Biochem., Physics, and Engl.	Molecular Bio., Math, Stats., Business, Writing Skills, Computer Science, Sculture, Art, Social Science, History, Literature, Economics, Philosophy, and Psych.	Two lecture courses, 4 sem. hrs each req for Bio. One must be General Bio. w/Lab. The other course must be Human Anatomy and Physiology or vertebrate Zoology. Both must include labs with vertebrate dissection. No listed information on AP credits. Contact admissions.

OHIO

School	Required	Recommended	Notes
Case Western Reserve University School of Dental Medicine	Chem. w/Lab, OChem. w/Lab, Bio. w/Lab, Physics w/ Lab, and Engl.	Sciences strongly recommended: Stats., Biochem., Microbio., Genetics, Anatomy, Physio., Advanced Cell Bio., Histology, Neuroscience, Engineering coursework. Social Science: Ethics, Business, Psych., Sociology, Epidemiology, and Cultural Anthropology. Humanities: Art, Music, Dance, and Media. Mastery of foreign languages (including ASL) highly encouraged.	AP credits accepted as long as they are listed on undergraduate transcript.
The Ohio State University College of Dentistry	Engl. 1 & 2, Physics 1, Chem. 1 & 2, OChem. 1 & 2, Bio. 1 & 2, Microbio., Biochem., Physio., and Anatomy (dissection important).	N/A	9 out of the 13 prerequisites are required. If a lab is required as part of a course, then OSU requires the lab. If the lab is a separate course then OSU does not require it. No listed information on AP credits. Contact admissions.

OKLAHOMA

School	Required	Recommended	Notes
UNIVERSITY OF OKLAHOMA COLLEGE OF DENTISTRY	Bio. w/Lab, Chem. w/Lab, OChem. w/ Lab, Biochem., Physics w/Lab, Psych, and Engl. Comp or Writing Intensive.	N/A	No listed information on AP credits. Contact admissions.

OREGON

School	Required	Recommended	Notes
Oregon Health & Science University School of Dentistry	Bio. w/Lab, Chem. w/Lab, OChem. w/ Lab, Physics w/Lab, Human Anatomy & Physio. w/Lab, Biochem. w/Lab, and Engl. Comp.	Microbio., Cell Bio., Molecular Bio., Genetics, Histology, and Neuroscience. Other recommended courses: Social and Behavioral Sciences, Humanities, and Fine Arts (Sculpture and 3D drawing).	AP credits accepted as long as they are listed on undergraduate transcript.

PENNSYLVANIA

School	Required	Recommended	Notes
The Maurice H. Kornberg School of Dentistry, Temple University	Bio. w/Lab, Chem. w/Lab, OChem. w/ Lab, Physics w/Lab, and Engl.	Highly recommended: Biochem., Physio., Anatomy, and Histology	No listed information on AP credits. Contact admissions.
University of Pennsylvania School of Dental Medicine	Bio. w/Lab (Zoology accepted), Chem. w/Lab, OChem. w/ Lab, Physics w/Lab, Biochem., Math (Calc. preferred, Stats or college-level Math accepted), and Engl.	Anatomy, Microbio., Physio., and Aadditional coursework in Physical Chem.	No listed information on AP credits. Contact admissions.
University of Pittsburgh School of Dental Medicine	Engl./Writing Intensive, Bio. w/ Lab, Physics, Chem. w/Lab, OChem. w/ Lab, and Biochem.	Anatomy	AP credits accepted as long as they are listed on undergraduate transcript.

PUERTO RICO

School	Required	Recommended	Notes
University of Puerto Rico School of Dental Medicine	Spanish, Engl., Bio. or Zoology w/ Lab, Physics w/ Lab, Chem. w/Lab, OChem. w/Lab, Social and Behav. Sciences.	Highly recommended: Biochem. or Molecular-Cellular Bio., Histology, Physio., Anatomy, Microbio., Genetics, Psych., and Ethics.	No listed information on AP credits. Contact admissions.

SOUTH CAROLINA

School	Required	Recommended	Notes
Medical University of South Carolina James B. Edwards College of Dental Medicine	Chem. w/Lab, OChem. w/Lab, Bio. or Zoology w/ Lab, Physics w/Lab, Science Electives (see Recommended), Engl., and Math.	Science Electives: Microbio., Biochem., Anatomy, Physio., Genetics, etc.	AP credits accepted as long as they are listed on undergraduate transcript.

TENNESSEE

School	Required	Recommended	Notes
Meharry Medical College School of Dentistry	Bio. or Zoology w/Lab, Chem. w/Quantitative Analysis w/Lab, OChem. w/Lab, Physics w/Lab, Engl. Comp., Biochem., and Calc. or Stats.	Strongly recommended: Anatomy/ Physiology, Microbio., and Histology/Cell Bio. Other recommended courses: Genetics, Molecular Bio., and Pharmacology.	AP credits accepted as long as they are listed on undergraduate transcript. Strongly advised that no more than 16 credit hours of prerequisite courses be satisfied with AP credit.
University of Tennessee Health Science Center College of Dentistry	Engl. Comp., Bio. w/Lab, Chem. w/ Lab, OChem. w/ Lab, Physics w/ Lab, Biochem., and at least 1 of the following: Histology, Microbio., or Comparative Anatomy (Human Anatomy accepted if taken with lab)	N/A	AP credits accepted as long as they are listed on undergraduate transcript.

TEXAS

School	Required	Recommended	Notes
Texas A&M College of Dentistry	Engl., Stats., Chem., OChem., Physics, Biochem., Bio. w/ Lab (Must include: Anatomy w/ Lab, Physio., and Microbio.)	Histology, Neuroscience, Cellular and Molecular Bio., Immunology, and Biochem. 2	No listed information on AP credits. Contact admissions.
Texas Tech University Health Sciences Center El Paso Woody L. Hunt School of Dental Medicine	Bio., Microbio., Biochem., Chem. w/ Lab, OChem. w/Lab, Physics w/Lab, Stats, and Engl.	N/A	AP credits accepted as long as they are listed on undergraduate transcript.
The University of Texas School of Dentistry At Houston	Bio. w/Lab (including Microbio.), Chem. w/ Lab, OChem. w/Lab, Biochem., Physics w/Lab, Engl., and Stats.	Additional upper-level coursework strongly recommended	AP credits accepted as long as they are listed on undergraduate transcript.
Ut Health San Antonio School of Dentistry	Bio. w/Lab, Chem. w/Lab (see Notes), OChem. w/Lab, Biochem., Physics w/Lab, Engl., and Stats.	N/A	Chem. prerequisite should include familiarity with analytic and volumetric techniques. AP credits accepted as long as they are listed on undergraduate transcript.

438

School	Required	Recommended	Notes
Roseman University of Health Sciences College of Dental Medicine – South Jordan, Utah	Bio. w/Lab, Chem. w/Lab, OChem. w/ Lab, Physics w/ Lab, Biochem., Communication course (see Recommended).	Communication: Engl., Composition, Creative, Business, Technical, or Scientific Writing, Lit. or Philosophy, Communication coursework focused on Speech/Debate, Journalism, Psych., or Theater.	No listed information on AP credits. Contact admissions.
University of Utah School of Dentistry	Anatomy (Human or Comparative), Biochem., Bio., Chem., Ochem., Engl. Comp./ Tehnical Writing, Physics, Physio., and Microbio. w/Lab.	Business, Cell Bio., Communications, Computer Science, Ethics, Histology, Molecular Bio./Genetics, Additional Bio., Chem., and/or Physics, and 3D Art.	Up to 3 AP credit hours accepted per prerequisite. AP credits must be listed on undergraduate transcript.

VIRGINIA

School	Required	Recommended	Notes
Virginia Commonwealth University School of Dentistry	Bio. w/Lab, Chem. w/Lab, OChem. w/ Lab, Physics w/Lab, Biochem., Math/ Stats., and Engl.	Upper-level bio., Behavioral Science coursework, and courses involving the use of psychomotor skills.	AP credits accepted as long as they are listed on undergraduate transcript.

WASHINGTON

School	Required	Recommended	Notes
University of Washington School of Dentistry	Chem., OChem., Biochem., Physics, Bio. or Zoology, and Microbio.	N/A	AP credits accepted as long as they are listed on undergraduate transcript.

WEST VIRGINIA

School	Required	Recommended	Notes
West Virginia University School of Dentistry	Engl. Comp. and Rhetoric, Bio. or Zoology w/Lab, Chem. w/Lab, OChem. w/Lab, Physics w/Lab, Comparative or Human Anatomy, and Biochem.	Cellular and Molecular Bio., Physio., Microbio., Embryology/ Developmental Bio., Genetics, and Psych.	AP credits only accepted for Engl.

WISCONSIN

School	Required	Recommended	Notes
Marquette University School of Dentistry	Chem. w/Lab, OChem. w/Lab, Bio. w/Lab (see Recommended), Physics w/Lab, Engl., Biochem., and Electives (see Recommended).	Bio: Zoology and Comparative Vertebrate Anatomy preferred. 4 Semester Hours of Botany may apply towards this requirement. Pre-dental electives: Anatomy, Cell Bio., Genetics, Microbio., and Physio. Other recommended courses: Speech, History, Philosophy, Sociology, Political Science, Econ., Psych., and Foreign Language.	No listed information on AP credits. Contact admissions.

DENTAL SCHOOLS IN THE U.S. BY CITY/STATE

Dental Schools	City	State
University of Alabama at Birmingham School of Dentistry	Birmingham	AL
Midwestern University College of Dental Medicine-Arizona	Glendale	AZ
Arizona School of Dentistry & Oral Health	Mesa	AZ
California North State College of Dental Medicine	Elk Grove	CA
Loma Linda University School of Dentistry	Loma Linda	CA
Herman Ostrow School of Dentistry of USC	Los Angeles	CA
University of California, Los Angeles, School of Dentistry	Los Angeles	CA
Western University of Health Sciences College of Dental Medicine	Pomona	CA
University of California, San Francisco, School of Dentistry	San Francisco	CA
University of the Pacific Arthur A. Dugoni School of Dentistry	San Francisco	CA
University of Colorado School of Dental Medicine	Aurora	CO
University of Connecticut School of Dental Medicine	Farmington	CT
Howard University College of Dentistry	Washington	DC
Lake Erie College of Osteopathic Medicine School of Dental Medicine	Bradenton	FL

Dental Schools	City	State
Nova Southeastern University College of Dental Medicine	Davie	FL
University of Florida College of Dentistry	Gainesville	FL
Dental College of Georgia at Augusta University	Augusta	GA
The University of Iowa College of Dentistry & Dental Clinics	Iowa City	IA
Southern Illinois University School of Dental Medicine	Alton	IL
University of Illinois at Chicago College of Dentistry	Chicago	IL
Midwestern University College of Dental Medicine-Illinois	Downers Grove	IL
Indiana University School of Dentistry	Indianapolis	IN
University of Kentucky College of Dentistry	Lexington	KY
University of Louisville School of Dentistry	Louisville	KY
Louisiana State University Health New Orleans School of Dentistry	New Orleans	LA
Boston University Henry M. Goldman School of Dental Medicine	Boston	MA
Harvard School of Dental Medicine	Boston	MA
Tufts University School of Dental Medicine	Boston	MA
University of Maryland School of Dentistry	Baltimore	MD
University of New England College of Dental Medicine	Portland	ME
University of Michigan School of Dentistry	Ann Arbor	MI
University of Detroit Mercy School of Dentistry	Detroit	MI

Dental Schools	City	State
University of Minnesota School of Dentistry	Minneapolis	MN
University of Missouri-Kansas City School of Dentistry	Kansas City	MO
Missouri School of Dentistry & Oral Health	Kirksville	MO
University of Mississippi Medical Center School of Dentistry	Jackson	MS
University of North Carolina at Chapel Hill Adams School of Dentistry	Chapel Hill	NC
East Carolina University School of Dental Medicine	Greenville	NC
University of Nebraska Medical Center College of Dentistry	Lincoln	NE
Creighton University School of Dentistry	Omaha	NE
Rutgers, The State University of New Jersey, School of Dental Medicine	Newark	NJ
University of Nevada, Las Vegas, School of Dental Medicine	Las Vegas	NV
University at Buffalo School of Dental Medicine	Buffalo	NY
Touro College of Dental Medicine at New York Medical College	Hawthorne	NY
Columbia University College of Dental Medicine	New York	NY
NYU College of Dentistry	New York	NY
Stony Brook University School of Dental Medicine	Stony Brook	NY
Case Western Reserve University School of Dental Medicine	Cleveland	OH
The Ohio State University College of Dentistry	Columbus	OH

Dental Schools	City	State
University of Oklahoma College of Dentistry	Oklahoma City	OK
Oregon Health & Science University School of Dentistry	Portland	OR
The Maurice H. Kornberg School of Dentistry, Temple University	Philadelphia	PA
University of Pennsylvania School of Dental Medicine	Philadelphia	PA
University of Pittsburgh School of Dental Medicine	Pittsburgh	PA
University of Puerto Rico School of Dental Medicine	San Juan	PR
Medical University of South Carolina James B. Edwards College of Dental Medicine	Charleston	SC
University of Tennessee Health Science Center College of Dentistry	Memphis	TN
Meharry Medical College School of Dentistry	Nashville	TN
Texas A&M College of Dentistry	Dallas	TX
Texas Tech University Health Sciences Center El Paso Woody L. Hunt School of Dental Medicine	El Paso	TX
The University of Texas School of Dentistry at Houston	Houston	TX
UT Health San Antonio School of Dentistry	San Antonio	TX
University of Utah School of Dentistry	Salt Lake City	UT
Roseman University of Health Sciences College of Dental Medicine – South Jordan, Utah	South Jordan	UT
Virginia Commonwealth University School of Dentistry	Richmond	VA

Dental Schools	City	State
University of Washington School of Dentistry	Seattle	WA
Marquette University School of Dentistry	Milwaukee	WI
West Virginia University School of Dentistry	Morgantown	WV

DENTAL SCHOOLS IN THE U.S. BY AVERAGE DAT SCORE

Dental Schools	Avg. DAT
Meharry Medical College School of Dentistry	18
University of Puerto Rico School of Dental Medicine	18
West Virginia University School of Dentistry	18
Howard University College of Dentistry	18.1
Missouri School of Dentistry & Oral Health	18.8
University of Mississippi Medical Center School of Dentistry	19
University of New England College of Dental Medicine	19
Arizona School of Dentistry & Oral Health	19.1
Midwestern University College of Dental Medicine-Illinois	19.4
Southern Illinois University School of Dental Medicine	19.5
Creighton University School of Dentistry	19.6
University of Oklahoma College of Dentistry	19.6
Roseman University of Health Sciences College of Dental Medicine – South Jordan, Utah	19.7
University of Missouri-Kansas City School of Dentistry	19.8
East Carolina University School of Dental Medicine	19.9
Indiana University School of Dentistry	19.9
University of Colorado School of Dental Medicine	19.9
Dental College of Georgia at Augusta University	20
Lake Erie College of Osteopathic Medicine School of Dental Medicine	20
Loma Linda University School of Dentistry	20
Marquette University School of Dentistry	20
Medical University of South Carolina James B. Edwards College of Dental Medicine	20
Tufts University School of Dental Medicine	20
University of Detroit Mercy School of Dentistry	20

Dental Schools	Avg. DAT
University of Kentucky College of Dentistry	20
University of Louisville School of Dentistry	20
Western University of Health Sciences College of Dental Medicine	20
Midwestern University College of Dental Medicine-Arizona	20.1
University of Nebraska Medical Center College of Dentistry	20.1
University of Tennessee Health Science Center College of Dentistry	20.1
Louisiana State University Health New Orleans School of Dentistry	20.2
UT Health San Antonio School of Dentistry	20.2
Herman Ostrow School of Dentistry of USC	20.3
Boston University Henry M. Goldman School of Dental Medicine	20.4
Oregon Health & Science University School of Dentistry	20.4
University at Buffalo School of Dental Medicine	20.4
University of Nevada, Las Vegas, School of Dental Medicine	20.4
University of Maryland School of Dentistry	20.8
University of Minnesota School of Dentistry	20.8
Case Western Reserve University School of Dental Medicine	20.9
University of Washington School of Dentistry	20.9
Nova Southeastern University College of Dental Medicine	21
NYU College of Dentistry	21
Texas A&M College of Dentistry	21
The Ohio State University College of Dentistry	21
The University of Iowa College of Dentistry & Dental Clinics	21
University of Connecticut School of Dental Medicine	21
University of Illinois at Chicago College of Dentistry	21
University of Utah School of Dentistry	21
Virginia Commonwealth University School of Dentistry	21
The Maurice H. Kornberg School of Dentistry, Temple University	21.1
The University of Texas School of Dentistry at Houston	21.2
University of Alabama at Birmingham School of Dentistry	21.2
Touro College of Dental Medicine at New York Medical College	21.3
University of Michigan School of Dentistry	21.4
Rutgers, The State University of New Jersey, School of Dental Medicine	22
University of California, San Francisco, School of Dentistry	22
University of Florida College of Dentistry	22

Dental Schools	Avg. DAT
University of North Carolina at Chapel Hill Adams School of Dentistry	22
University of Pittsburgh School of Dental Medicine	22
University of the Pacific Arthur A. Dugoni School of Dentistry	22
University of Pennsylvania School of Dental Medicine	22.1
Stony Brook University School of Dental Medicine	22.2
Columbia University College of Dental Medicine	23
University of California, Los Angeles, School of Dentistry	23
Harvard School of Dental Medicine	23.8
California North State College of Dental Medicine	N/A
Texas Tech University Health Sciences Center El Paso Woody L. Hunt School of Dental Medicine	N/A

DENTAL SCHOOLS BY IN-STATE TUITION

Dental Schools	In-State Tuition	Out-of-State Tuition	COA (O)
West Virginia University School of Dentistry	$25,506.00	$56,574.00	$56,574.00
Dental College of Georgia at Augusta University	$26,344.00	$64,778.00	$64,778.00
Howard University College of Dentistry	$28,000.00	$65,000.00	$81,924.00
University of Alabama at Birmingham School of Dentistry	$28,000.00	$65,000.00	$81,924.00
Louisiana State University Health New Orleans School of Dentistry	$28,418.00	$57,146.00	$83,981.00
University of Oklahoma College of Dentistry	$30,137.00	$66,162.00	$66,162.00
The University of Texas School of Dentistry at Houston	$30,869.00	$47,510.00	$92,744.00
Texas A&M College of Dentistry	$31,697.00	$42,497.00	$71,061.00
University of Puerto Rico School of Dental Medicine	$32,702.00	$32,702.00	$49,886.00
East Carolina University School of Dental Medicine	$33,495.00	$33,495.00	$68,794.00

Dental Schools	In-State Tuition	Out-of-State Tuition	COA (O)
University of Missouri-Kansas City School of Dentistry	$34,152.00	$68,066.00	$68,066.00
University of Tennessee Health Science Center College of Dentistry	$34,972.00	$73,732.00	$110,944.00
University of Kentucky College of Dentistry	$35,228.00	$75,178.00	$116,226.00
University of Michigan School of Dentistry	$35,691.00	$53,540.00	$90,156.00
Indiana University School of Dentistry	$36,767.00	$81,885.00	$107,240.00
Stony Brook University School of Dental Medicine	$36,900.00	$62,950.00	$113,444.00
University at Buffalo School of Dental Medicine	$36,900.00	$62,950.00	$113,557.00
University of Connecticut School of Dental Medicine	$38,437.00	$76,191.00	$109,391.00
University of Colorado School of Dental Medicine	$38,784.00	$64,086.00	$112,586.00
Texas Tech University Health Sciences Center El Paso Woody L. Hunt School of Dental Medicine	$39,171.00	$59,171.00	$95,031.00
UT Health San Antonio School of Dentistry	$39,514.00	$50,314.00	$76,366.00
University of Nebraska Medical Center College of Dentistry	$40,450.00	$84,325.00	$130,720.00
University of Florida College of Dentistry	$41,720.00	$68,200.00	$104,014.00
University of Maryland School of Dentistry	$42,080.00	$78,236.00	$78,236.00
University of Louisville School of Dentistry	$42,299.00	$79,771.00	$79,771.00
University of Mississippi Medical Center School of Dentistry	$43,440.00	$85,494.00	$109,670.00
The Ohio State University College of Dentistry	$44,209.00	$87,629.00	$112,341.00
University of North Carolina at Chapel Hill Adams School of Dentistry	$45,748.00	$87,784.00	$100,273.00
University of Minnesota School of Dentistry	$46,192.00	$78,998.00	$96,680.00
University of California, Los Angeles, School of Dentistry	$46,577.00	$58,822.00	$101,512.00
Southern Illinois University School of Dental Medicine	$47,373.00	$47,373.00	$62,869.00
University of Utah School of Dentistry	$50,133.00	$86,340.00	$86,340.00
Rutgers, The State University of New Jersey, School of Dental Medicine	$50,154.00	$50,154.00	$81,262.00

Dental Schools	In-State Tuition	Out-of-State Tuition	COA (O)
University of Pittsburgh School of Dental Medicine	$50,370.00	$60,398.00	$102,712.00
The University of Iowa College of Dentistry & Dental Clinics	$50,791.00	$75,929.00	$94,065.00
University of California, San Francisco, School of Dentistry	$51,904.00	$64,149.00	$104,991.00
University of Illinois at Chicago College of Dentistry	$52,474.00	$80,964.00	$100,964.00
Lake Erie College of Osteopathic Medicine School of Dental Medicine	$55,130.00	$55,130.00	$99,881.00
Virginia Commonwealth University School of Dentistry	$57,911.00	$90,281.00	$127,938.00
University of Nevada, Las Vegas, School of Dental Medicine	$59,836.00	$99,571.00	$99,571.00
The Maurice H. Kornberg School of Dentistry, Temple University	$61,452.00	$69,398.00	$103,878.00
Oregon Health & Science University School of Dentistry	$61,868.00	$89,628.00	$113,678.00
University of Washington School of Dentistry	$64,258.00	$93,762.00	$120,908.00
Harvard School of Dental Medicine	$64,984.00	$64,984.00	$99,939.00
Meharry Medical College School of Dentistry	$66,503.00	$66,503.00	$100,816.00
Medical University of South Carolina James B. Edwards College of Dental Medicine	$69,010.00	$104,885.00	$140,055.00
Marquette University School of Dentistry	$69,950.00	$78,610.00	$103,502.00
University of Detroit Mercy School of Dentistry	$74,260.00	$74,260.00	$115,334.00
Creighton University School of Dentistry	$77,856.00	$77,856.00	$103,263.00
University of New England College of Dental Medicine	$78,575.00	$78,575.00	$96,575.00
Case Western Reserve University School of Dental Medicine	$78,612.00	$78,612.00	$107,012.00
Tufts University School of Dental Medicine	$79,200.00	$79,200.00	$123,570.00
University of Pennsylvania School of Dental Medicine	$79,409.00	$79,409.00	$123,521.00
Nova Southeastern University College of Dental Medicine	$80,932.00	$81,741.00	$129,465.00

Dental Schools	In-State Tuition	Out-of-State Tuition	COA (O)
Boston University Henry M. Goldman School of Dental Medicine	$82,500.00	$82,500.00	$85,393.00
Western University of Health Sciences College of Dental Medicine	$83,378.00	$83,378.00	$116,924.00
Touro College of Dental Medicine at New York Medical College	$86,255.00	$86,255.00	$117,925.00
Missouri School of Dentistry & Oral Health	$87,382.00	$87,382.00	$87,382.00
Roseman University of Health Sciences College of Dental Medicine – South Jordan, Utah	$92,181.00	$92,181.00	$92,181.00
Loma Linda University School of Dentistry	$93,275.00	$93,275.00	$110,870.00
Arizona School of Dentistry & Oral Health	$93,912.00	$93,912.00	$93,912.00
NYU College of Dentistry	$95,968.00	$95,968.00	$95,968.00
Columbia University College of Dental Medicine	$97,027.00	$97,027.00	$122,767.00
Midwestern University College of Dental Medicine-Arizona	$97,048.00	$97,048.00	$125,617.00
Midwestern University College of Dental Medicine-Illinois	$99,078.00	$99,078.00	$127,586.00
University of the Pacific Arthur A. Dugoni School of Dentistry	$114,720.00	$114,720.00	$132,400.00
Herman Ostrow School of Dentistry of USC	$122,154.00	$122,154.00	$152,123.00
California North State College of Dental Medicine	N/A	N/A	N/A

DENTAL SCHOOLS BY OUT-OF-STATE TUITION

Dental Schools	In-State Tuition	Out-of-State Tuition	COA (O)
University of Puerto Rico School of Dental Medicine	$32,702.00	$32,702.00	$49,886.00
East Carolina University School of Dental Medicine	$33,495.00	$33,495.00	$68,794.00
Texas A&M College of Dentistry	$31,697.00	$42,497.00	$71,061.00
Southern Illinois University School of Dental Medicine	$47,373.00	$47,373.00	$62,869.00
The University of Texas School of Dentistry at Houston	$30,869.00	$47,510.00	$92,744.00

Dental Schools	In-State Tuition	Out-of-State Tuition	COA (O)
Rutgers, The State University of New Jersey, School of Dental Medicine	$50,154.00	$50,154.00	$81,262.00
UT Health San Antonio School of Dentistry	$39,514.00	$50,314.00	$76,366.00
University of Michigan School of Dentistry	$35,691.00	$53,540.00	$90,156.00
Lake Erie College of Osteopathic Medicine School of Dental Medicine	$55,130.00	$55,130.00	$99,881.00
West Virginia University School of Dentistry	$25,506.00	$56,574.00	$56,574.00
Louisiana State University Health New Orleans School of Dentistry	$28,418.00	$57,146.00	$83,981.00
University of California, Los Angeles, School of Dentistry	$46,577.00	$58,822.00	$101,512.00
Texas Tech University Health Sciences Center El Paso Woody L. Hunt School of Dental Medicine	$39,171.00	$59,171.00	$95,031.00
University of Pittsburgh School of Dental Medicine	$50,370.00	$60,398.00	$102,712.00
Stony Brook University School of Dental Medicine	$36,900.00	$62,950.00	$113,444.00
University at Buffalo School of Dental Medicine	$36,900.00	$62,950.00	$113,557.00
University of Colorado School of Dental Medicine	$38,784.00	$64,086.00	$112,586.00
University of California, San Francisco, School of Dentistry	$51,904.00	$64,149.00	$104,991.00
Dental College of Georgia at Augusta University	$26,344.00	$64,778.00	$64,778.00
Harvard School of Dental Medicine	$64,984.00	$64,984.00	$99,939.00
Howard University College of Dentistry	$28,000.00	$65,000.00	$81,924.00
University of Alabama at Birmingham School of Dentistry	$28,000.00	$65,000.00	$81,924.00
University of Oklahoma College of Dentistry	$30,137.00	$66,162.00	$66,162.00
Meharry Medical College School of Dentistry	$66,503.00	$66,503.00	$100,816.00

Dental Schools	In-State Tuition	Out-of-State Tuition	COA (O)
University of Missouri-Kansas City School of Dentistry	$34,152.00	$68,066.00	$68,066.00
University of Florida College of Dentistry	$41,720.00	$68,200.00	$104,014.00
The Maurice H. Kornberg School of Dentistry, Temple University	$61,452.00	$69,398.00	$103,878.00
University of Tennessee Health Science Center College of Dentistry	$34,972.00	$73,732.00	$110,944.00
University of Detroit Mercy School of Dentistry	$74,260.00	$74,260.00	$115,334.00
University of Kentucky College of Dentistry	$35,228.00	$75,178.00	$116,226.00
The University of Iowa College of Dentistry & Dental Clinics	$50,791.00	$75,929.00	$94,065.00
University of Connecticut School of Dental Medicine	$38,437.00	$76,191.00	$109,391.00
Creighton University School of Dentistry	$77,856.00	$77,856.00	$103,263.00
University of Maryland School of Dentistry	$42,080.00	$78,236.00	$78,236.00
University of New England College of Dental Medicine	$78,575.00	$78,575.00	$96,575.00
Marquette University School of Dentistry	$69,950.00	$78,610.00	$103,502.00
Case Western Reserve University School of Dental Medicine	$78,612.00	$78,612.00	$107,012.00
University of Minnesota School of Dentistry	$46,192.00	$78,998.00	$96,680.00
Tufts University School of Dental Medicine	$79,200.00	$79,200.00	$123,570.00
University of Pennsylvania School of Dental Medicine	$79,409.00	$79,409.00	$123,521.00
University of Louisville School of Dentistry	$42,299.00	$79,771.00	$79,771.00
University of Illinois at Chicago College of Dentistry	$52,474.00	$80,964.00	$100,964.00
Nova Southeastern University College of Dental Medicine	$80,932.00	$81,741.00	$129,465.00
Indiana University School of Dentistry	$36,767.00	$81,885.00	$107,240.00

Dental Schools	In-State Tuition	Out-of-State Tuition	COA (O)
Boston University Henry M. Goldman School of Dental Medicine	$82,500.00	$82,500.00	$85,393.00
Western University of Health Sciences College of Dental Medicine	$83,378.00	$83,378.00	$116,924.00
University of Nebraska Medical Center College of Dentistry	$40,450.00	$84,325.00	$130,720.00
University of Mississippi Medical Center School of Dentistry	$43,440.00	$85,494.00	$109,670.00
Touro College of Dental Medicine at New York Medical College	$86,255.00	$86,255.00	$117,925.00
University of Utah School of Dentistry	$50,133.00	$86,340.00	$86,340.00
Missouri School of Dentistry & Oral Health	$87,382.00	$87,382.00	$87,382.00
The Ohio State University College of Dentistry	$44,209.00	$87,629.00	$112,341.00
University of North Carolina at Chapel Hill Adams School of Dentistry	$45,748.00	$87,784.00	$100,273.00
Oregon Health & Science University School of Dentistry	$61,868.00	$89,628.00	$113,678.00
Virginia Commonwealth University School of Dentistry	$57,911.00	$90,281.00	$127,938.00
Roseman University of Health Sciences College of Dental Medicine – South Jordan, Utah	$92,181.00	$92,181.00	$92,181.00
Loma Linda University School of Dentistry	$93,275.00	$93,275.00	$110,870.00
University of Washington School of Dentistry	$64,258.00	$93,762.00	$120,908.00
Arizona School of Dentistry & Oral Health	$93,912.00	$93,912.00	$93,912.00
NYU College of Dentistry	$95,968.00	$95,968.00	$95,968.00
Columbia University College of Dental Medicine	$97,027.00	$97,027.00	$122,767.00
Midwestern University College of Dental Medicine-Arizona	$97,048.00	$97,048.00	$125,617.00
Midwestern University College of Dental Medicine-Illinois	$99,078.00	$99,078.00	$127,586.00

453

Dental Schools	In-State Tuition	Out-of-State Tuition	COA (O)
University of Nevada, Las Vegas, School of Dental Medicine	$59,836.00	$99,571.00	$99,571.00
Medical University of South Carolina James B. Edwards College of Dental Medicine	$69,010.00	$104,885.00	$140,055.00
University of the Pacific Arthur A. Dugoni School of Dentistry	$114,720.00	$114,720.00	$132,400.00
Herman Ostrow School of Dentistry of USC	$122,154.00	$122,154.00	$152,123.00
California North State College of Dental Medicine	N/A	N/A	N/A

COMPREHENSIVE HEALTH CARE SERIES

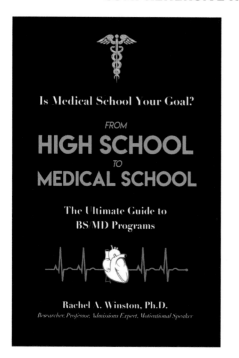

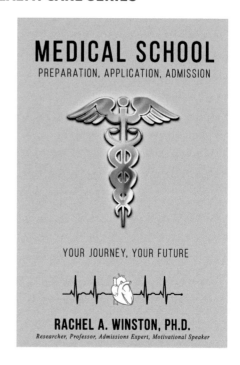

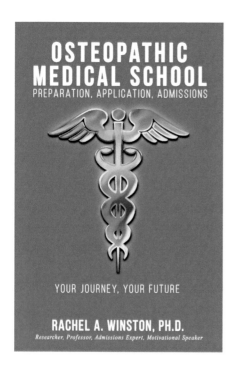

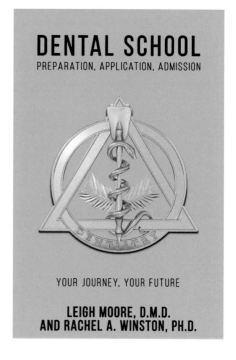

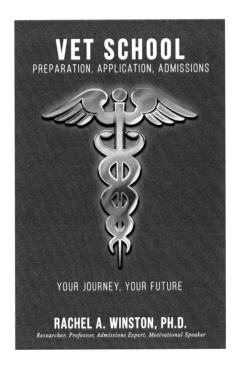

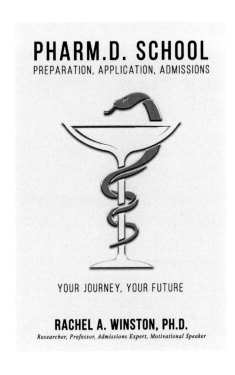

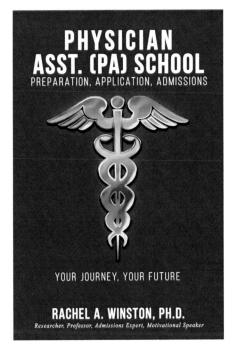

FOR MORE INFORMATION

bsmdguide.com

medschoolexpert.com

Purchase books at Lizard-publishing.com

INDEX

A

B

C

D

E

F

G

H

I

J

L

P

R

S

T

U

V

W

Z